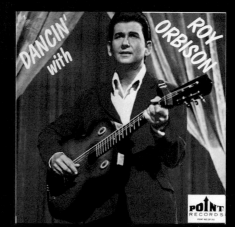

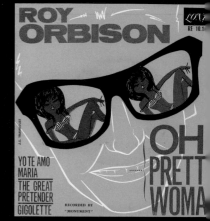

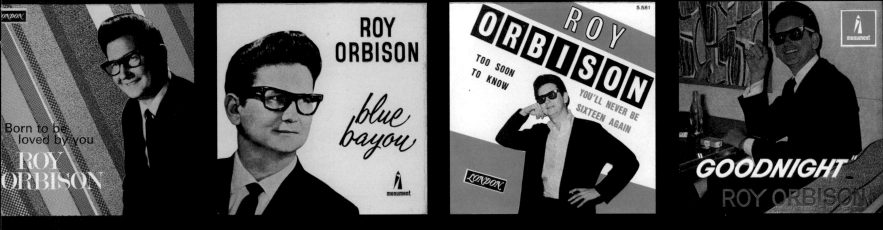

The Authorized

ROY ORBISON

by his sons **ROY Jr., WESLEY, & ALEX ORBISON**

with Jeff Slate

Concept, Curation and Research by Marcel Riesco

CENTER
STREET

Center Street
Hachette Book Group
1290 Avenue of the Americas, New York, NY 10104
centerstreet.com
twitter.com/centerstreet

First Edition: October 2017

Center Street is a division of Hachette Book Group, Inc. The Center Street name and logo are
trademarks of Hachette Book Group, Inc.

The publisher is not responsible for websites (or their content) that are not owned by the publisher.

The Hachette Speakers Bureau provides a wide range of authors for speaking events.
To find out more, go to www.HachetteSpeakersBureau.com or call (866) 376-6591.

Print book interior design by Timothy Shaner, NightAndDayDesign.biz

Project manager Christopher Measom, NightAndDayDesign.biz
Project manager for Roy's Boys,LLC, Chelsie Lykens

ISBNs: 978-1-4789-7654-7 (hardcover), 978-1-4789-7655-4 (ebook)

Printed in the United States of America

LSC-Willard

10 9 8 7 6 5 4 3 2 1

Frontice: Roy Orbison photographed by Sheila Rock in 1987. **Following pages**: Roy's 1969 José Ramirez flamenco guitar (see page 198 for another view).

For Roy, Barbara, and Claudette

and

Orbie Lee, Nadine, Grady, Sammy,

Roy DeWayne, and Anthony King

CONTENTS

PEOPLE OFTEN

ASK ME HOW

WOULD I LIKE TO

BE REMEMBERED

AND I ANSWER

THAT I WOULD

SIMPLY LIKE TO BE

REMEMBERED.

—ROY ORBISON

INTRODUCTION

by Wesley, Roy Jr.,
and Alex Orbison

It's hard to believe

that our father has been gone for nearly thirty years. To the world, Roy Orbison was a legend, but to us he was simply Dad. Whether he was hanging out around the house, holed up in the "purple room"—the office where he'd work on new music—hamming it up with friends, legends like Johnny Cash, George Harrison, or Carl Perkins, or simply cracking jokes and playing games with us, he never lost the humility he had from growing up hard in West Texas. But though we thought of him as Dad first, even to us he was something more than just a father. Even in our small world at home, we knew he was special.

Remarkably, the story of our dad's life has never been told. Not the real story, that is. So this book is the first step in setting the record straight. But it also gives us the ability to provide some insight into what our dad was like, with us, growing up, and with his famous friends.

In putting together this book, the memories really came flooding back for all of us. We laughed and cried and recalled things together that had long been forgotten. But one of our favorite memories is of a visit the producer Jeff Lynne, who along with Dad was a member of the supergroup the Traveling Wilburys, made to our lake house in Hendersonville, Tennessee. We were just next door to Dad's pal Johnny Cash, and it was a busy place. Dad did business there, and if the door of his third floor office was closed, we knew he was writing or working on demos and shouldn't be disturbed. But the house was also a refuge where Dad could just be himself, and more often than not people would just be hanging about, palling around with him, or simply waiting for him to finish whatever he was doing. Or sometimes just to wake up.

One day, this guy with a thick English accent, sunglasses, and curly hair visited the house. Jeff Lynne had ar-

Previous pages: Roy during the filming of the "In Dreams" video, 1987. **Opposite**: Roy in his Ford Thunderbird in Hendersonville, TN, May 1961.
Right: Barbara and Roy with their sons, Roy Jr. and Alex, at home in Hendersonville, TN in the late 1970s.

Above: Class of '55—Johnny Cash, Jerry Lee Lewis, Roy Orbison, and Carl Perkins—at the Sun Studios in Memphis, September 1985. **Opposite**: The Traveling Wilburys—George Harrison, Jeff Lynne, Tom Petty, Roy Orbison, and Bob Dylan—in Encino, CA, May 1988.

rived for a meeting with Dad because he'd begun producing records after leaving his group, the hugely successful Electric Light Orchestra, and he really wanted to make a record with Dad. Jeff would go on to single-handedly shape the sound of music in the late 1980s as a result of his work on George Harrison's *Cloud Nine* and Tom Petty's *Full Moon Fever*, not to mention Dad's *Mystery Girl* album and, of course, those Traveling Wilburys records, but to us he was just another guy sitting on our couch waiting for Dad.

Wild, young kids at the time, we'd met Jeff at the door when he arrived, and he had played with us for a bit, chasing Roy Jr. under the pool table. But we'd been having a fight with wet paper towels, trying to pummel one another, or one of our mom's friends who was visiting, and poor Jeff had no idea what he was in for. As he went to wait for Dad, we went into a nearby bathroom, loaded up our paper towel bombs, and resumed our battle. Just as Dad came down the stairs, we let loose with a furious storm, and one of the bombs nailed Jeff.

Dad sure wasn't too pleased, but Jeff took it in stride, and after we made our apologies, everything went back to normal and Dad and Jeff disappeared to talk shop.

Dad had just made the *Class of '55: Memphis Rock & Roll Homecoming* album with Johnny Cash, Jerry Lee Lewis, and Carl Perkins, which was sort of a Sun Records version of the Wilburys, but that was really unlike him, because it felt to everyone like a step backward. Dad was a songwriter, first and foremost, and he sure wasn't sentimental. He was always looking forward. If you asked him what his best song was, he'd surely tell you "The next one." But we had no idea how important Jeff, or any of the other guys around at the time, such as Rick Rubin and T Bone Burnett, would be to Dad's career. Once they stepped in our door, they were just guys there to visit Dad, and we sure didn't think much of it.

Even a few years later, after we'd moved to Malibu, when Dad seemed busier than ever before and the director David Lynch and Jeff and George and Tom and Bob Dylan were around a lot, daily life for us didn't change all that much. It was only later, after Dad was gone, that we realized that his story reads like the treatment for an almost unbelievable movie, conjured up by some highly imaginative Hollywood screenwriter.

Dad was born in rural Texas in 1936, when having a radio, let alone a guitar, in the house was a luxury. But he had talent and drive and, of course, that amazing voice. Maybe that was enough, but how does a kid who grew up deep in the heart of West Texas end up with millions of fans around the world, including some of the greatest artists of the twentieth century, including Elvis, John Lennon, and Bruce Springsteen? We're pretty sure that the hand of fate guided Dad's life, both for good and for bad.

It certainly played a part the day Dad crossed paths with Johnny Cash for the first time, when they both appeared on a local Texas television show and Dad pleaded with the rising star to put in a good word for him with his label boss, Sam Phillips, at Sun Records. Even though Johnny's recommendation didn't seem to amount to much in Sam's eyes, soon Dad was headed to Memphis. And although Sun didn't quite make Dad a star, he worked hard and became a great performer and guitar player and, crucially, an amazing songwriter. He scored big when the Everly Brothers recorded his song "Claudette," and after he signed with the revered Monument Records, the hits just kept coming. "Oh, Pretty Woman," "Only the Lonely," "Crying," "Blue Bayou," "It's Over," and the groundbreaking, operatic "Running Scared," plus constant touring—as he did in England with the Beatles as his opening act—endeared Dad to the public. But hard times followed close behind, and the next thirty years were a roller coaster for all of us.

Dad was a survivor, and the tireless touring and dedication to his songwriting craft during his so-called wilderness years sowed the seeds that led to a career renaissance unheard of in the entertainment business. By the 1980s, when David Lynch used Dad's classic "In Dreams" in a key scene of his breakout movie *Blue Velvet* and subsequently directed a video of the song, introducing Dad to the ravenous MTV Generation, it felt to all of us like we were on some sort of rocket ship. The now-legendary *Roy Orbison and Friends: A Black and White Night* television special and an album with the Traveling Wilburys followed, but with Dad at the center of perhaps the only true supergroup ever, tragedy struck one last time.

Dad's untimely death from a heart attack in December 1988 seemed to put an end to a career on the ascent. But he left behind two albums worth of material, and one of the songs, "You Got It," is the song that, to this day, no matter where any one of us goes, people know, as much as or even more than "Oh, Pretty Woman."

We're going to refer to Dad as Roy throughout this book, because that's how the story of this amazing man, incredibly gifted singer, songwriter, and guitarist should be told. We all—our family and you, his fans—lost him way too early. This book and his story are our gift to you, so we can all remember him the way he was, which is truly amazing enough.

—November 2017

Prologue

A BLACK AND WHITE NIGHT

PROLOGUE

Los Angeles's Ambassador Hotel

was a shadow of its former glory. It had hosted six Academy Awards ceremonies, Marilyn Monroe had begun her modeling career at poolside there, and Robert Kennedy had gone there to celebrate after winning the California presidential primary in June 1968, before he was tragically gunned down in a pantry just off the ballroom where he had given his victory speech. By 1987, the once brilliant black-and-red carpets were worn and faded, and the gold and cream–colored paint was peeling. Over the years, a succession of owners had tried to make the Ambassador's club, the infamous Cocoanut Grove, the hot spot it had been in the early 1960s but without success. Still, it held an iconic status in Hollywood lore and retained its allure as a once great nightclub, even as it struggled to reinvent itself.

Meanwhile, across town in Malibu, Roy Orbison was driving his family nuts. He would sit for hours on end picking at his guitar, looking for the new sound that might show him the way forward. He'd been blessed with having the enormously popular band Van Halen record his 1960s classic "Oh, Pretty Woman," and the money he had earned as a result had allowed him to cut back on the public appearances he had always disliked: car shows and oldies circuit performances. He was fifty-one; ancient in rock and roll terms at the time. Maybe he was through, he wondered aloud to friends, but he had no desire to let up. Over the previous two decades, he had kept at his songwriting and recording schedule. Like any ambitious performer, he harbored dreams of finding just one more showbiz break.

Then, seemingly out of nowhere, he was catapulted back into popular consciousness when his song "Crying," a duet with k.d. lang, was featured in the movie *Hiding Out*, and then "In Dreams" was used to devastating effect in David Lynch's startling film *Blue Velvet*. The previous year, he'd reunited with his pals from Sun Records—Johnny Cash, Carl Perkins, and Jerry Lee Lewis—on the album *Class of '55*, to modest accolades. But after three decades in the business, and even after he had turned Lynch down the first time, he knew that the exposure from Lynch's use of his almost forgotten song in a movie that had captured the public's attention was as golden an opportunity as he'd ever seen. On the heels of Lynch's film, Roy dusted off the

Previous pages and opposite: Film stills from "Roy Orbison & Friends: A Black & White Night" concert, Cocoanut Grove, Los Angeles, CA, September 30, 1987.

7

rerecordings he had made in 1986 of some of his biggest hits, added "In Dreams" to the mix, and released *In Dreams: The Greatest Hits* to capitalize on the movie's success, with an arresting music video directed by Lynch for the title track that intercut clips from *Blue Velvet* with Roy performing the song.

It did the trick; he was back on the charts and back in the spotlight.

Roy was the godfather to a whole host of artists who had grown up with his music in the 1960s and had become stars in their own right in the 1970s. Bruce Springsteen, Jackson Browne, Elvis Costello, and Bonnie Raitt were all major stars as the 1980s wound down. They were also die-hard disciples of Roy's music.

Perhaps the way forward wasn't so far off from what Roy had always been doing. He just needed a way to get the most out of his position as a newly rediscovered elder statesman of rock.

That's when the ace producer T Bone Burnett, whom Roy had worked with on *In Dreams*, and Roy's wife, Barbara, came to him with an idea: Why not find a special location and invite some of those big-name fans to do a filmed concert with Roy? After a bit of brainstorming, they also hit upon the idea of shooting the special in black and white, which would make it stand out and give it a distinct, instantly classic look. Roy was immediately sold. He'd wanted to capture one of his concerts to showcase his remarkable catalog of songs and had recently filmed *Roy Orbison Live in Texas* at a 1986 concert in Houston, but it hadn't lived up to Roy's expectations. This seemed like an opportunity to right that wrong.

Barbara and T Bone took the idea to some contacts at HBO's Cinemax. The pair liked the prospect of working with Cinemax because they knew the channel's *Sessions* series created by Stephanie Bennett, the wife of Jim Mervis, who had managed Roy a few years prior. Bennett, the head of Delilah Films, which was behind the film *Hail! Hail! Rock 'n' Roll*, celebrating Chuck Berry and featuring the Rolling Stones's Keith Richards and Roy, seemed perfect for the job.

Roy Orbison and Friends: A Black and White Night, as they pitched Cinemax, would be a unique, star-studded concert, in which Roy would be accompanied onstage by other popular performers at the Cocoanut Grove nightclub. Even in its relatively run-down state, the once ritzy, Moroccan-influenced design of the Cocoanut Grove, complete with Arabian doors and artificial

Above: Roy and Barbara, Malibu, CA, September/October 1988. **Opposite**: Roy and T Bone Burnett on September 29, 1987 rehearsing for the "Roy Orbison & Friends: A Black & White Night" concert.

You are Cordially Invited to Attend
An Evening in Black & White
with

Roy Orbison
and Friends

Wednesday September 30th
at 6pm

The Cocoanut Grove at
The Ambassador Hotel
3400 Wilshire

Attire: Black & White & Formal

palm trees left over from the filming of Rudolph Valentino's 1921 film *The Sheik*, would look fantastic on film and give the show a classic feel for what would surely be a memorable evening.

Cinemax quickly came on board.

The Ambassador Hotel opened in 1921. It was a stunning place, designed by the renowned architect Myron Hunt on more than twenty-three acres of prime real estate at 3400 Wilshire Boulevard. As the result of a series of legal battles and the ever-changing Hollywood nightlife scene, the former centerpiece of the Wilshire corridor and treasure of Los Angeles had been left to deteriorate by the time Roy's Cinemax special was filmed. But the hotel and facilities were used with such regularity as sets for film and television that it had come to be known as the Ambassador Studios.

As Roy drove onto the hotel's grounds, along the elongated driveway and past the gardens, to the front parking lot just off Wilshire, he thought he'd stepped into a time machine. A red-carpeted entrance led to an impressive glass entryway. Inside, a grand staircase wound up to the second floor, where through a series of black-carpeted rooms with mirror-lined walls, just before the coat check, you'd find the hidden doors that led to the backstage area.

The Cocoanut Grove itself was down a walkway, via ramps with handrails that led to a slightly sunken, surprisingly small multilevel room. On the right was the unusually low stage, with a dance floor just in front of it. Unfortunately, there would be no dancing during *A Black and White Night*. For the filming, the production team decided to build out the stage to accommodate the large band assembled to accompany Roy, and the expanded stage covered much of the dance floor. The remaining dance floor space was populated with tables.

Around the room were two elevated, railed tiers with tables for optimal viewing of the stage, and there were ramps on either side of the stage where usually there would be steps. From

WHY NOT FIND A SPECIAL LOCATION AND INVITE SOME OF THOSE BIG-NAME FANS TO DO A FILMED CONCERT WITH ROY?

Roy's vantage point onstage the room looked unusually small, with a cramped control room wedged at the back.

Behind the stage, a small doorway led to the backstage area, where there were four small dressing rooms. Roy used the biggest one, which was furnished with a tiled countertop and a sink, mirrors with ample lights across the tops, and several couches.

A Black and White Night was the last great concert at the Cocoanut Grove. Considering how large it looms in Roy's legend now, the show was arranged just like anything else on his schedule, just after he came back from touring and recording the song "Life Fades Away" for the film *Less than Zero*—in which it was used to soundtrack the death of Robert Downey Jr.'s character—and before he went back on tour in Europe. It was seemingly the same kind of lightning bolt of luck that often struck when Roy was at work that made it the legendary event it became.

Planned on relatively short notice, the single day of rehearsals took place on Tuesday, September 29, 1987, at the Cocoanut Grove itself, with all the band members and Roy going through the songs. The TCB—Taking Care of Business—Band, which accompanied Elvis Presley from 1969 until his death in 1977, provided the powerful backing. Glen D. Hardin, who had been a member of the house band of the popular 1960s television show *Shindig!* was on piano; the celebrated James Burton, who had lent his distinctive Fender Telecaster sound to not just Elvis but Ricky Nelson and the *Shindig!* band, was on lead guitar; Jerry Scheff, who'd played with the Doors and many others before taking the job with the King, played stand-up bass; and the monstrous-sounding Ronnie Tutt was behind Roy on the drums.

Besides the all-star sidemen assembled to back Roy, a host of musicians who were stars in their own right made the proceedings all the more special. Burnett put the rest of the lineup

Opposite: Concert invitation. **Above**: Vintage artwork advertising the Cocoanut Grove and a photo of the Ambassador Hotel in Los Angeles circa 2001.

11

Roy and Bruce Springsteen rehearse for the concert,
September 29, 1987.

Above: k.d. lang and Roy, promo photo for their Grammy-award winning duet, "Crying," 1987.
Opposite: Images from "Roy Orbison & Friends: A Black & White Night" concert, featuring Elvis Costello, James Burton, J. D. Souther, k.d. lang, and Bruce Springsteen, September 30, 1987.

together with the help of the songwriter J. D. Souther, who corralled people they had both worked with. In truth, each one was a fan of Roy's, and Burnett and Souther knew they'd be there—no matter how big the star—not for themselves but to support the main attraction.

Bruce Springsteen, who was at the height of his fame, played guitar and sang; the incredibly gifted songwriter Tom Waits played acoustic guitar and organ; the huge Orbison fan Elvis Costello played acoustic guitar, organ, and even harmonica (on the only live recording of Roy's song "Uptown"); and T Bone Burnett, who was, of course, the musical director, also played acoustic guitar. Rounding things out, Jackson Browne, Souther, and Steven Soles were the male background singers, while k.d. lang, Jennifer Warnes, and Bonnie Raitt provided the female backing. Alex Acuña played percussion, and Mike Utley, who had worked with Roy before, played keyboards and was the band director.

Originally, T Bone and Barbara had conceived a program in which everyone would perform his or her favorite Orbison classic, but the thought of trying to deliver the goods, with their hero right in front of them, proved too daunting a request, even for the megastars taking part. Still, the rehearsal was exciting for all involved, and the contagious exuberance poured over into suggestions from everyone.

"I've got an idea," Bruce Springsteen said midway through the proceedings. He described his scheme to have the band members bring their playing down to almost a whisper during the middle of Roy's "Dream Baby," before roaring back with a powerful ending. They ran through it, and everyone agreed that the results were stunning.

J. D. Souther, who mercilessly rehearsed probably the most amazing group of backing vocalists ever assembled prior to the full band rehearsal, continued to crack the whip, especially on "Blue Angel," which was, sadly, cut, along with "Blue Bayou" and "Claudette," from the original broadcast due to time constraints, and a string quartet worked hard on the beautiful touches to what everyone there could tell was shaping up to be a marvelous night.

The performance itself took place on Wednesday, September 30, 1987, and was billed as a tribute to Roy's more than thirty-year contribution to rock and roll. Filmed entirely in black and white and directed by Tony Mitchell, before an audience of devoted Orbison admirers, including Billy Idol, Kris Kristofferson, and Patrick Swayze, the final result was magnificent and stands to this day as a lasting document of what a charismatic performer Roy Orbison was.

Roy and the band tore through a set list of some of the greatest songs in the history of rock and roll, sung with gusto by one of its architects: "Only the Lonely," "Dream Baby," "Blue Bayou," "Ooby Dooby," "Leah," "Running Scared," "Uptown," "In Dreams," "Crying,"

"Candy Man," "Go Go Go (Down the Line)," "Mean Woman Blues," "Claudette," "It's Over," "Oh, Pretty Woman" and "Blue Angel" were all performed that night, and Roy had never sounded better.

Roy also debuted two new songs that he'd just recorded for his forthcoming album during the one-hour show—which actually took about three hours to film—and they fit seamlessly into the set list next to some of his best-loved songs. His take on Billy Burnette and David Mal-loy's "(All I Can Do Is) Dream You" and "The Comedians," penned by Elvis Costello for his hero, were both stunning.

Roy's guitar playing was fluid and stinging, and his voice was as fresh in 1987 as it had been on the original recordings of the many hits the band played that night. T Bone and Barbara had agreed that although some of the arrangements would be updated for live performance, there would be no trace of fake, synthesized strings or the distorted guitar sound so popular at the time. Instead, the band surrounding Roy was the real deal. A stand-up bass, grand piano, and real strings complemented the rhythm section and Roy's crystal clear voice. The sound was natural and loose, and the magic they created was transmitted straight onto the film as the cameras rolled.

The man himself was pleased with the performance. "It was a great night," he recalled a few months later. "Barbara and I wanted to do a television special, and she put it together with T Bone Burnett and they came up with the idea of it being black and white. It was fabulous; we had a great time. It was wonderful."

Not surprisingly, *A Black and White Night* introduced Roy to a whole new generation of fans. An album version of the concert, released in October 1989, was a huge hit, and Roy's performance of "Oh, Pretty Woman," released as a single, won the Grammy for Best Male Pop Vocal Performance in 1991. (It was also nominated for Best Live Performance.)

"Roy's voice, which had seemed fragile during rehearsals, suddenly sounded sure and beautiful," Elvis Costello said later about performing with his childhood hero. "He let loose on crescendo after crescendo, delivering a fine rendition of 'The Comedians,' one of the few new songs in the show. As I recall, we all got home from the filming pretty late, only to be shaken out of bed a few hours later by a major earthquake."

Previous pages: Roy and Bruce Springsteen during the guitar solo of "Down the Line." **Above**: Roy singing "Only the Lonely." **Opposite**: (top) Roy, sons Alex and Roy Jr., wife Barbara, and Billy Idol. (bottom) Roy with Patrick Swayze and Lisa Niemi before the concert.

The California Department of Conservation reported, "An earthquake of magnitude 6.1, located 10 miles east of the Los Angeles city Civic Center, occurred on Thursday, October 1, at 7:42 a.m." It was the day after the filming.

The Ambassador was permanently damaged, and the audio of the concert was feared to have been lost or ruined. Luckily, it was found safe and sound.

"A chandelier fell on the tapes, and with all the mess from the earthquake we couldn't find them for more than twenty-four hours," Roy recalled. "If that tape had been destroyed, I would have been singing an extended version of 'Crying.' We could never have gotten all those guys together again."

"The purity in his voice is something that you don't hear much at all anymore, and how effortlessly he sings," Springsteen said after the performance at the Cocoanut Grove. "You stand there and think, 'Gee, is he gonna hit that note?' No matter how many times you've heard him sing it on the records or you've seen him play it, you're not sure. But he always hits it. There is no singing like that left anymore, and it's a beautiful, beautiful thing."

"I can remember, we were doing *A Black and White Night*, when I was going to do the little harmony part with him, when I come to sing with him. . . . He moved his guitar, which was sort of this grand gesture," Springsteen remembered years later. "He was almost not there. You couldn't see his eyes. His mouth barely moved. And yet you were hearing this sound that was coming straight from his center to yours. It was always stirring. He never became like a nostalgia act and his songs never sounded like oldies, even if he did them exactly—and he did do them the way the records were cut—because he had some element within him that allowed him to be in the present, and he was able to do that just through his artistry. You're hearing something that was so beautiful and so present. He treated those songs with great respect."

Springsteen, a master himself, was clearly in awe of Roy as a performer and, especially, as a singer. "When he sings 'Crying,' or any of those songs, what amazes me about them is that it

THERE IS NO SINGING LIKE THAT LEFT ANYMORE, AND IT'S A BEAUTIFUL, BEAUTIFUL THING.

—BRUCE SPRINGSTEEN

Previous pages: J. D. Souther, Jennifer Warnes, Jackson Browne, Bonnie Raitt, k.d. lang, Steven Soles, Tom Waits, Mike Utley, James Burton, Jerry Scheff, Roy Orbison, and Ron Tutt. **Above**: Roy in the spotlight. **Opposite**: Top Row: James Burton, Glen D. Hardin, Jennifer Warnes, Jerry Scheff, J. D. Souther, k.d. lang, T Bone Burnett, Ron Tutt, and Steven Soles. Third Row: Tom Waits, Bonnie Raitt, Jackson Browne. Second Roy: Roy Orbison. First Row: Elvis Costello, Bruce Springsteen.

is happening in the present," he said about his hero not long before Roy died. "He is not doing an oldies tune. You know, [they sound] totally modern. Also, it is happening now because it is emotionally happening now for him. When he sings that stuff, he closes his eyes, and wherever he goes, that's where he is."

The Cinemax special aired on Sunday, January 3, and was a huge success. It became one of the top-selling concert videos of all time and has been used by PBS stations ever since to assist in fund-raising, eventually being responsible for the single most successful drive in PBS history.

Before a wrecking ball leveled the Ambassador Hotel in 2005, a public auction was held in its gardens. The stage lights and the tables and chairs seen in *A Black and White Night* sat on the lawn among the items waiting to be sold. It was a sad end for the grand hotel, with so much Hollywood history and so many Hollywood secrets. Though the hotel and "old Los Angeles," may be gone and a heart attack took Roy in December 1988, the music he made at the Cocoanut Grove with his all-star cast that night in 1987 will live forever.

Chapter 1

FROM WINK TO THE BRINK

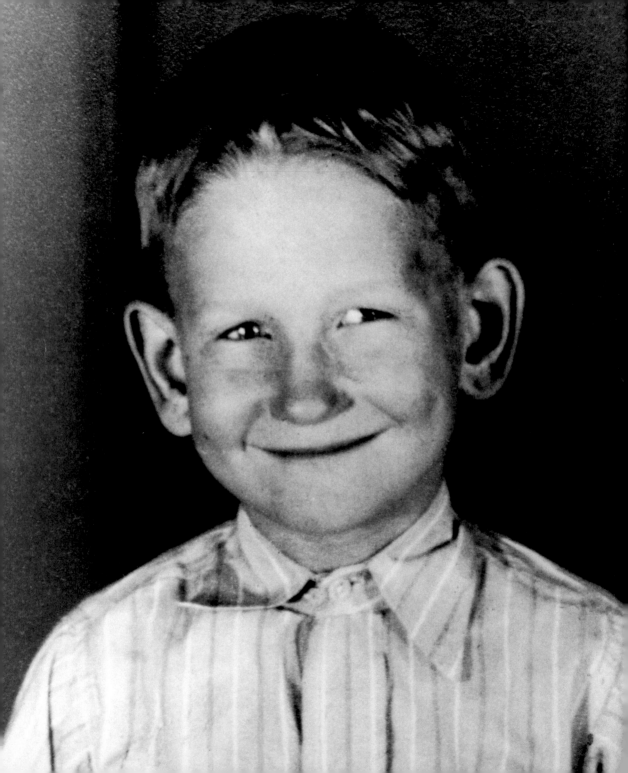

WHEN I WAS SIX YEARS OLD, MOM AND DAD GAVE ME A GUITAR FOR MY BIRTHDAY, AND DADDY TAUGHT ME THE CHORDS TO "YOU ARE MY SUNSHINE."

—ROY ORBISON, 1988

In 1936, the town of Vernon

was much like any other Texas town. There was a trolley, a fire department, three newspapers, two flour mills, two ice factories, and a courthouse, plus the Plaza Theatre and the big Wilbarger Hotel, not to mention eight churches, in the town where the St. Louis, San Francisco and Texas Railway joined the Fort Worth and Denver lines. Vernon's population was estimated at 9,137 in 1936, but on Thursday, April 23, 1936 at 3:50 p.m., Roy Orbison made it 9,138.

Roy Kelton Orbison, with light blue eyes and hints of sandy blond hair, was born at Christ the King Hospital on the corner of Lamar and Pease Streets, right on the Chisholm Trail, "where they drove the cattle from Texas through to Kansas," Roy later recalled. "That trail was the main street in Vernon."

The Orbisons had a rear apartment at 930 Maiden Street but moved to 1912 Eagle Street after Roy was born. As the family grew, they bounced around, from a ten-dollar-a-month apartment on Pease Street and finally to Bowie and then Pearl Street.

Roy's mom, Nadine, was a nurse, and kept their home spotless for her pride and joy, while his father, Orbie Lee, worked as an attendant at the local filling station and as a mechanic at Vernon Storage and Battery Co. on Cumberland Street. But what Orbie Lee truly loved to do was sing, and Roy would forever remember his sweet, soft singing voice.

As their son would soon enough, Orbie Lee and Nadine both wore glasses, and his mother shared Roy's soft-voiced nature. "She was very soft spoken, extremely so, with the cutest southern drawl," Janna Frodsham, the daughter of Nadine's brother Royal, whom Roy was named for, would recall.

Previous pages: Archive photo of a traveling medicine show caravan. **Opposite**: A young Roy, early 1940s. **Above**: Roy's parents, Orbie Lee and Nadine, in Wink, TX.

27

Above: Nadine's parents, Royal Shultz and Maude Chappell, in Wise County, TX, 1913. **Opposite**: (top) Roy and lifelong pal Orbie Lee Harris playing street football in Wink, TX, circa 1948. (bottom left) The Wink Kittens (Wink Junior High School football team), Roy Orbison, Orbie Lee Harris, and Barna Richards (standing), 1950. (bottom right) Roy playing street football with brother Grady Lee Orbison and friends Melvin Harris and Orbie Lee Harris, Wink TX, circa 1948.

In 1936, the town of Vernon was much like any

other Texas town. There was a trolley, a fire department, three newspapers, two flour mills, two ice factories, and a courthouse, plus the Plaza Theatre and the big Wilbarger Hotel, not to mention eight churches, in the town where the St. Louis, San Francisco and Texas Railway joined the Fort Worth and Denver lines. Vernon's population was estimated at 9,137 in 1936, but on Thursday, April 23, 1936 at 3:50 p.m., Roy Orbison made it 9,138.

Roy Kelton Orbison, with light blue eyes and hints of sandy blond hair, was born at Christ the King Hospital on the corner of Lamar and Pease Streets, right on the Chisholm Trail, "where they drove the cattle from Texas through to Kansas," Roy later recalled. "That trail was the main street in Vernon."

The Orbisons had a rear apartment at 930 Maiden Street but moved to 1912 Eagle Street after Roy was born. As the family grew, they bounced around, from a ten-dollar-a-month apartment on Pease Street and finally to Bowie and then Pearl Street.

Roy's mom, Nadine, was a nurse, and kept their home spotless for her pride and joy, while his father, Orbie Lee, worked as an attendant at the local filling station and as a mechanic at Vernon Storage and Battery Co. on Cumberland Street. But what Orbie Lee truly loved to do was sing, and Roy would forever remember his sweet, soft singing voice.

As their son would soon enough, Orbie Lee and Nadine both wore glasses, and his mother shared Roy's soft-voiced nature. "She was very soft spoken, extremely so, with the cutest southern drawl," Janna Frodsham, the daughter of Nadine's brother Royal, whom Roy was named for, would recall.

By 1941, when Roy was five years old, his teacher, A. K. Hamblen, whose brother Stuart had written the popular songs "It Is No Secret" and "This Ole House," noticed Roy's singing voice as different from the other children's around him and encouraged him to sing. When Orbie Lee asked young Roy what he was going to be when he grew up—a policeman, or a fireman, say—Roy replied, "I'll be a singer," with a certainty that belied his years.

Those days were also when Roy got the scar on his left cheek. After carving a wooden knife, he proudly ran to show his mother what he'd done. As he was running toward her, Roy fell, and the knife went right through his cheek.

In 1942, the Orbisons packed up and headed for Fort Worth, where Orbie Lee and Nadine found work in the munitions and aircraft factories that had been expanded as a result of the United States entering World War II, and Roy started first grade at the Denver Grade School.

"I was deeply involved with music from an early age," he recalled in 1975. "There would have been so many influences that would have been impossible to trace."

When he was ten, he saw Lefty Frizzell perform. It changed his life. "The first live stage show I ever saw was Bill and Joe Callahan, and the next live show I ever saw was Lefty Frizzell, when I was ten years old," he remembered wistfully years later. After that concert, he saw Lefty's Cadillac parked outside the venue. By all accounts, that image made as much of an impression as the music he had heard that night.

"The first singer I ever heard on the radio that really slayed me was Lefty Frizzell," he told interviewer Dave Booth. "He had this technique which involved sliding syllables together that really blew me away."

Inspired, Roy wrote his first song. "I don't remember it, but I remember the title," he recalled. "It was called 'A Vow of Love.' I really wasn't mature enough to follow that through, I don't think. I wrote it in front of my grandmother's house, and then I dropped that altogether, because I just hadn't been through enough to write a good song."

Roy bounced around—he was sent to live with family during a polio outbreak—attending third grade in Floydada, Texas, and the fourth grade in Wink. But the family landed back in Vernon, and Roy attended Parker Grade School. In 1946, a medicine show, with its traveling horse-and-buggy, peddling miracle medications between a variety of acts, came to town.

"I played a medicine show, Jay, when I was ten years old," Roy told Jay Leno on *The Tonight Show* in 1987. "They sold this elixir that was supposed to cure everything, and they sold candy and told a few rude jokes, and then they had a talent contest. And I shared the prize. A fifteen-year-old boy and I both tied, and we shared the $15 prize. I got $7.50 of that, and then I had to give my buddy half of that, because he was my manager."

Roy sang "Mountain Dew" and "Jole Blon." Orbie Lee Harris, a childhood friend, whom Roy jokingly referred to as his "manager," carried his guitar.

With the war over and a baby brother, Samuel Keith, joining the family on June 28, 1946, the Orbisons moved out west to Wink, Texas, for good. There was plenty of work there, and Roy settled in to fifth grade at the Wink School. For most kids, starting over yet again would have been hard. But by all accounts, Roy adapted quickly, singing and playing his guitar at the school assemblies.

Wink was an oil-boom town, with one of the best high schools around and an unbeatable football team. Wink's main drag was anchored by the Rig Theatre, but the rest of the town was made up of small houses and shacks. "If you wink, you miss it," the locals would say.

Opposite: Lefty Frizzell, singing for radio station WSM, home of the Grand Ole Opry, Nashville, TN, circa 1955. **Above**: (top) Roy with partner in crime Orbie Lee Harris holding final report cards for 6th grade, Wink, TX, 1948. (bottom) The Rig Theatre, Wink, TX, circa 1939.

"If you saw the film *Giant*, it was filmed eighty miles out of Wink," Roy told *Rolling Stone* in 1988.

There's nothing. No trees, no lakes, no creeks, a few bushes. Between Wink and Odessa, where I used to drive all the time, one of the towns is called Notrees, Texas. And it has trees. But Wink was an oil-boom town. There was one movie theater, two drugstores, one pool hall and one hardware store, and that was about it. In fact, the Sears, what you did was go to this little office and look at the catalog. It's really hard to describe, but I'll give you a few more things: it was macho guys working in the oil field, and football, and oil and grease and sand and being a stud and being cool.

I got out of there as quick as I could, and I resented having to be there, but it was a great education.

Above: Downtown Wink, TX, in the 1940s.
Opposite: (top) Roy's high school yearbook photo, 1950. (bottom) The Day Drug Store before demolition, Wink, TX.

THE FIRST THING HE'D PICK UP IN THE MORNING, EVEN BEFORE HE GOT OUT OF BED, WAS THAT GUITAR.

—JAMES MORROW, THE WINK WESTERNERS

The Orbisons settled at the Townsend Apartments, on the main drag, just a few blocks from the beautiful Rig Theatre, which Roy frequented as a youngster, though they still moved around a bit, living for a time in nearby Kermit and Andrews, Texas.

Young Roy sang for nickels and dimes at the local drugstore. The Day Drug store was a busy place after everybody got off work, and Roy would stand there and sing every day after school, as well as at the Derrick Hotel, which was run by the parents of a childhood friend, Bobby Blackburn.

In 1948, Roy made a new friend, James Morrow.

"We both played guitars and we would get together after school in the evenings and play and he'd sing and we did that until about 1952," Morrow recalls. "We would dream—you know how kids are—we'd just dream about one of these days being big and famous. But Roy was single-minded. He didn't think anything but music. The last thing he'd lay down at night was his guitar right at the edge of the bed. The first thing he'd pick up in the morning, even before he got out of bed, was that guitar."

The 1950 Wink School yearbook shows a blond Roy wearing a striped sweater. Friends recall that Roy used to play his guitar in the hallways at school, often drawing a small crowd while singing songs such as "Crawdad Hole" or "Mountain Dew."

Meanwhile, James Morrow and Roy would get together each day after school at Morrow's house across the street from the school. One of the local kids who often joined them was Billy Pat "Spider" Ellis, who'd bought a pair of drumsticks he'd use to keep the rhythm on Morrow's mom's couch.

Soon the trio met Richard West, who had a piano, and the gang moved headquarters and started hanging out at Richard's house.

"Roy and James had been messin' around over at James's house and worked up a few tunes," West recalls. "They came over to my house. I got over to the piano, and Roy said, 'Yeah, that sounds pretty good. Maybe we ought to get us a band started!' That's just about what happened."

Determined to push things forward, Morrow enlisted a classmate, Charles Evans, to play the bass, wrangling the use of an upright bass that belonged to the Wink High School band.

Wink High School's Glee Club was another pursuit of Roy's, and his April 1951 rendition of "When Yuba Plays the Tuba" is recalled by his classmates with fondness. He was also a keen

Roy Orbison Reporter

33

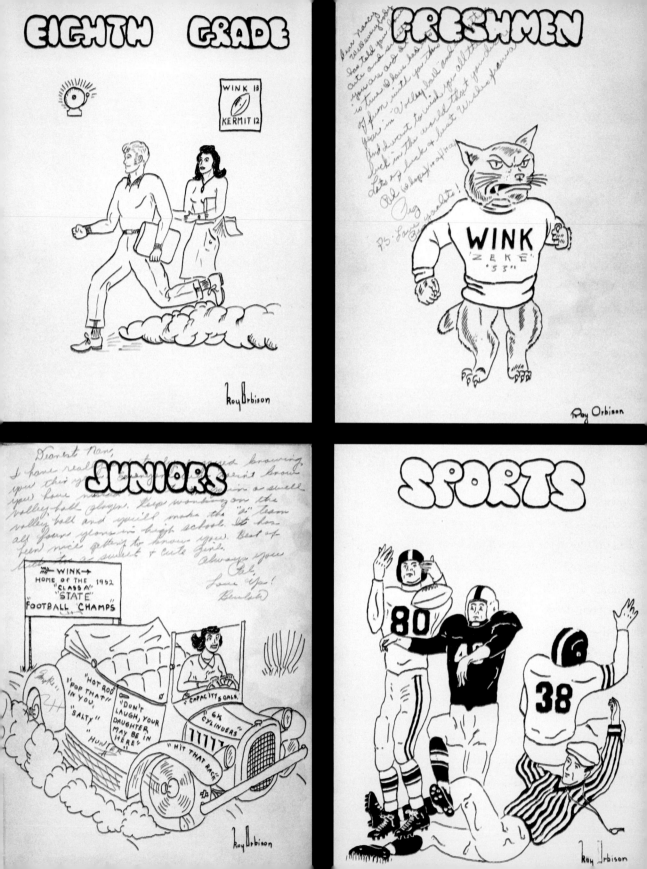

artist and designed the artwork that would grace the high school yearbook. But it was his nascent band that was really getting his attention.

"Thinking back, I think our first public appearance, if you wanna call it that, was at a school auditorium assembly there in the high school," Billy Pat Ellis recalls. "Some of the kids there at school had come to listen while we would practice, and word got around. Eventually we were invited to be part of an assembly and play some music. Roy sang a Lefty Frizzell song. We played that, and Mr. Lipscomb, who was the superintendent, invited us to go down to the Lions Club luncheon to entertain the local dignitaries. Our repertoire was about three songs, maybe four or five. The next thing I remember happening was Mr. Lipscomb was running for district governor of the Lions Club and he invited us to go to the different towns to entertain the local dignitaries."

After playing a Lions Club luncheon in McCamey, Texas, the group was offered $300 to play an upcoming dance. Considering that the minimum wage at the time was $1.25 per hour, Roy and company were elated.

With their scant repertoire, the group, consisting of Richard West on piano, Charlie Evans on bass, James Morrow on mandolin, Billy Pat Ellis on drums, and Roy on guitar and singing, hunkered down in the high school band hall and canteen, where their classmates and even teachers would come down and watch as they rehearsed enough songs to make up an evening's worth of music.

"We worked up a lot of songs in a quick amount of time," Billy Pat recalls. "After that we played a few dances here and there, plus football games and a few assemblies at the high school. And we realized, 'Hey, we have something unique going here.'"

Eva June Harben, their science teacher, is credited with giving them their name: the Wink Westerners.

DANCE
AMERICAN LEGION HALL
Wink, Texas
Saturday Night, March 20th
9:00 p.m. to 1 a.m.
MUSIC BY
"THE WINK WESTERNERS"
Admission $1.00 Per Person
Everybody Welcome!

THE WINK WESTERNERS
James Morrow, Billy Pat Ellis, Roy Orbison, Charles Evans, Richard West.

By the early 1950s, Wink had grown into a small but thriving community, with a winning football team that had put it on the map. The young Roy Orbison was a fixture of that community, too. In 1951, he began appearing regularly on KERB in Kermit, Texas, located about seven miles northeast of Wink, and by 1953, the Wink Westerners had their own radio show on KERB, one day a week before school, sponsored by local businessmen. While the show promoted their local performances at clubs and dance halls such as the Winkler County

Opposite: Roy's illustrations for the Wink High School yearbook, 1953. **Above**: (top) Newspaper clipping, 1954. (bottom) The Wink Westerners. (from left to right): James Morrow, Billy Pat Ellis, Roy Orbison, Charles Evans, and Richard West, Wink High School cafeteria, 1953.

Above: Newspaper advertisement for the Slim Whitman appearance at the Rig Theatre, Wink, TX, 1954. **Opposite**: The Wink Westerners with Slim Whitman (from left to right): Billy Pat Ellis, Roy Orbison, Richard West, Slim Whitman, James Morrow, and Charles Evans, Wink, TX, 1954.

Community Center, Kermit American Legion, the McCamey Lions Club, the Blue Room in Wink, and the Archway Club in Monahans, it also forced the band to expand their repertoire and hone their collective skills. Soon they were being featured on the *KERB Jamboree* on Saturday afternoons, playing songs such as "Kaw-liga," "Mexican Joe," "Caribbean," and "Under the Double Eagle," alongside local country and western bands.

"Country and western music, the blues, Dixieland jazz, growing up with those three types of music probably resulted in what we played," James Morrow remembers. "We played for high school dances, we played for dances in some of the clubs, like Eagle Clubs, American Legion, VFW, and some of the honky-tonks, like the Archway Club. But even as young as we were, we never had any problem with the law enforcement."

"We didn't know how we was going to be accepted or anything with all those pool players and gamblers in there playing dominos and cards," Richard West recalls. "All of a sudden here comes a shower of nickels and dimes. They'd started throwing money at us."

"Well, I guess they like us," West said to his bandmates.

On Friday, July 3, 1953, Roy and the Wink Westerners appeared in a photograph in the *Vernon Daily Record*, just before the young combo attended the 36th International Lions Club Convention in Chicago, and the following year, on April 7, 1954, the band backed up Slim Whitman when he came to town for a show at the newly renovated Rig Theatre. Things were moving fast for the fledgling musicians.

As he tried to find his own voice and style, Roy became even more endeared with Lefty Frizzell, even signing Charles Evans's yearbook "Roy 'Lefty' Orbison." But he'd also discovered Columbia Records producer Mitch Miller's stable of artists, who included Frankie Laine, Guy Mitchell, Johnnie Ray, Rosemary Clooney, and the Four Lads, most of whom were recording country and western hits for the northern and international pop markets, and Roy bought himself a 1953 Gibson Les Paul Goldtop with a wraparound tailpiece.

Meanwhile, to help make ends meet, he worked for the county, shoving tar or working in the oil fields, chopping steel and weed or painting water towers.

"When I graduated from Wink High School, I wanted to go to college," he recalled of those days under the hot Texas sun. "We played for these dances, but we didn't make a great deal of money, so we all decided to get jobs. So we started working for El Paso Natural Gas Company, sixteen hours a day, seven days a week. When I say sixteen hours a day, it was twelve a day and four hours of playing at a club. Those days didn't last very long, about four or five weeks. Got enough money to go to the University of North Texas, for the tuition. But after it

was over, it was a good experience. But I hadn't planned on doing labor anyway. I planned on being an artist."

Roy, Billy Pat, Richard West, and a classmate from Wink, Joe Ray Hammer, signed up to attend North Texas State College in Denton that fall. Roy studied history and English, even though his original plan had been to study geology.

"My dad wanted me to study geology," he told David Letterman. "But that's the only course I flunked: geology. So I changed my major then."

"While we were up there in north Texas, I remember Roy, he'd practice on the guitar all the time instead of studying books like he should be, and he came up with all these pretty chords," Billy Pat Ellis remembers of his college days with Roy. "He really progressed a lot with his guitar at college. And we met a guy named Wade Moore, who was in the fraternity there. And he and a guy named Dick Penner had written a couple of songs. One was 'Ooby Dooby,' and the other was 'Wild Woman.' Roy got to play with them, and they became friends."

Roy was especially fond of Moore and Penner's song "Ooby Dooby."

Roy and the boys returned home for Christmas and played the local New Year's Eve dance on December 31, 1954. Shortly before midnight, he and his fellow Wink Westerners kicked off "Shake, Rattle and Roll," only to find that the dance hall clock was running eight minutes slow. They gamely continued playing the song until the stroke of midnight. Roy would later say that the power of the backbeat during that eight minutes converted him to the church of rock and roll forever.

Then, after he'd returned to Denton for the spring 1955 semester, Roy heard Elvis Presley perform at the *Big D Jamboree* in Dallas. The regional showcase drew the best of Shreveport and

WE HAD TO DO IT TO STAY IN BUSINESS, THE DANCING BUSINESS. . . . SO WE HAD MEXICAN SONGS, WE HAD COUNTRY, AND EVEN INSTRUMENTAL VERSIONS OF BIG-BAND STUFF. —ROY ORBISON

the Grand Ole Opry and touring bands as visiting talent, and the *Big D* was the pride of Dallas from the late 1940s up until the early 1960s. Though it was neither as fabled nor as long lived as the Grand Ole Opry or even its friendly nearby rival, the *Louisiana Hayride*, the *Big D Jamboree* was an important second-tier radio "barn dance." Broadcasting in its heyday on Dallas's KRLD, the *Jamboree* gained a national slot on CBS radio's *Saturday Night Country Style*, on which Roy would one day perform.

"I didn't have that much money at the university, so we listened to the *Big D Jamboree* and one night the announcer said, 'We have a young man who just arrived in a pink Cadillac, here he is, Elvis Presley,'" Roy remembered many years later of Presley's April 16, 1955, appearance. Hearing the future King of Rock and Roll perform his signature hit, "That's All Right," had a profound effect on Roy, as did the fact that Elvis was making $40 a night.

More determined than ever, Roy and Billy Pat headed back to Wink after they'd finished their first year at North Texas State College and reunited with Charles Evans and James Morrow.

"There was the four of us, James, Charles, me, and Roy," Billy Pat Ellis recalls. "We got the band together again."

The Wink Westerners performed regularly all summer, and when school resumed in the autumn of 1955, Roy, Billy Pat, and James enrolled at nearby Odessa Junior College, while Charles Evans left the band to enroll at Texas Tech in Lubbock. Their efforts paid off in the fall of 1955, when the Wink Westerners appeared, along with other local country and western bands, on a Saturday-afternoon television show on KMID-TV Channel 2 out of Midland.

"At the time, I had been singing six hours a night, every song from any country artist, if they were popular," Roy recalled later of their preparation to take KMID's *Jamboree* by storm. "We had to do it to stay in business, the dancing business. We did all the pop records and everything that anybody would listen to, so we had Mexican songs, we had country, and even instrumental versions of big-band stuff."

In addition, the Wink Westerners added some teen-oriented numbers to their repertoire, including "That's All Right Mama," "Rock Around the Clock," and, of course, "Ooby Dooby," while Roy perfected his guitar solos, a trademark of the budding Rockabilly style.

"Pioneer Furniture had a contest," James Murrow recalls. "They had a bunch of bands that'd come together and play, and they were going to pick a band out of that group that they were going to sponsor."

Above: Roy, friend Melvin Harris, and brother Grady Lee Orbison, Wink, TX, circa 1955.

39

Roy's group was a smash and was given its own thirty-minute show on Friday nights at seven on KMID-TV beginning on January 6, 1956.

"The prize was that you got to appear on television," Roy recalled many years later. "So we won the contest, and the man who sponsored the thing, owned the furniture store, well, I talked him into letting us have a television series, a regular thing, locally, just so that we could get enough exposure so that if we did play anywhere, someone would come see us."

That show was also called *Jamboree*, and Roy and the gang began living in a rented duplex at 3202 Walnut Street in Odessa, while they continued to attend Odessa Junior College.

"We had a 30-minute show, and we did songs like 'Ooby Dooby' and 'Maybellene,' Presley stuff, Fats Domino, Little Richard, and anything we wanted to do, and we were sponsored by a furniture company, Pioneer Furniture," Roy told Dave Booth in 1980. "We had a fellow that did the commercials, but I did all the emceeing and everything else."

A month earlier, and with Elvis Presley's sound still fresh in his mind, Roy and the gang had traveled to Dallas for a recording session, and they found themselves one bitter winter day in December 1955 at a small, makeshift recording studio on the outskirts of Dallas owned by Jim Beck. Beck had been instrumental in the discovery of Lefty Frizzell and other country stars for Columbia Records, and Roy jumped at the chance to record with Beck at the same studio as his musical hero.

The group recorded "Ooby Dooby," together with "Hey, Miss Fannie," originally recorded by the Clovers; the recordings feature Billy Pat Ellis on drums; their old Wink buddy who was now living in Odessa, Jack Kennelley, on bass; James Morrow on guitar; and Roy on electric guitar and vocals. "Hey, Miss Fannie" featured a duet with their pal Johnny "Peanuts" Wilson, who had recently joined them.

With the brief session completed, Roy was convinced that they'd be signed to Columbia Records. But Roy wrecked his dad's car on the way home, a harbinger of the bad news that was soon to come. When Jim Beck played the recording for

Don Law, the head of Columbia's country division, Law was unimpressed. Eventually, he gave the acetate to the newly signed Sid King, the leader of Sid King & the Five Strings. King and his band recorded the song in March 1956 and released the track on Columbia Records.

Meanwhile, the band continued to perform around the area. As a result of the Friday-night *Jamboree* success, Pioneer Furniture agreed to sponsor another show, *The Teen Kings Show*—Roy's group was now called the Teen Kings in order to get away from seeming like a country and western group and to appeal to its growing teenage audience—on KOSA-TV, a new television station out of Odessa, beginning on Saturday, March 31, 1956.

That winter "The Memphis Flash," as Elvis Presley was known at the time, came to town to perform. The two had met briefly the previous October, and Roy had followed Presley's meteoric rise and admired his undeniable charisma. Elvis had made an impression on Roy, who became more determined than ever, in the wake of the future King's hit record "That's All Right," to record his own material, not like in the ramshackle session in Dallas but properly this time.

That's when Presley's Sun Records labelmate Johnny Cash came through West Texas and appeared on Roy's TV show to promote his area concert.

Hailing from Arkansas, Cash had worked in the cotton fields as a boy and sung from an early age. He'd spent time in the army in Germany, where he had formed his first band, moving later to Memphis, where he sold appliances until, as he would later say, he just couldn't take it anymore.

Cash headed for Sam Phillips's Sun Records, recording "Hey Porter" and "Cry, Cry, Cry," which were released on June 21, 1955, and met with reasonable success on the country music Hit Parade. His second single, "Folsom Prison Blues," came out in December of the same year and put his name on the country music map.

Opposite: Roy pointing out Wink, TX, on a map.

Above: The Wink Westerners (from left to right): Richard West, James Morrow, Roy Orbison, Charles Evans, and Billy Pat Ellis, Wink, TX, May 1955.

Cash was in Midland, Texas, on October 12 and Odessa on October 14, 1955, on a package tour with Elvis Presley, Wanda Jackson, Jimmy Newman, Porter Wagoner, and Floyd Cramer, and circled back through Roy's neck of the woods on December 2, 1955, and February 4 and 17, 1956.

Warming up to the Man in Black, and with seemingly nothing left to lose, Roy made the fateful request of help from Cash during Cash's final visit. He asked him for advice on how he could get a record deal, and Cash gave him Sam Phillips's telephone number in Memphis.

"Elvis came through Odessa, and Johnny Cash, and they were with Sun Records," Roy recalled. "The Odessa Coliseum held about ten thousand people, and when they booked the show, either the *Louisiana Hayride* or the *Big D Jamboree*, whoever booked it, they would come on my show to plug their performance. We were invited to do the show as well, which was once about every two or three months. We went over really well at the concerts. At one particular concert, I asked Johnny about Sun Records—how it was and everything—and he gave me an address and a phone number and everything. So I called Sam Phillips, and I said, 'I talked to Johnny Cash, and he said I should call you about getting on the label.' And he said, 'Well, Johnny Cash doesn't run this operation, I do, thank you very much,' and hung up."

Johnny Cash would later give Roy some more advice: that if he changed his name and lowered his voice, he might make it in the business. Roy would tease the man who would become one of his closest friends about that advice till the day he died.

Opposite: The Wink Westerners (from left to right): Billy Pat Ellis, James Morrow, Roy Orbison, Charles Evans, and Richard West, Wink High School cafeteria, Wink, TX, 1953. **Above**: First promo photograph of Teen Kings (from left to right): Billy Pat Ellis, Roy Orbison, James Morrow, Johnny Wilson, and Jack Kennelley, May 1956.

SUN
RECORDS

U-192
VOCAL

OOBY DOOBY
(Moore & Penner)
ROY ORBISON
& TEEN KINGS
242

TENNESSEE

Chapter 2
THE SUN YEARS

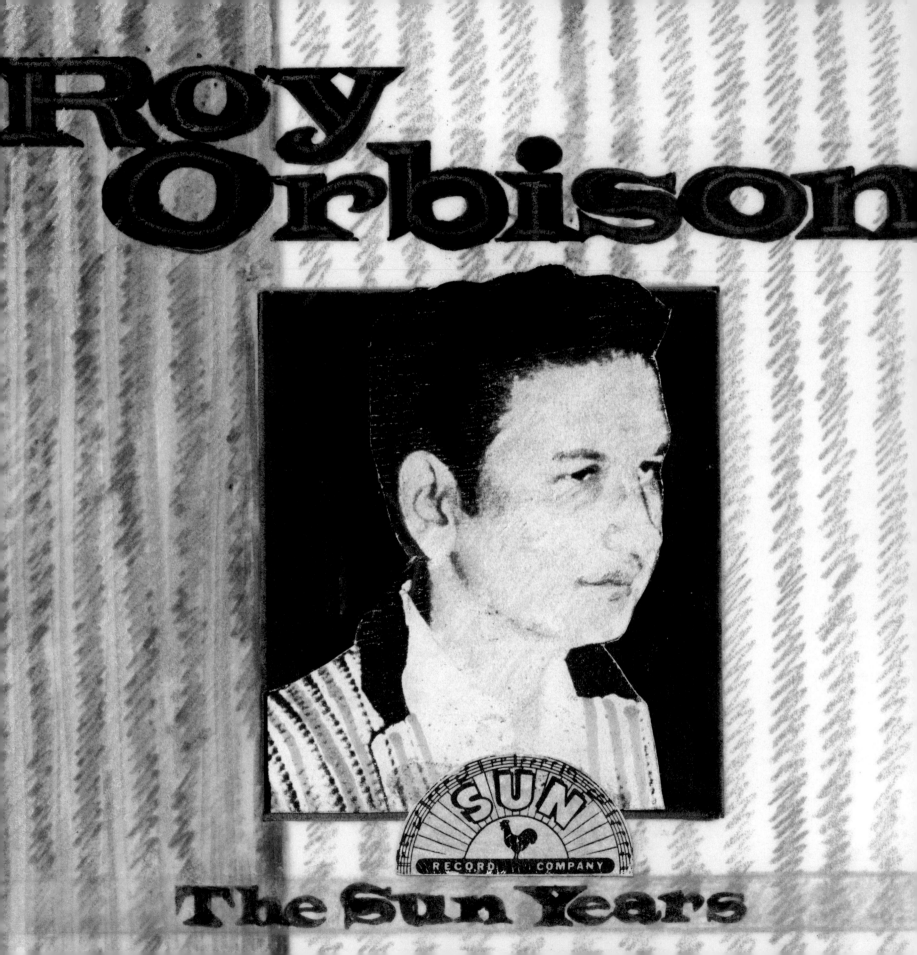

"You've gotta help me, Mr. Cash," Roy pleaded. "I just can't seem to catch a break."

Roy Orbison was desperate. He knew his single, the undeniably catchy "Ooby Dooby," recorded at Norman Petty's studio in Clovis and released on the local Odessa label Je-Wel Records, had hit potential and felt his shot at the big time slipping away. Now, with one of his heroes, the country music star Johnny Cash, appearing as a guest with Roy and the Teen Kings on the same local West Texas television show, Roy made his case.

Cash, along with Elvis Presley, Carl Perkins, Jerry Lee Lewis, and a host of other groundbreaking artists, would forever be known as part of the venerable Sun Records stable of that era. Roy loved the records the label's owner, the irascible Sam Phillips, was making, and felt that if only he could get himself and his band in front of the great man, his future wouldn't be reduced to driving a truck around the dusty roads of West Texas.

"How do I get on records?" Roy pleaded. Cash knew that Roy had a single out and was generating some heat locally, but he also knew that what young Roy was really asking was how could he get signed to *Sun* Records.

"I'll see what I can do," Cash intoned in his deep drawl. "Sam sure is a tough customer, but you hang in there, kid."

It was all the encouragement Roy needed. Three anxious days later, armed with the number Cash had given him, he called Phillips. He dropped Cash's name liberally, if gingerly, into the conversation. Johnny Wilson, the guitarist in Roy's backing group the Teen Kings, stood next to Roy expectantly, trying to hear what was going on. There was some shouting on the line, and then Wilson heard it go *click*. Roy looked at him blankly—stricken.

"What did he say?" Wilson asked.

Opposite: Hand-colored Sun Records album art mockup taken from Rhino Records' 1989 *The Sun Years*. **Right**: Roy and Sun Records founder, Sam Phillips, at the new Sam Phillips Recording studio in Memphis, TN, 1961.

Above: Roy and Billy Pat Ellis, possibly August 1956.
Opposite: (top) The Teen Kings playing at the Jal Jamboree, Jal, NM, 1956. (bottom) The Teen Kings (left to right): Jack Kennelley, James Morrow, Roy Orbison, Billy Pat Ellis, and Johnny Wilson, on tour, fall 1956.

"He said"—Roy paused and gulped—"'Tell Johnny Cash that he doesn't run Sun Records.'"

Roy was sure that was that. But then, as it so often did for Roy, fate intervened.

A local record store owner and small-time concert promoter, Cecil "Poppa" Holifield, knew Philips from way back. He'd occasionally booked Roy, as well as Elvis Presley, around the small but significant areas of Odessa and Midland, Texas, and Roy pestered him until Poppa got on Phillips's case about Roy. He played Phillips the record over the phone and told the Sun Records owner that he couldn't keep "Ooby Dooby" in stock in his record store. Then he sent Phillips a copy of the record. It worked.

The next thing Roy knew, he and the Teen Kings were on the road, jammed along with their equipment into the Oldsmobile Delta 88 that Roy had borrowed from his father, cruising as fast as they could manage to the little storefront at 706 Union Avenue in Memphis, Tennessee—the home of Phillips's Memphis Recording Service and his already legendary Sun Studio.

Roy and the Teen Kings arrived in Memphis late on Monday, March 19, 1956. With Texas sand still covering their boots, they were greeted by Sam and his secretary, Marion Keisker, and the next day they recorded a new version of "Ooby Dooby." Next, Roy and company tried their hands at "Trying to Get to You," but Phillips balked. Elvis had recently recorded it, and it just wasn't working, as far as he was concerned. After flipping through Phillips's boxes of records for something suitable to record as a flip side to "Ooby Dooby," Roy and the Teen Kings ran through a song by Roy and drummer Billy Pat Ellis, "Go, Go, Go" (later retitled "Down the Line"), which they had written during their stay at North Texas State College the year before.

"Stop! What's that you're playing? Play that again," Phillips called out from the control room. Phillips rolled tape, and Roy and the Teen Kings' "big-time" recording career was off to a fine start.

Roy played a black 1956 Gibson Les Paul Custom with Alnico and P-90 pickups on the session, and his playing on every take of "Ooby Dooby" retained the same structure and style. The song's sudden stops in Roy's instantly recognizable guitar riff make it one of the most memorable ever to come out of Sun Studios.

Although abandoned, two versions of "Trying to Get to You" have survived, showcasing the mandolin so prevalent on live recordings of the Teen Kings but almost completely absent from the groups' Sun recordings. Sadly, no alternate takes of "Go! Go! Go!" have surfaced, as it was almost certainly recorded in a single take.

With the irresistible single of "Ooby Dooby" and "Go! Go! Go!" in the can, the Teen Kings were on top of the world as the session wrapped up, and they headed downtown to the Claridge Hotel on North Main Street.

Soon Roy and his bandmates returned to Wink and school, but as "Ooby Dooby" scaled the charts and the band's promotional schedule became more demanding, they left before graduating and never looked back.

"Sun Records' distribution network was regional," Roy recalled. "It was Texas, Arkansas, Mississippi, and Alabama, really. But what they had was something no other company had, and it wasn't what you might think or what you might have read. It was that in the tradition of country music stars—who would make records or be on the Grand Ole Opry or some other show—they would go out and hit the road. [It was] the only place in the world where people would make a rock record and then go on tour. So if Johnny Cash—if Elvis

and everybody—hadn't come to Odessa to play and sing, I would've never known how to get in touch with Sun Records. It says Memphis, Tennessee, but there's no phone number."

More than being just another label, even with Elvis gone to RCA, Sun carried a certain cachet, too.

"After I recorded 'Ooby Dooby' at Sun, I went on a nationwide tour myself," Roy said later. "Everyplace I went, they said, 'Who do you record for?'" When he told them Sun, every single one of them was in awe. Just being on the label meant you were a star.

By July, "Ooby Dooby" had sold 250,000 copies and had reached Number 59 on the charts. In the May 19, 1956, edition of *Billboard*, the record industry trade magazine, "Ooby Dooby" got a favorable write-up, stating that "Orbison's spectacular, untamed quality spells big action for both sides of this new disking. The top side is already getting healthy initial reaction and regardless of competition, figures to cash in for plenty of loot in the rural sectors. The flip is wild, swingin' country blues with an impressive flavor. Either one here."

Above: (top) Roy jamming with James Morrow (second from left) and unidentified friends, circa 1955. **Left**: Canadian Quality single of "Ooby Dooby." Picture shows B-side "Go! Go! Go!" Quality Records was Sun Records' faithful ally in Canada.
Opposite: Various early news clippings and photos of the Teen Kings.

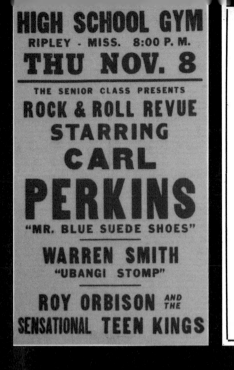

VOLUME 19   NUMBER 45   FIVE CENTS PER COPY   WINK, WINKLER COUNTY, TEXAS

HIT RECORD MAKERS—The Teen Kings of Odessa, formerly the Wink Westerners, have a sure-fire hit record in "Ooby Dooby" and "Go, Go, Go," according to Billboard and The Cash Box Magazines. The record was made early in April for Sun Record Co. in Memphis and is heading for top place in the nation, the magazines forecast. It is a western rhythm rock 'n roll. Pictured are left to right, front row: Johnny Wilson, Roy Orbison, leader; Cecil Hollifield, their sponsor, who arranged the record-making; back row,

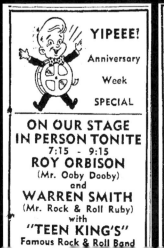

They were right. "Ooby Dooby" was a solid A-side, and "Go! Go! Go!" was a classic rock-abilly barnburner that proved its staying power when Roy's future labelmate Jerry Lee Lewis went on to record the song two years later.

Billed as "the new sensation," Roy and the Teen Kings embarked on a grueling tour, traveling all the way from Canada to El Paso in Roy's father's '55 Oldsmobile and guitarist Johnny Wilson's '55 Chevrolet Bel Air, with a trailer attached, bringing up the rear. By the end of May, they found themselves in one of the poshest venues they'd ever played. Along with fellow Sun artists Johnny Cash and Carl Perkins, who had appeared on the nationwide *Perry Como Show* the day before, they entertained a crowd of 5,000 at Richmond, Virginia's luxurious Mosque theater.

After a series of one-nighters, the band members found themselves back in Memphis on Friday, June 1, at the city's Overton Park Shell. By that time, the Teen Kings had honed their stage act. While Roy delivered the goods at center stage, the band put on a wild show behind him. They'd developed choreographed moves, looking one way, then the other way, then up and down, all while the song was going on. Audiences loved it. That night, along with Carl "Mr. Blue Suede Shoes" Perkins, Johnny Cash, Warren Smith, and Eddie Bond, Roy and the Teen Kings found themselves with a Number One record on the local charts and Elvis himself in the crowd.

"Elvis came backstage," Roy recalled later. "He said, 'Marvelous show.' And he said, 'I'll tell you one thing, you were just that good that I'll never appear onstage with you.' It was a nice compliment. That was his nice way of saying that he liked what I did."

"We went to a few parties and things together," Roy remembered of the King. "And one night we went by to pick up Elvis's girlfriend, and he had a new purple Cadillac with purple fur and everything in it. And I think he was making $20 million a year at the time. And he knocked on the door, and the girl said, 'I'm sorry, you are too late,' turned around, and walked back in. We all went on to his house and had Pepsi-Colas and potato chips, and I couldn't believe that some woman would turn down a date with Elvis Presley."

Roy also recalled getting together to party and jam. "We didn't know that all these history-making events were taking place, I guess because we were too caught up with what we were doing," he said. "Jerry Lee would walk in and sit down at the piano, and I would say, 'Do you know 'If You've Got the Money, I've Got the Time,' for instance, and he'd sing and play it." They were really just kids having fun.

A few weeks later, in mid-June, Roy and the Teen Kings appeared on KCMC-TV in Texarkana, Texas, where the host, Cowboy John, interviewed Roy and Johnny Cash. Though the

ELVIS CAME BACKSTAGE AND SAID, "MARVELOUS SHOW. I'LL TELL YOU ONE THING, YOU WERE JUST THAT GOOD THAT I'LL NEVER APPEAR ON STAGE WITH YOU."

—ROY ORBISON

Opposite: Sun Records single #242, "Ooby Dooby," released May 1, 1956.

event does provide us with the earliest known photo of the friends and labelmates, Roy and Johnny were disappointed that Elvis, who had been expected to join them, was a no-show.

Soon, *The Ed Sullivan Show* expressed an interest in booking Roy. Though the appearance never materialized, Roy and the Teen Kings were on their way. Because of "Ooby Dooby"'s huge sales, along with Carl Perkins and Johnny Cash, Roy and the boys became the best-selling artists on Sun.

"Ooby Dooby" finally dropped from the charts on August 4, and soon Sam Phillips was on Roy's case to deliver a follow-up single. That follow-up was recorded during one of their stays in Memphis in the late summer. The songs, "You're My Baby" and "Rockhouse," seemed like just the thing that Roy and the Teen Kings needed to keep the momentum going.

Johnny Cash had given Roy a song called "Little Woolly Booger" while on tour together, which Roy refashioned as "You're My Baby," though there's some confusion as to how the flip side, "Rockhouse," came about. The copyright claims "Orbison-Jenkins," although the two never sat down to write the song together. Harold Jenkins, who later became famous as Conway Twitty, was trying to get a shot at recording for Sun Records at the time and had made a few recordings there. He had written and recorded a song called "Rockhouse," which was the

WELL YA WIGGLE TO THE LEFT,
YOU WIGGLE TO THE RIGHT
DO THE OOBY DOOBY WITH ALL OF YOUR MIGHT

theme song for his band, the Rockhousers. That was also about the time that Roy recorded his own song called "Rockhouse." By all accounts, Roy's "Rockhouse" was written about a spot back near home in Wink—at the Archway in the town of Monahans, which was made of rocks—and though the songs are different, they do have similarities. Both are about a rockin' club made out of rocks, where the music is loud. The most likely scenario is that Roy heard the song at Sun and refashioned it to his liking, duly earning his cowriter credit.

The single of "You're My Baby" backed with "Rockhouse" was released on September 24 as Sun number 251. Although *Billboard* gave it a favorable review, probably owing to its primitive, countrified sound, it failed to make the charts.

Meanwhile, the tour went on, with a series of one-night stands and local radio and television appearances. The surviving recordings of those appearances show Roy and the Teen Kings in fine form, performing rocking versions of "Ooby Dooby," "Go! Go! Go!," and "Rockhouse," along with a couple of original instrumentals, a few popular tunes such as "Rip It Up," released by Little Richard in June 1956, "Singing the Blues," a then-current hit by Guy Mitchell, and Chuck Berry's "Brown Eyed Handsome Man," which had been released in September of that year, among others. More than the Sun recordings, they're evidence of the raw energy the Teen Kings displayed onstage.

Roy was also writing songs whenever he could. If he found himself with a free moment—in hotel rooms between tour dates or even when the group stopped alongside the road—he would sit and pick at his guitar, trying to come up with new material. As a result, his songwriting started to flourish, and he had some new songs to play for Sam Phillips the next time he saw him, including "Sweet and Easy to Love," "Devil Doll," and "So Long, I'm Gone."

Roy's next recording session was on December 14, and by all accounts he was looking to change his sound. He wasn't happy with the direction in which Sam Phillips was pushing him, and he felt he'd outgrown the Teen Kings; with the days of hard life on the road taking their toll, they surely must have known. Before the session began, while Roy and Sam were next door at Taylor's Cafe, the Teen Kings packed up their gear and drove back to Texas without saying a word. With some good times, great records, and thousands of grueling miles behind them, it was all over.

"Sam Phillips decided he wanted to push a name and not a band," Teen King Jack Kennelley recalled later. "We were all in a conspiracy against Roy," fellow Teen King Billy Pat Ellis added. "We had finished up a tour and didn't have anything else booked. It was in December, and I remember we were at the Sun Records studio and we had it all planned out that when Roy was gone

Opposite: (left to right) Johnny Cash, Cowboy John Garner, and Roy Orbison on KCMC-TV in Texarkana, TX, July 16, 1956, before a *Louisiana Hayride* appearance the same night. **Above**: Promo poster for Roy's first chart hit, "Ooby Dooby," as printed in *Billboard* magazine.

we were just gonna cut out. I remember Sam Phillips and Roy were at the little café next door that they used to go to, and we loaded up, and just pulled out without saying a word."

When Roy and Sam returned to the studio, they were shocked to find the rest of the band gone. Sam tried to persuade Roy to go ahead with the session, but Roy balked and the recording date was called off. Roy stayed on in Memphis, bunking at Sam Phillips's house, but he wouldn't record again for several months. Then, in February, he returned to Sun to record "Sweet and Easy to Love," "Devil Doll" and "Fools Hall of Fame," using Sun studio musicians and some backup singers from Odessa called the Four Roses.

"Roy asked us to go with him to cut a couple of singles at a studio in Memphis," singer David Bigham recalled. "We did both songs in about four or five takes. We had rehearsed them prior to going to Memphis, so everyone knew their parts, which made the sessions very easy. But after the sessions, he said they didn't like the sound."

With Sam busy elsewhere, Cowboy Jack Clement, who had also engineered the "Rockhouse" session, sat in the control room. The Sun studio musicians that day were Roland Janes on guitar, Jimmy Van Eaton on drums, Stan Kesler on bass, and Jimmy Smith on piano. Between 1956 and 1963, those musicians were part of the "Sun band" and recorded with virtually everyone who walked through the studio's doors. Roland was one of the anchors of that band, and in those seven years he played on the majority of Jerry Lee Lewis's 150-plus Sun recordings, was a founding member of Billy Lee Riley and His Little Green Men, and backed up a host of lesser-known Sun artists, such as Charlie Rich, Sonny Burgess, and Barbara Pittman. He also backed Roy on most of his remaining Sun sessions, though Roy still always played lead guitar.

"Sweet and Easy to Love" backed with "Devil Doll" was released in March 1957 as Sun number 265 in both 45 RPM and 78 RPM formats. The label read "Roy Orbison and the Roses." *Billboard* picked "Devil Doll" as the hot side and reviewed it on April 20, calling it "a swingy song, with an unusual lyric. Orbison chants this solidly. It's backed with chorus and an instrumental combo that contributes a fine beat. Will get attention."

The single sold only a few thousand copies, though, and, as Roy's previous release hadn't even made the charts, Sam's attention moved on to other acts. The recordings, however, marked the change in style Roy had been looking for. They sport beautiful vocal work by the Roses, who would be with him for the next year, and tighter musicianship, not to mention better production overall.

Below: The Roses—Robert Linville, Ray Rush, and David Bigham—in a promo photo circa 1957.
Opposite: Norman Petty in his studio. Roy recorded his first single release here, "Trying to Get to You" backed with "Ooby Dooby," released on Je-Wel Records briefly before the Teen Kings' first Sun Records single.

Roy never really lived in Memphis, but after the Teen Kings left him, he decided to stay in town. In 1957, he appeared on the local TV hit show *Top Ten Dance Party* on WHBQ in Memphis, hosted by Wink Martindale and Susan Bancroft. Though he continued touring, he typically returned to Memphis, staying with Sam Phillips, Johnny Cash, or Carl Perkins while there. He also spent quite a bit of his free time hanging around the studio, though his own recording sessions were few and far between. During 1957 and 1958, he did, however, play and sing on a number of records by other artists, including Jerry Lee Lewis's "Fools like Me."

"I don't think people generally know how good a guitar player Roy was," Sam Phillips recalled years later. "He used a lot of the bass strings. He would do a lot of combination string stuff, but it was all real good. Also, Roy had probably the best ear for a beat of anybody I recorded outside of Jerry Lee Lewis. Roy would take his guitar by himself, and if we had a session going, he would come in early and pick an awful lot, just warming up and getting his fingers working. His timing would amaze me, with him playing lead and filling in with some rhythm licks. I would kid him about it: 'Roy, what you're trying to do is to get rid of everybody else and do it all yourself?' But Roy just hated to lay his guitar down. He was always either writing or developing a beat or an approach to what he was doing. He was totally preoccupied with making records at that time."

In early 1957, Roy pitched one of his new songs, "So Long, I'm Gone," to fellow Sun artist Warren Smith. Smith's recording entered the *Billboard* charts on June 10, peaking at Number 72 on June 17. For Roy, more than anything, it meant that much-needed royalties would be coming his way. He also kept playing on package tours with other Sun artists.

ROY HAD PROBABLY THE BEST EAR FOR A BEAT OF ANYBODY I RECORDED OUTSIDE OF JERRY LEE LEWIS. —SAM PHILLIPS

"I remember Roy minded his own business," remembered Sun labelmate Jerry Lee Lewis, who would soon become a superstar on the heels of a huge promotional push by Phillips. "He always kept to himself, pretty much. He might come by just to say hello, hug your neck real nice, and get out of your hair. He was that kind of person. He was a pretty nice guy, and he sang his butt off."

Roy later remembered the package shows with fondness. But after touring with fellow rockers Eddie Cochran and Gene Vincent, he also became more determined than ever to develop his craft.

"When I was on tour in '56, '57, with Eddie Cochran and Gene Vincent, all around on these package shows, there would be acts with only one song," Roy later recalled. "I never wanted to be in the position where the only thing I could do was something I had already done. So I started writing songs. When I first started touring with guys like Eddie and Gene, I wondered where the material would come from to sustain their success. I just figured I'd write my own. On the road to becoming a true and deserving professional, my songwriting ability came along to go with my singing. It was a blessing and a gift."

"I met Claudette at the television station in Midland," Roy said of an encounter that would change his life.

Roy and Claudette Frady were introduced by Jack Kennelley at KMID-TV at the end of 1955, while he and the Teen Kings had their weekly TV show there. She was born on September 5, 1941, in Odessa, Ector County, Texas.

"We used to call good-looking women 'queens.' So I went to check the mail, I think it was, and I saw this good-looking girl and I went back and told the rest of the group. They hadn't packed up yet. I said, 'Boy, there's a queen outside, you gotta come see this.' So we all went out, and the bass player said, 'Yeah, that's my date for today.' So we got in the car and he put his big bass fiddle in the car, then he kissed her good-bye and that was it. And then she used to call the apartment—by then I was living in Odessa—and wanted to talk to the bass man. And I told her she couldn't, and she thought I was very rude. And I'd say, 'I was just teasing you,' and I'd let her talk to him. Then he started dating someone else, and I started dating her. So that was in 1956. And then I got this call from the management company to go on this first tour. So I left West Texas and my sweetheart and all that and went on tour. I told her I was gonna go be a personality, I was gonna be a star or something. And I said, 'When I get back, if we're still cool, we'll get married.' So in 1957 we were married."

Above: (top) Claudette Frady and Roy Orbison pose outside Roy's house in Wink, TX, 1956. (bottom) Roy's parents, Orbie Lee and Nadine, with Claudette.

To my beloved Roy,
All my love forever,
Claudette

According to Sam Phillips, it was Claudette who helped Roy get over things when the Teen Kings split up in December 1956. "He called her up, and she came in town," he remembered. "They stayed a long time. I said, 'Look, you're not company in my house. You get up and do, you cook and here's where the eggs are and there's where this is, you know, and feel at home.' They weren't married at the time, and they didn't sleep together when they stayed with us."

Years later, Sam's son Knox, who was twelve at the time, remembered the time fondly. "We had a pinball machine and pool table in the den and a big dining table in the kitchen," he said of the family home in Memphis. "We all sat around the table and talked for hours, and Roy played pinball with me and let me win some games. All the kids in the neighborhood were in awe of Claudette. She was the most beautiful thing that had ever walked around this vicinity, especially when she wore her green-and-gold dress. One night Elvis Presley showed up unannounced, and Mother and Claudette fixed a big meal, despite the hour."

Carl Perkins remembered Roy carrying a picture of Claudette in his wallet and calling her every day while they were on tour, and he gave his friend some advice.

"You're gonna fool around and be out here on the road, and you're gonna go back to Wink one of these times, and as pretty as she is, some ol' long-legged cowboy's gonna have her around the waist," Perkins told Roy. "If she loves you like you say she does, and if you love her like I'm believin' you do, you better go back to Wink and forget how you gonna live. That will fall in place. Instead of that hamburger you chewin' on there, tear it in two and give Claudette half of it. And both of you can live on love and half a hamburger. It'd work. You can do it."

Roy took the advice. During 1957, Roy and Claudette alternated staying with Carl, Johnny Cash, Sam Phillips, and their parents in West Texas, and they finally got married on June 21, 1957, at a ceremony at the Church of Christ in Kermit. Soon after, Claudette was pregnant.

In September, Roy's first UK release, "Hillbilly Rock," hit the stores. The four-track extended play record featured Roy's first two Sun singles, "Ooby Dooby" and "Go! Go! Go!," "You're My Baby," and "Rockhouse." Though it didn't sell much at first, it would be reissued several times between 1957 and 1965 and hinted at the huge success Roy would find in Great Britain.

By October, Roy was back in Memphis for five days of recording sessions at Sun, his first as a married man. The sessions, which took place on the sixteenth, seventeenth, nineteenth, twenty-first, and twenty-second, were his first in months, and Sam Phillips was clamoring for a new single. Sun regulars Roland Janes on guitar, Stan Kesler and Sid Manker on bass, Otis Jett on drums, Jimmy Smith and Jimmy Wilson on piano, and Martin Willis on tenor sax ac-

Opposite: "To my beloved Roy. All my love forever, Claudette," circa 1957. **Above**: (top) Claudette and Roy in Wink, TX, circa 1957. (bottom) Claudette at home beside a portrait of her soon-to-be-husband, September 1956.

companied Roy, and the sessions were engineered by Cowboy Jack Clement and had Bill Justis as musical director.

Clement and Justis convinced Roy to record two of their own compositions. "I came to town to record, and Jack and Bill Justis teamed up to record me," Roy recalled. "I had two or three songs written, and they said, 'Let's have a bite to eat.' As we were eating, Bill and Jack both said, 'Look, the material you brought is not up to par. We've got a couple of songs that we think are really right for you.' So we went back to the studio, and I cut a couple of the worst recordings in the history of the world!"

The kicker was that Clement infamously told Roy never to record a ballad and that his voice just wasn't suited to them.

Roy detested the songs, "Chicken Hearted" and "I Like Love," but with them already in the can and Clement and Justis on his case, Phillips insisted on releasing the single.

The other songs recorded during the sessions were knockouts but sadly sat in the can, unreleased, for years. Roy's rockin' "Mean Little Mama," which became a rockabilly classic, was fantastic, and its release might have changed his fortunes and set his relationship with Sun on a far different path had it seen the light of day. The other songs, "Problem Child" and Roy's "A True Love Goodbye," were also far superior to his imminent single.

Sun number 284, "Chicken Hearted" backed with "I Like Love," was released in December 1957 and was a flop. On the heels of the Jerry Lee Lewis monster smash "Great Balls of Fire," it just could not compete.

Not surprisingly, Roy was growing disillusioned with Sun. He wanted to do his own thing—and record the new songs he'd been writing furiously—but really it came down to business.

"They had us on a three percent thing, when it was common practice in the industry to pay five percent," Roy said later. "Johnny and Elvis and Jerry Lee and all of us were on three percent, and everything we wrote, naturally, Sam Phillips published. I remember being in New Mexico, playing a show, and a fella named Slim Willet, who wrote a song called 'Don't Let the Stars Get in Your Eyes,' asked me, 'How is your BMI running?' and I said, 'I don't understand the question.' He said, 'When they play your record on a radio station, they are supposed to pay you.' And he told me how much he made on 'Don't Let the Stars Get in Your Eyes.' I told Carl Perkins about it, and he said, 'I don't believe that, I'm going straight to Memphis right now, you wanna go?' and I said, 'Yes.' But by that time we had all decided to leave."

Opposite: The "Hillbilly Rock" EP, Roy's first release in the UK, September 1957. **Above**: Roy Orbison on set for BBC television show, *Top of the Pops*, England, 1964.

65

Roy and Carl raced to Memphis to talk to Sam Phillips about what Roy had discovered: that BMI—Broadcast Music, Inc.—one of the three performing rights organizations in the United States, paid songwriters performance royalties. The confrontation did not go well.

Still, Roy went back into Sun Studio on Saturday, January 4, and again on Friday, January 10, 1958. That time he was there to record demos of some of the new songs he had written, including "You Tell Me," "I Give Up," "One More Time," "Love Struck," "The Clown," and "Claudette." There was no doubt about it; given that clutch of fantastic songs, it was obvious that his writing was developing in leaps and bounds.

Meanwhile, with Claudette back at home, six months pregnant, he needed to pay the bills. So, on March 2, he found himself in Hammond, Indiana, for two shows at the Hammond Civic Center. On the bill were the Everly Brothers and also Warren Smith, Carl Perkins, and Don Gibson. The hand of fate was also present, though Roy couldn't have known it at the time.

Backstage after the show, Don and Phil Everly told Roy they'd liked "Ooby Dooby." Roy was equally impressed with the duo and told them he loved their records, too. Soon everyone was pitching songs. As he was about to leave, Phil Everly asked Roy if he had some songs they might consider recording. "I said, 'I've got *one* song,'" Roy recalled later. "I sat down and sang it for them, and they liked it very much and wrote the lyrics down on top of a shoebox. Took it back to Nashville and recorded it."

The song was "Claudette," and it became the B-Side to the Everlys' smash "All I Have to Do Is Dream," as well as a hit for them in its own right.

Not long after that, Jerry Lee Lewis recorded Roy's "Go! Go! Go!" for the B-side of his soon-to-be-smash-hit "Breathless," rechristening the track "Down the Line." The single was released as Sun number 288 in February 1958; combined with the success of the Everly Brothers, Roy was fast becoming a hot commodity as a songwriter.

"I think I had come of age," Roy recalled of the period. "I didn't know that there was money in writing. So the success of 'Claudette' prompted me to start writing more seriously. Financially, it was very rewarding."

All that couldn't have happened at a better time. Roy's first son, Roy DeWayne Orbison, was born on Friday, April 18, 1958, in Winkler County, Texas, but soon Roy was back on the road, trying to keep his family afloat. The royalties just weren't coming in. On top of that, the Everly Brothers' management had told Roy that unless Acuff-Rose, Phil and Don's publisher, was allowed to publish "Claudette," the deal to include the song as a B-side on their next single was off. Roy knew that connecting with the venerable Acuff-Rose company would open doors for him in a way that Sam Phillips never could.

So Roy confronted Phillips. "Mr. Phillips, I know you've got the publishing on 'Claudette,'" he began. "I've got the chance to get the Everly Brothers to record it, but they are under contract to a Nashville publishing company, and if they do it they'll have to have the publishing rights, otherwise they won't do it."

"'Okay, Roy,' Phillips said. "You go ahead. We'll work out a deal."

The "deal" he was talking about unfortunately required Roy to sign over the rights to all his songs recorded during his years at Sun to Phillips, except for "Claudette." It was a lousy deal by any stretch, and even today, every Sun Records rerelease credits Roy's songs to Sam Phillips. But Roy wanted out and agreed.

At Sun, Roy was not only one of a stable of young rockabilly artists who became lost in the shuffle after his first hit and wasn't getting paid; the combination, on top of all the hard hours on the road, was simply too much.

In the end, most of the recordings Roy made for Phillips and Sun wouldn't see the light of day until years later, when Phillips sought to take advantage of Roy's hard-won stardom. Though Roy's years at Sun didn't make him the star that Elvis, Johnny Cash, Carl Perkins, and Jerry Lee Lewis became, it put him into enviable company. And in many ways, Roy fared better than his labelmates.

As the 1960s dawned, Elvis was driving an army jeep in Germany, Johnny Cash had become a victim of his addictions, Carl Perkins's career had stalled after the smash success of "Blue Suede Shoes" and a nearly deadly subsequent car crash, and Jerry Lee Lewis, after marrying his teenage third cousin, had become a pariah. But Roy was on the cusp of superstardom, with a Sun pedigree under his belt to boot.

Releasing "Oh, Pretty Woman" and headlining tours of the United Kingdom with the Beatles were in the not-so-distant future. Though Roy couldn't have imagined it at the time, as a result of his hard work and dedication, he would need the black shades that would soon become his trademark more than ever in the years to come.

Opposite: (top) Claudette with Johnny Horton at one of Roy's performances, 1957. (bottom) Claudette and Roy with their first son, Roy DeWayne, Wink, TX, summer 1958. **Above**: British sheet music for the Everly Brothers's recording of Roy Orbison's "Claudette."

ROY WAS ON THE CUSP OF SUPERSTARDOM, WITH A SUN PEDIGREE UNDER HIS BELT TO BOOT.

Chapter 3

THE MONUMENT YEARS
AND STARDOM IN THE UNITED KINGDOM

From the beginning, Roy had been lost amid the stable of stars in the making at Sun

Records. Elvis, Johnny Cash, Jerry Lee Lewis, even Carl Perkins, were easy for the overworked, understaffed Sam Phillips to market. Still, losing Roy was one of the true regrets of his storied career. "I really have to take the blame for not bringing Roy to fruition," he recalled. "It's still my regret that I didn't do more promotion for him."

"The money had something to do with it, getting paid or not getting paid," said Roy of the split with the man who had given him his big break. "By the time I left Sun, I wanted to sing the material I eventually wound up singing a couple of years later. It's the reason Presley left. It's the reason we all did."

Wesley Rose, the president of Acuff-Rose, had proposed a broader deal, according to which Roy would leave Sun and join Acuff-Rose in Nashville as a staff songwriter, while they tried to land Roy a better record deal with a label that had bigger budgets for recording and more staff for promotion. To Roy it seemed like a dream come true.

Released from his Sun Records contract, Roy was suddenly on his way. The Everly Brothers' version of "Claudette" was released in short order. About two weeks later, with the song blanketing the airwaves, Roy called Wesley Rose. "How's the record doing?" he asked. "Oh, it sold a half a million already," Rose replied. "Have I made any money?" Roy asked. "Why, yes, you have," Rose told the thrilled Roy, who promptly asked for $500. Rose told him it would be in the mail immediately.

Rose appeared to be a man of his word. In their first meeting he had told Roy that if things didn't work out between them, they could simply tear their contract up. Roy felt good about the new situation, a far cry from battling tooth and nail with Sam Phillips over every penny.

Acuff-Rose, headquartered at 2510 Franklin Road in the Melrose district of Nashville, was formed in 1942 by Grand Ole Opry superstar Roy Acuff and veteran songwriter Fred Rose, a respected talent scout. The publishing firm specialized in country music and quickly became one of the genre's most successful publishers.

Previous Pages: Roy on tour in the UK with Gerry and the Pacemakers and the Beatles, 1963.
Opposite: Claudette, Roy, and Roy DeWayne, Hendersonville, TN, May 1961.

FRED FOSTER, THE MAN WHO'D STARTED MONUMENT IN 1958 . . . WOULD MAKE ROY A STAR.

Wesley Rose started off life as an accountant in Chicago and was working with Standard Oil Company when his father, Fred Rose, invited him to join Acuff-Rose in 1945. After Fred Rose's passing in 1954, Wesley became Acuff-Rose's president.

In April 1958, Roy hit the road with superstar Patsy Cline. Rose had booked Roy on the Country Music Spectacular, featuring Cline, Justin Tubb, Carl Perkins, and Bob Wills and His Texas Playboys, one of Roy's earliest inspirations. They traveled through Nebraska and Iowa. Afterward, Roy hit the road in Texas and New Mexico with Johnny Cash and Don Gibson.

Meanwhile, Rose was hard at work on Roy's behalf. Hot on the heels of the success of "Claudette," he secured a recording contract with RCA Victor and legendary country guitarist Chet Atkins, whom Roy had been pestering for months for a chance to work together.

"We did some pretty good records, but they were typical Nashville at that time, and we didn't reach out and try to do something different," Atkins would later recall. "I blame myself for that. I should have seen the greatness in him and the quality of his voice."

Atkins had been named RCA's manager of operations in Nashville in early 1957. Feeling limited by the label's old studios on McGavock Street, he and Steve Sholes, who was first the head of RCA's country division, and then RCA's pop singles manager, convinced the label to build a new studio. Located on the corner of 17th Avenue and Hawkins, it would become the first major label facility in town.

The studio was housed in a small building, with offices occupying the front and a long hallway that led to a control room and then the studio itself. The second story contained an echo chamber. It was considerably larger than Sun Studio, though, with walls covered in one-foot-square acoustic tiles all the way to the ceiling. The control room sported a custom-made RCA broadcast-type tube mixing console and single-track Ampex tape machines. Most of the microphones used were top-of-the-line German-made Neumanns. For its time the studio was state of the art.

Flush with the royalties from "Claudette," in June Roy bought a Cadillac, moved to Nashville with Claudette and the baby, and rented a second-floor apartment at 8th Avenue South, close to the Acuff-Rose offices, not far from what is now Music Row.

After one last session at Sun in early September, Roy's first RCA session was scheduled for Monday, September 29, 1958. Three songs were recorded, including "Seems to Me," "Sweet and Innocent," and "I'll Never Tell." None of the songs recorded during that session had been written by Roy; they were chosen by Wesley Rose. Many of the musicians who recorded with Roy that day would end up playing with him for the next decade. Chet Atkins produced the session and played guitar, as did Ray Edenton and Walter "Hank" Garland, with Jerry Byrd on bass, Buddy Harman on drums, and Floyd Cramer on piano. The Jordanaires sang backup vocals.

"Seems To Me" and "Sweet and Innocent" were released the following month, and the single was "Pick of the Week" in *Billboard* on October 20. As on his Sun recordings, Roy's voice sounded shy, thin, and fragile.

Roy started building a catalog for Acuff-Rose, cutting demos of the songs he was churning out, including "Daylight," "I'm to Blame," "Little Boy Blue," "Defeated," and "Night Owl." Another song, "Almost Eighteen," was by far the best of the bunch and was recorded during his second session with Atkins for RCA; it was released as a single in January 1959.

Times were tough for Roy and Claudette, though. They'd gone through Roy's "Claudette" royalties, and with Roy off the road, money was tight. New to Nashville, their social life was virtually nonexistent, so the pair were relegated to the occasional drive-in movie or industry event, such as the DJ convention that Roy attended with Johnny Cash in November.

Finally, after a few months of practically starving and two flop singles, Roy sold his beloved Cadillac. He, Claudette, and their baby moved back to West Texas, and Roy went back out on the road.

Despite those disappointments, Roy headed into the studio on his birthday, Thursday, April 23, 1959, for what was to be his final RCA session. He brought with him two original songs, "With the Bug," an adaptation of an old Teen Kings number, and "Paper Boy," which later on he would refer to as partially autobiographical, since he had been a paperboy early in his life.

"When I had the Teen Kings, we had this number called 'The Bug,' where we had an imaginary bug we would throw on each other," Roy recalled in 1988. "When it hit you, you had to shake and stuff. So I shook for a while, but I wasn't very successful at it. That phase of the career didn't last too long."

"I can't do what I need to do for you," Atkins told the frustrated singer when Roy's final RCA recordings were shelved.

By chance, Wesley Rose soon ran into Fred Foster, the man who'd started Monument in 1958. Asked by Roy's manager if he'd like to sign the struggling singer, Foster jumped at the chance. The move would make Roy a star.

Foster was born in Appalachia on July 26, 1931. After moving to Washington, DC, at seventeen, while working in a small restaurant he met a customer named Ben Edelman, a music

Above: Roy with Monument Records founder and life-long friend, Fred Foster, May 1961. **Following pages**: Roy at the Riverside Ballroom in Phoenix, AZ, September 29, 1960.

Above: Roy pioneered the concept of the isolated vocal booth using a coat rack and blankets inside RCA Studio B in Nashville during the "Blue Angel" session, August 8, 1960. **Opposite**: (top) Roy Orbison, Fred Foster, and the Nashville A-Team, including Bob Moore on bass, Harold Bradley on guitar, and the Anita Kerr singers recording at RCA Studio B in Nashville during the "Blue Angel" session. (bottom) Promo advertisement for Roy's single "Uptown."

publisher, which led Foster to a job as a promotion man for Mercury Records. After finding what he knew was his life's calling, Foster gathered his life savings, and in September 1958 he started Monument Records. A string of hits followed.

Meanwhile, Foster had met Wesley Rose in Baltimore and had kept in touch with the publisher. A few weeks later Rose called Foster.

"Do you know who Roy Orbison is?" Rose asked.

"Well, if he's the guy that did that thing called 'Ooby Dooby' and that other thing called 'Rockhouse,' I know who he is,' Foster replied.

"Would you like to have him? I'm taking him off RCA," Rose said. Foster jumped at the chance.

The songwriter Boudleaux Bryant once said of the jump from the world-renowned RCA to the upstart independent label Monument that "Roy probably thought it was like trading a mule for a picture of a racehorse." In fact it was a match made in heaven.

In short order, "Paper Boy" and "With the Bug," among Roy's first recordings for Monument, were released in September 1959. Billboard gave "Paper Boy" four stars, calling it, "a sad ballad nicely performed by Orbison." It was yet another important step forward.

Soon Roy was collaborating with fellow Texan Joe Melson, a partnership that began with "I'm Lost," "Too Bad," "Cry Baby," and "Show Me So" and would come to include roughly a hundred other Orbison-Melson songs written for Acuff-Rose over the next couple of years. Along the way, Roy was developing his chops as a singer and a writer. But it was "Uptown" that turned the tide.

"Look, I think we've got something really good here, but we are gonna have to use strings," Roy told Foster of the song he'd just written. Although Wesley Rose had balked at the cost, Foster readily agreed. He hired Anita Kerr to write an arrangement and contracted four players from the Nashville Symphony for the session.

"I don't know if his confidence had been shaken by being on RCA and then pulled off or dropped or whatever happened, but he was sort of timid and not really projecting really well," Foster recalled later. "We got to 'Uptown' and we had strings now and everything, and I was really having trouble. And I asked Bill Porter, the engineer, what would happen if we put Roy over in the corner and pulled the coat rack in front of him to keep the band out of his microphone. He said 'I don't know, we can try.' So not only did we pull the coat rack over and put coats in it, but there were blankets back in the maintenance room, and we got those so we really isolated that corner. It worked great."

"Uptown" became Roy's first hit for Monument, albeit a modest one, named "Pick of the Week" by *Billboard* on November 30, 1959.

"Roy's voice was very thin-sounding in the beginning," engineer Bill Porter wrote in his liner notes for the *All-Time Greatest Hits of Roy Orbison*. "It didn't have much body to it, and you couldn't make it stand out in the mix, especially in those big arrangements with strings and voices. I had to come up with some way to fatten up his voice. I used some slap echo on his vocals basically, taking a slap back from the 3-track machine with his voice on one track, and fed it back into the console with a slight repetitive echo. It was the first time I ever used that technique on Orbison recordings. This was very subtle and his voice got better over the years, I eventually didn't need it anymore."

"'Only the Lonely' wasn't the original title of the song," Roy told the Australian journalist Glenn A. Baker of the Orbison-Melson masterpiece that would finally put Roy on the map. "I called Fred and said, 'Okay, here's what it's called' and he said, 'Pat Boone just released a song called that.'" Frustrated, the pair knocked out "Only the Lonely" in ten minutes. "We'd already worked on the other song for months," said Roy. "I called Fred and I said, 'Look, here is the title of the song. I don't care if it's out now, if it was out yesterday, if it was a smash, if it is a smash right now. It don't make any difference, this is what it's called.'"

The pair headed for Nashville on Sunday, March 20, 1960, driving a borrowed watermelon truck. On the way they stopped by Graceland to play the song for Elvis, who was fresh out of the army and in need of material. Leaving a note with the guard at the gate, Roy got a reply that Elvis would have to see them in Nashville. The Everlys would also pass on the song.

Ready to cut the song as soon as he arrived in Nashville, Roy was frustrated to find that Elvis had the studio booked solid for the next three days.

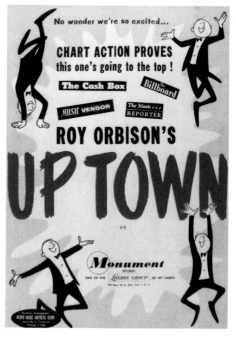

No wonder we're so excited...

CHART ACTION PROVES this one's going to the top!

The Cash Box   Billboard
MUSIC VENDOR   The Music REPORTER

ROY ORBISON'S

UP TOWN

Monument RECORDS
ONE OF THE *LONDON GROUP* OF HIT LABELS

Above: Dynamic songwriting duo, Joe Melson and Roy Orbison, at Roy's home, Hendersonville, TN, May 1961. **Opposite**: Promo advertisement for Roy's song, "Only the Lonely," written with Joe Melson.

"I had to wait three days, cooling my heels, while my good friend was in there with all the money in the world, and I didn't have a dime to my name," Roy would recall in 1980.

"By the time I finally got to record 'Only the Lonely' I was ready to do it because there was something that was keeping everybody away from me, and everybody away from that song," Roy said of the session that began on Friday the twenty-fifth. "I figured that maybe the song would be Top 20—that was what I guessed—but I didn't tell anybody."

Using the lessons he'd learned on their previous session, engineer Bill Porter started building his mix around the vocals, rather than the rhythm section. It established the soft, breathy sound that became a trademark of Roy's music.

"Only the Lonely" was the first song to truly probe the potential of Roy's voice, and it established his unique style. Roy's voice was crystal clear, and the falsetto at the end of the song was remarkable. With the instantly recognizable "dum-dum-dum-dumbee-duwaaa" backing vocals swapped out by Foster from another Orbison-Melson composition, the song sounded unlike anything that had ever come out of Nashville before. Ironically, with its signature lush production, strings, and highly developed background vocal harmonies led by Joe Melson, in "Only the Lonely," Roy and Foster had just invented what would come to be called the Nashville Sound.

"Only the Lonely" was released on May 9, 1960, the day before Roy began a tour with singer Jimmy Clanton at the La Jolla Club in Tucson, Arizona. It started strong in some eastern markets such as Boston and Baltimore, where Foster had connections, and entered the charts on June 6 at Number 88, after Roy appeared on *Dick Clark's Saturday Night Beechnut Show* out of New York City, still sporting his natural blond hair and without the glasses that he needed to see and that would become his trademark. It then jumped into the Top 10 at Number 6 on July 11, finally peaking at Number 2 on July 25, staying on the charts for twenty-one weeks in the United States and twenty-four weeks in the United Kingdom, making it the longest-charting single of Roy's career.

"Blue Angel," written with Joe Melson and recorded in August, followed on the heels of "Only the Lonely." It was another song with an elaborate, big-ballad style and a driving beat,

and with Roy peaking in falsetto, "Blue Angel" and "Only the Lonely" would in many ways come to define his impact on rock and roll.

When Roy's royalties for the songs began to trickle in, he bought a pearl white Ford T-Bird and moved to Nashville for good, settling at 118 Cumberland Shores Drive in Hendersonville, Tennessee, about a half hour outside the Music City.

"I talked it over with my wife, and she said, 'Well, we'll have to do it sometime. It might as well be now,'" he recalled later. "I bought a car, a Thunderbird that had been in a car crash so it was cheap, and we loaded everything we had into the car. It didn't take up much room. I had more songs than anything else. And we headed off for Nashville, not knowing what might come of it."

With Roy about to go on tour and demand at an all-time high, Monument needed more songs. Although he was only just settling into his new home and life with Claudette and Roy D., he headed into the studio again.

He recorded "(I'd Be) a Legend in My Time" and "I Can't Stop Loving You," written by Don Gibson; "Bye Bye Love," written by Boudleaux and Felice Bryant; "Cry," made famous by the singer Johnnie Ray; and "Twenty Two Days" by Gene Pitney. Roy contributed "I'm Hurtin'" and "Come Back to Me (My Love)," the song that had inspired the "dum-dum-dum-dumbee-doowah" in "Only the Lonely."

"I'm Hurtin'" was picked to be the next single, and after the session Roy had enough songs in the can for his first-ever long-playing album.

The sessions were a marathon and kept Roy away from home, much to Claudette's chagrin. But just a few days after they concluded, he embarked on his first West Coast tour. Playing the same Gretsch White Falcon guitar as he had on Dick Clark's show, he played fifteen dates across California, Arizona, New Mexico, and Texas. On the same bill on the Amarillo, Texas, date was a group called the Whirlwinds, led by a local singer named Bill Dees, who would play an important part in Roy's later career.

Meanwhile, "I'm Hurtin'" backed with "I Can't Stop Loving You" was released on December 5, 1960, featuring Roy's first picture sleeve, a photo of him sitting in a car at a drive-in in Madison, Tennessee, which was also used for the cover of his *Lonely and Blue* album, released a month later. On the cover he sports the dyed black hair he'd begun to favor as a way of cultivating a cool, rockabilly look, but is pictured without glasses. By the end of 1960, his look would evolve, as well as his sound. The totally new, innovative form of pop music he and Fred Foster would create would become known as the Orbison Sound and would go on to inspire countless imitators.

Opposite: Roy at RCA Studio B in Nashville during the "Blue Angel" session. August 8, 1960.
Above: "Another Great Hit!" from Roy Orbison and Joe Melson, "Blue Angel," promo advertisement.

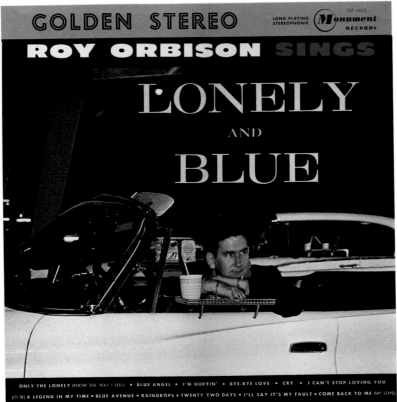

GOLDEN STEREO

LONG PLAYING STEREOPHONIC **Monument** RECORDS SM 14002

ROY ORBISON SINGS

LONELY AND **BLUE**

ONLY THE LONELY (KNOW THE WAY I FEEL) • BLUE ANGEL • I'M HURTIN' • BYE-BYE LOVE • CRY • I CAN'T STOP LOVING YOU
(TO BE) A LEGEND IN MY TIME • BLUE AVENUE • RAINDROPS • TWENTY TWO DAYS • I'LL SAY IT'S MY FAULT • COME BACK TO ME (MY LOVE)

Above: Roy's first Monument album, *Lonely and Blue*, 1961. **Opposite**: Roy at RCA Studio B in Nashville during the "Running Scared" session, February 27, 1961.

Not long after moving to Nashville, Roy had begun dying his hair jet black. He even toyed with the idea of growing a beard. But after settling on dyed black hair and glasses, Roy showed up at a photo session on December 1 sporting the look he would be forever associated with.

Meanwhile, his new single, "I'm Hurtin'," stalled at Number 27 on the charts. Roy was furious and attributed the poor showing to Sam Phillips, who had released some of Roy's unreleased tracks done for Sun, combined with previously released tracks, all overdubbed with new instrumentation and released as *Roy Orbison at the Rockhouse*, in competition with his new recordings.

"I remember when my first Monument album was ready to come out, I went and visited Sam Phillips in Memphis to let him listen to it and clear out a couple of points," Roy recalled. "Sam was sitting around with his brother, Jud. And Sam said, 'Shoot, I've got enough stuff on you to release an album myself, and I'm gonna do it and it will outsell your Monument album.' Jud just looked at him and said, 'Sam, are you crazy?'"

Roy and Fred Foster grew worried. They needn't have bothered.

Roy and Joe Melson wrote "Running Scared," inspired by Maurice Ravel's "Bolero," after a pep talk from Fred Foster and prepared it for Roy's next recording session, scheduled for February 27, 1961.

"'Running Scared' approaches classical music dynamics," engineer Bill Porter recalled. "The intro started out real soft, and the song built and built as the arrangement went on. In fact, it was so muted to start that if you had your radio turned down low, you almost didn't hear it at all. I wanted so much to capture that sound, and I changed my balance concept about three different times, trying to get that dynamic going."

Roy believed that "Running Scared" was the turning point in his career, not least because it was the moment when his voice, at least on record, became the voice with which he will be forever associated. As the song reached its climax, at the point he would normally have reached for a falsetto note, he was forced to sing full voice to match the dynamics of the session musicians. Not without some trepidation, he did it, with remarkable results.

After the final take, Foster turned to Porter, worried that the engineer hadn't captured the magic, and said, "If you didn't get that, it's all over for you."

Wesley Rose, though, didn't have faith in "Running Scared" and insisted that Boudleaux Bryant's "Love Hurts" go on the flip side as insurance. He needn't have worried. Fred Foster took both songs to Howard Miller, a top-rated DJ in Chicago, and asked him to play them on the air and let him know the response. He was in a cab on the way to the airport when he heard Miller on the radio saying "I have to call Fred Foster and tell him it's 'Running Scared' one hundred to one."

"Running Scared" was released on March 27, 1961. Reviewers agreed it had the earmarks of a runaway hit. The single entered the *Billboard* charts on April 10 at Number 71, going all the way to Number 1 on June 5 and staying on the US charts for a total of seventeen weeks. In the United Kingdom, it made it to Number 9 and remained in the charts for fifteen weeks.

For the next couple of months, Roy was busy writing and recording material for his next album. The Orbison-Melson team was at its peak, writing some of their best songs ever. "After All," "Little Black Book," "You Gotta Know What You Want," "Remember When," "Because," and "A Thousand Times Yes" are just a few examples of the remarkable songs the pair were turning out that, though fantastic, never made it past the demo stage, as they were so prolific at the time. Roy also recorded "She Wears My Ring," "Sunset," "The Great Pretender," and "Candy Man," as well as "Crying," "Lana," and an early version of "Blue Bayou" during sessions in June 1961.

"We were singing along, and Joe Melson said, 'Once again, I'm crying,'" Roy recalled of the song that would make him a superstar. "I was worried about it because we had just come out with 'Running Scared' and everybody said you shouldn't follow a ballad with a ballad. It was not difficult to write, it was difficult to conjure that song up. When that song came out, I don't think anyone had accepted the fact that a man should be able to cry when he wants to cry."

"We forgot about making money. We forgot about everything except 'We've got to make this as good as it can be,'" Fred Foster remembered of those days.

"I wasn't taught how to write a song," Roy said. "No one taught me that. As I started writing, it was all personal choice and personal preference, to write what sounded good to me, and a lot of the songs start and never stop, they don't have an instrumental break."

> I WASN'T TAUGHT HOW TO WRITE A SONG . . . A LOT OF THE SONGS START AND NEVER STOP, THEY DON'T HAVE AN INSTRUMENTAL BREAK.
>
> —ROY ORBISON

Opposite: Roy and Claudette aboard *Claudette*, the boat named for her, Hendersonville, TN, 1961.

That was the case of "Crying," a characteristic that became very common to Roy Orbison songs. As in the case of "Running Scared" and many to follow, "Crying" was constructed melodically, lyrically, and musically, rather than according to a typical songwriting template or formula. It's a complex song, with no pattern to follow. Its structure is completely unique and its style pioneering. Like "Running Scared," it has no bridge or instrumental break, and it flows from beginning to end without any repetition of words or chord changes.

But breaking with convention as both a singer and songwriter would become a hallmark of Roy's career, and "Crying" would go on to touch listeners around the globe.

Meanwhile, work continued on Roy's album. During those sessions, the B-side of "Crying," "Candy Man," was recorded. For it Roy wanted a harmonica and asked around in the studio if anybody could play it. With no one able to play the part satisfactorily, Charlie McCoy was summoned to the studio in the middle of the night to lend his harmonica talents to "Candy Man." He and saxophonist Boots Randolph worked up the arrangement.

"If you give an artist a place to paint and some good canvas and brushes, paint, and some

sunlight, then he'll paint you a picture," Roy recalled of the atmosphere at his sessions around that time.

McCoy's harmonica was just what he was looking for.

"Crying" and "Candy Man" were picked out as the strongest songs of the sessions and were released as a single in mid-July, even while "Running Scared" was still on the charts. Billboard called Roy's new single "a fine follow-up to his recent smash hit 'Running Scared.' 'Crying' features an expressive reading on a moving country-flavored ballad."

Demand for the single was tremendous—"Crying" rose to Number 2, while "Candy Man" hit Number 25—making it Roy's first double-sided smash.

Roy's first tour on foreign soil, apart from the brief Canadian trek with the Teen Kings in 1956, was to Australia. In September 1961, he shared the bill with Ray Peterson, Dion, Jack Scott, and a local star, Johnny Chester.

"The tour didn't turn out so good," Roy would recall. "There weren't that many people there, but they were enthusiastic to see us."

Above: A selection of the many Roy Orbison singles from Monument Records.

The show, titled The All Star Rock Show, was presented by Jim Noall, who was booking musical acts for the Embers Club in Melbourne. Roy's tour was the first of seven All Star tours in Australia and the cities on the tour were Brisbane, Melbourne, and Sydney.

Roy loved Australia, and he kept returning over the years, as did his father, Orbie Lee. He told Australian radio years later, "I'm crazy about Australia. When I first went there, I took my father with me, and he said, 'If I was ten years younger, I'd stay here and never go back.'"

Roy also discovered that his prescription sunglasses, which would become part of his trademark look, could be worn onstage to great effect. Murray Robertson, the pianist for the backing band, wore them, and Roy liked the look. Worried that the prescription glasses he needed to see properly might seem uncool for a rocker, Roy realized that the prescription shades he normally wore only at home might be just the thing he was looking for to complete his look.

"Roy, we can't have another big ballad, we need to have an up-tempo song," Fred Foster pleaded with Roy upon his return. Foster didn't want to follow up "Running Scared" and "Crying" with yet another ballad. "Dream Baby" was his answer.

"He tried, he couldn't write it," Foster recalled. "I checked every publisher in New York and LA that I'd ever done anything with, and I called [the songwriter] Cindy Walker in Texas. I told her what I needed, and she said, 'I only have a couple of tunes, I'll look around in the catalog.' So the next morning she called me and said, 'I found two things that might do.'"

Foster played "Dream Baby" for Roy. Halfway through, he said, "Mercy! Let's do it!" He cut the song on Tuesday, January 9, 1962, in RCA's Studio B.

"Dream Baby" has a country swing, but it's also pure, uptempo Roy Orbison, with a beat that owes more to Ray Charles's music than anything else. It entered the *Billboard* charts on February 17 and peaked at Number 4 on March 31. In the United Kingdom it reached the Number 2 spot, where a new group called The Beatles, from the northern port of Liverpool, recorded a version for their first radio appearance on March 8, 1962.

Roy's second Monument album was released in January 1962. Entitled *Crying*, it was a compilation of singles and other tracks recorded during 1961. It reached the Number 21 position in the United States and stayed in the charts for thirty-one weeks. *Roy Orbison's Greatest Hits* quickly followed in late July, peaking at Number 14 in September and staying in the charts for an amazing 140 weeks.

On May 31, 1962, Roy flew to London with Wesley Rose to scout venues for a possible tour. While there, he performed a show for Roy Orbison Fan Club members and invited journalists.

Opposite: Roy Orbison as photographed by legendary Nashville photographer Walden S. Fabry. **Above**: Jim Noall All Star Rock Show poster, Australia, September 1961.

ROY REALIZED THAT THE PRESCRIPTION SHADES HE NORMALLY WORE ONLY AT HOME MIGHT BE JUST THE THING HE WAS LOOKING FOR TO COMPLETE HIS LOOK.

Roy signs autographs for waiting fans in Worthing, England while visiting friend Peter Gray's garage, April 8, 1967.

"I've performed there once a year since '62," Roy remembered years later about his visits to England. "I learned from Buddy Holly that it was marvelous, and he was trying to tell the Everly Brothers how great it was, and then they came back and said it was marvelous. So I wanted to see firsthand what it was like, and then of course I went over in 1963 for the Beatle tour."

But Roy was soon back in Tennessee, and on June 29 Claudette gave birth to their second baby, Anthony King Orbison.

Roy started touring more steadily now, and he was away more often, so with two babies at home, finding time to write with Joe Melson became difficult. Meanwhile, Joe wasn't enjoying the recognition or success he was looking for in his own singing career. He'd signed with Acuff-Rose's Hickory label in 1960 but had struggled to score a hit. Now he wanted to take his songs with Roy in a more classical direction that Roy wasn't any too comfortable with. He started writing with another artist, Dan Folger. The Orbison-Melson songwriting duo was slowly coming apart.

As a result, Roy started writing on his own. The first two efforts put on tape were "Leah" and "Working for the Man." "Leah," although not a true story, came to Roy after a trip to Hawaii. "Working for the Man" was based on Roy's experiences working in the West Texas oil fields.

"'Boy, if he had a daughter and I'd marry her, then I would own the company and I'd be in good shape,' that was untrue," Roy recalled of the lyrics. "But the rest of the story is true. It was just a collection of my memories of that period, which were distasteful at times.

"I only write what I like to listen to," he said of his songwriting at the time. "I normally don't listen to the radio and other music, so I'm not influenced by that. If I get an urge to hear a nice ballad, I come up to the studio and write one, or attempt to write one. And if I wanna hear something that really rocks, then I come up and do that as well. But I'm not really prolific anyway. I only write about ten or twelve songs a year. I write many more than that, but I wouldn't let them out.

"It takes about an hour after you sit down before anything comes to you. Sometimes it's good and sometimes it's bad, but if you remember it the next day, or the next time you're in the studio, then you're in good shape. Because if you've remembered it, maybe somebody else will.

"It's the loneliest type of work that you can do, but very satisfying," he continued. "I still do play the guitar just to relax. It's a good companion, the guitar. You can't take a piano with you. And I think that's why the guitar is so important to all kinds of music. You can take the old guitar wherever you go."

"Leah" and "Working for the Man" were recorded on August 14 and released in September. "Two fine songs," wrote *Billboard*, noting that "Working for the Man" was "a smartly styled work song that reaches a powerful climax" while "Leah" was "a Hawaiian-flavored ballad that has a strong vocal plus steel guitar and ukulele backing."

It would be Roy's second double-sided hit single, though it didn't reach the heights of "Crying," with "Working for the Man" peaking at Number 33 and "Leah" at Number 25.

With the new single just hitting the record store shelves, Roy toured the South and Midwest, and by September he was booked as part of the Grand Ole Opry Stars tour that was traveling across the country. Playing with stars such as Kitty Wells and Lester Flatt and Earl Scruggs well into October, such unlikely tours, put together by Acuff-Rose, would go a long way in accounting for Roy's being thought of as a country and western performer in the United States, despite his success on the pop charts and with a younger, more diverse audience.

Searching for the right image, Roy played a Fender Jaguar during those shows, after switching from the Gretsch White Falcon he'd recently favored. But soon he switched again, this time to a sunburst Fender Telecaster and then back to the White Falcon, which he had modified and custom painted black. The guitar would become known as the Orbison Custom.

As Roy traversed Canada as part of his seemingly endless string of live appearances, he also made a significant new fan.

"Years ago—'62 maybe. I saw Roy Orbison in Winnipeg," the legendary songwriter Neil Young wrote in his memoir.

Got to talk to him once outside a gig. He was coming out of his motor home with his backing band the Candymen. That had a profound effect on my life. I always loved Roy. I looked up to the way he was—admired the way he handled himself. That aloofness he had influenced me profoundly. It was the way he carried himself, y'know, with this benign dignity. . . . His music was always more important than the media. It wasn't a fashion statement. It wasn't about being in the right place at the right time making the right moves. That didn't matter to Roy. Just like it doesn't matter to me.

Anyway, I've always put a piece of Roy Orbison on every album I've made. His influence is on so many of my songs. . . . I even had his photograph on the sleeve of

I ALWAYS LOVED ROY. I LOOKED UP TO THE WAY HE WAS—ADMIRED THE WAY HE HANDLED HIMSELF.

—NEIL YOUNG

Opposite: "Working for the Man" promo advertisement and single.

Tonight's The Night for no reason, really. Just recognizing his presence. There's a big Orbison tribute song on *Eldorado* called *Don't Cry*. That's totally me under the Roy Orbison . . . spell. When I wrote it and recorded it I was thinking "Roy Orbison meets trash metal." Seriously.

Meanwhile, Roy's music had made a big impression on another fledgling songwriter. "His songs had songs within songs," Bob Dylan wrote in *Chronicles, Volume One*. " . . . Orbison was deadly serious—no pollywog and no fledgling juvenile. There wasn't anything else on the radio like him."

When Roy hit the studio on Friday, January 4, 1963, he had two new original songs: the remarkable "Falling" and "In Dreams," which he almost literally dreamed as he was falling asleep one night and would go on to be a Top 10 hit in the United States and United Kingdom and Number 1 in Australia—plus two written by Cindy Walker and another written by his old pal from West Texas Bill Dees, who would go on to become Roy's longest-serving collaborator.

William Marvin Dees was born on January 24, 1939, in Electra, Texas. He and his brothers, Mike and Val, sang and played together as kids, and Bill was playing the ukulele by the time he was twelve. During high school in Borger, Texas, he formed a vocal group called the Five Bops, which would later become the Whirlwinds, and recorded a single for Hamilton Records at Norman Petty's legendary studio in New Mexico. The Five Bops became local favorites and along the way played a few shows with Roy.

"First time I saw him, he was playing a show at the high school auditorium in Clovis, New Mexico," Bill told the Roy Orbison Fan Club years later. "His heels would come back—today, it would be considered a wild dance step—and he would lift his feet off the ground and land back with his heels again flat, playing the guitar at the same time. He would drop to one knee, and his long hair would fall over his glasses. He was doing hillbilly rock. A few years later we met up. I found out what a sincere, mild-mannered person he was."

After earning his stripes on the road, Bill ended up in Nashville in late 1962, when "Leah" was still hot, and reconnected with his old friend. Sponsored by Roy, he signed a five-year contract with Acuff-Rose, and the pair began collaborating.

Meanwhile, the secretary of the Roy Orbison Fan Club in England, Janet Martin, wrote to Roy with some exciting news: "You'll be touring with the Beatles, and everybody will get to see how good you are."

Opposite: Long-time UK Fan Club President Margaret Finch stuffs envelopes with fan club newsletters.
Above: (top) Promo advertisement for "Falling." (bottom) Roy and his long-time cowriter Bill Dees at Roy's new home closer to the lake in Hendersonville, TN, 1964.

oy The Joker Wins 'Em Over

AND HE'S GOT 4 DISCS IN THE CHARTS TOO!

hornrimmed spectacles

through my brain so fast I can't get it down on paper quick

Globe-trotter Roy

THAT great guy ROY ORBISON will soon become a world-wide household name, judging by his present amount of travelling. We met in June during his first British tour and it was good to se im here again recently (writes Geor Rooney.)

sked him what he had done since Ju nd where he would go after his curr ur. If it's a world trip you're interes just listen to this for an itinerary !

DISC, April 20, 1963   11

A few weeks before the start of his first-ever tour of Britain, and with 'In Dreams' still climbing the charts here,

ROY ORBISON talks to DISC from Nashville, Tennessee

Hits are gre

ROY STRIKE' RIGHT "OIL

Roy Orbison takes audience by storm

EW stars—British or American—could induce an audience to s for more immediately before the Beatles were due on stage. is just how highly Roy Orbison is scoring on his present Liverpool's two big groups.

y succeeds in one of the tasks any entertainer in n just now could face, for the s prove again on this tour that re currently the most exciting iners in the country. out a single movement Roy d the audience from the first of "Only The Lonely," wh initial hearing of that rbison sound. who also proves himse guitarist, played his a introduction to "C That preceded what I the big hit of his act Scared," for which he the final chorus ame the swinging version I Say," followed Dream Baby" and ord, "Falling," which week, ded off a terrific act wit s "—and was called bacl by the sustained applaus

pected, the Beatles virtu the roof, although little ard of them above the ney included " Som ever...

Other Guy," "Do You Want Know A Secret" and "Please P Me," before a tremendous rende of their current chart topper, " Me To You."

Gerry and the Pacemakers scored, as did newcom Crawford, I....

DISC, May 25, 1963

DISC, 161, Fleet St., London, E.C.4.

ROY GETS A STAR FAN

JOHNNY TILLOTSON, Hank Locklin, Chet Atkins, Floyd Cramer and Del Shannon have become honorary members of the Roy Orbison fan club.

Johnny says of Roy: "He always goes down real great with audiences. He's the type of performer that you just h, and applaud

TOP TEN

By Roy Orbison

LIMELIGHT by Mantovani and his Orchestra.—This beautiful Charles Chaplin melody ranks as my all-time favourite. I never tire of listening to it, particularly the Mantovani version.

IT'S ALL IN THE GAME by Tommy Edwards.—In my estima-tion, this is one of the best pop songs ever written. I've chosen the Tommy Edwards disc because it's the one I know best—after all, it was a hit twice in the States. But that doesn't mean to say I don't care for Cliff Richard's record—I think he sings it exceptionally well.

I CAN'T STOP LOVING YOU by Ray Charles. — And I can't stop loving this record—it's sensational ! I prefer Ray singing ballads, and of the many he has waxed, this is the most outstanding.

LONELY WINE by Les Baxter and his Orchestra—! Imagine this tune will be unfamiliar to most people in Britain, but it's achieved a fair degree of popularity in America, where it is virtually a standard ballad. I like the melody so much that I have recorded a lyric version for my new album.

THE STILL

One of the most consistent hit maker the last few years has been "The Big (above), who

Roy had been asked to tour England several times but had waited for the right moment. Originally booked for Duane Eddy, Roy's British tour kicked off on May 18.

"It was a mistake," Roy recalled later. "But it turned out to be a great mistake. The promoter who came over to America came to get Duane Eddy. The deal didn't go through, so he settled for me." It was the beginning of a long love affair between Roy and his fans in England.

It was also during that tour that Roy adopted dark prescription glasses for good. After first toying with wearing them onstage while on tour in Australia, he had considered wearing them regularly as part of his look. But after leaving his regular glasses on a plane after a flight to Dothan, Alabama, with ten days of concerts ahead of him before returning to Nashville and unable to see without glasses, he got used to the dark glasses and decided to keep wearing them. It was with those dark glasses that he embarked on his tour of England.

"I need these glasses," he told reporters. "I'm as blind as a bat without them."

When Roy got to London, "In Dreams" was Number 6 on the charts. The tour with The Beatles, plus fellow Liverpudlians Gerry and the Pacemakers, was a fantastic time for Roy. The Fab Four's first album, *Please Please Me*, had just been released, and Roy was flattered to learn that the group's smash hit of the same name had been inspired by "Only the Lonely."

"The boys wanted to close the show," Roy recalled later. "It was a Roy Orbison/Beatles tour, but they asked me if they could close the show. I said, 'Well, let's wait until after rehearsal.' And so we did the rehearsal, and I was doing mostly ballads and they were doing all up-tempo songs, from 'Twist and Shout' all the way to 'Love Me Do' on up to whatever record they had out at the time. They sounded a little rough at rehearsal, but it was all up-tempo, so I knew I should let them close the show, just for the show's balance. But I didn't let them know that straightaway. They asked me again, and I said, 'Well, I'm still thinking about it.' They said, 'Look, you're making all the money, let us close the show.' And they were right. I was making three times what they were making. So I said okay. But then opening night I was very scared, because a lot of American entertainers, great ones, had gone over to England and had not done so well. But after the fourteenth or fifteenth encore, I felt a lot better."

The four-week, twenty-one-show tour proved extremely popular.

Roy opened with "Only the Lonely," followed by "Candy Man," on which he played the

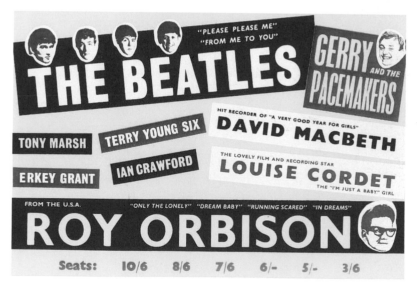

Opposite: Roy Orbison takes the UK by storm.

Above: (top) Album art for the *In Dreams* LP, 1963. (bottom) Show flyer for the Beatles, Roy Orbison, and Gerry and the Pacemakers, 1963.

Above: (top) Roy Orbison and George Harrison on the set of *A Hard Day's Night*, April 13, 1964. (bottom) Ticket stub for Roy Orbison and the Beatles, Walthamstow, England, May 24, 1963. **Opposite**: Ticket stub for the Beatles, Roy Orbison, and Gerry and the Pacemakers, May 26, 1963.

harmonica, "Running Scared," a swinging version of Ray Charles's "What'd I Say," and then "Dream Baby." He closed the show with "In Dreams."

"It was really hard to keep up with that man, he really put on a show," Ringo Starr remembers of the tour.

"The tour sold out in one afternoon," Roy said at the time. "One advert sold the tour out. And on opening night, I got to 'Running Scared,' and I did seven encores for 'Running Scared,' and then I got to 'In Dreams,' I think I did another six or seven encores there. Finally, I remember Paul and John grabbing me by the arms and not letting me go back on to take my curtain call. The crowd were yelling 'We want Roy!' and I was held captive by The Beatles, and they were saying, 'Yankee go home!'"

Standing on the side of the stage as Roy performed, George Harrison—the future Traveling Wilbury—turned to Paul McCartney and quipped, "So how're we gonna follow that?"

"So then I left the stage and I went backstage, and I said, 'Do you want me to step out and tell them to be quiet?'" Roy recalled. "And Paul said, 'No, we'll be all right.' When they came on, for the first two or three numbers the crowd was still shouting 'We want Roy! We want Roy!' And then, all of a sudden, a light scream was all you could hear, and it built to a very loud scream, and then that's all you could hear. They screamed all the way through the show and loved the Beatles, and me, too. That tour was a fantastic success. We had a great time."

"That tour, well, it made The Beatles and myself in Europe, and internationally, I guess," he said years later. "It was a really important tour, and with all these photographs around the world with the sunglasses, I was sort of stuck with that image."

In the middle of the tour, as "In Dreams" was dropping off the charts, "Falling" entered. Also written by Roy, it was another "Bolero"-style song, with a strong beat and a powerful ending. In England, "Falling" entered the charts on June 1, peaking at Number 9.

On the tour bus, huddled in the back during quiet moments throughout the long trips between shows, Roy was working on a guitar riff he couldn't get out of his head. *Da-da-da-da-daaa.* John Lennon, Paul McCartney, and George Harrison would look at one another and smile every time Roy played it. Even at that early stage in their careers, they knew the makings of a great song when they heard it.

EMPIRE
LIVERPOOL

THE BEATLES / ROY ORBISON / GERRY & THE PACEMAKERS

1st Performance 5-40

SUNDAY
MAY 26

GRAND CIRCLE
8/6

1 59

TO BE RETAINED

POP parade

ROY ORBISON.

ROY ORBISON, BESPECTACLED AND ORDINARY-LOOKING CHARACTER HAS BEEN MAKING HITS SINCE 1960. ROY IS ONE OF THE MOST SUCCESSFUL AMERICAN VISITORS. THOUGH HE WON'T INDULGE IN DRAMATICS, RIOT-RAISING OR WAY-OUT SHOWMANSHIP, HE JUST USES HIS SOARINGLY EFFECTIVE VOICE ...

- DRAWN BY -
- GORDON HOGG -

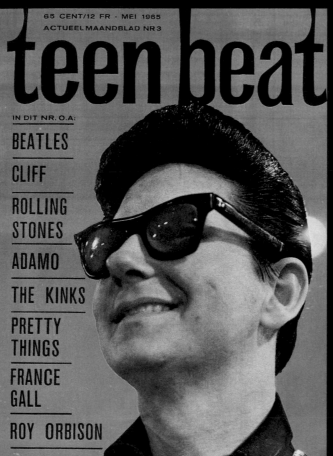

65 CENT/12 FR · MEI 1965
ACTUEEL MAANDBLAD NR 3

teen beat

IN DIT NR. O.A:

BEATLES

CLIFF

ROLLING STONES

ADAMO

THE KINKS

PRETTY THINGS

FRANCE GALL

ROY ORBISON

teenbeat
ROY ORBISON

Roy Orbison was a media darling in the UK.
Opposite: Roy Orbison illustration by British
cartoonist Gordon Hogg, circa 1964.

See how they've changed
—'One day they could be big' said Roy Orbison

THEN—The young and bright-eyed BEATLES pictured with GERRY and the PACEMAKERS and ROY ORBISON during a tour in 1963. ROY said at the time: "One day the BEATLES could become big in America". Little did he know.

Above: Roy on the British television show *Thank Your Lucky Stars*, October 1963. **Opposite**: Roy was an almost permanent feature on Australian and British television in the mid 1960s. Here he is in 1967 with his Gretsch Chet Atkins Country Gentleman guitar.

oy's tour with The Beatles ended on Sunday, June 9, at King George's Hall in Blackburn, and Roy headed back to the United States, where he was due to hit the road again during the Fourth of July weekend with a show in Iowa.

That same month, the *In Dreams* album was finally released, and Roy was the guest host on the weekly pop music television show *American Bandstand*. While *In Dreams* entered the US charts in August, staying on the list for twenty-three weeks and peaking at Number 35, in the United Kingdom it had an amazing run, peaking at Number 6 in December, with a total of twenty weeks in the Top 10 and fifty-eight weeks in the Hit Parade.

"Mean Woman Blues" backed with "Blue Bayou," the follow-up to "Falling," was released in August 1963 in the United States and in September in the United Kingdom. It became another double-sided smash on both sides of the Atlantic, as well as in Australia.

"'Blue Bayou' is basically just a story about wanting to go home," Roy said of what would become one of his most famous songs, one he'd written with Joe Melson back in 1961. "You are away from home, wanting to go back and do what it is that you do to relax. It is a semimythical place, but I've been to places like 'Blue Bayou' before."

With demand high, he returned to England, where he toured with Brian Poole and the Tremeloes, the Searchers, and Freddie and the Dreamers.

Although Roy had lost his voice and couldn't speak at his London press conference, there was work to do. Fred Foster had Decca Studio 2 booked for a September 11 session to record a Christmas song, "Pretty Paper," written by newcomer Willie Nelson. Foster rehearsed the arrangement with the assembled orchestra, and, though Roy was suffering from a 103-degree fever, he cut fantastic vocal after fantastic vocal during the session.

Finally recuperated in time for the start of the tour, Roy switched guitars to mark the occasion.

"I have a Gretsch White Falcon with a Gibson Super 400 neck on it," he said of the unique instrument he used, which he affectionately thought of as his "Frankenguitar." "I use steel guitar pickups with regular Gibson strings."

The guitar became part of Roy's image, and he would play it for several years; then, in late 1966, a guitar firm in Korea asked to make a replica of it and Roy sent it to the company, never to be seen again.

During the second British tour, Roy did a few TV and radio appearances. His *Ready, Steady, Go!* appearance aired on September 13, 1963. He also appeared on *Thank Your Lucky*

Stars with host Brian Matthew, the famed BBC presenter, and on the important *Saturday Club* radio show, also with Matthew.

The tour came to an end on Sunday, October 6, and Roy was on a plane to Nashville on Monday for a two-day rest before leaving again to tour Canada, followed by a trek to California, but not before the British promoter Peter Walsh had booked Roy for a Far East tour set for early 1964.

In November, Monument released a new single, "Pretty Paper" backed with "Beautiful Dreamer." "Pretty Paper," the song Roy had recorded while convalescing in London, peaked at Number 15 on January 11, becoming the highest-charting holiday song of the season.

In the wake of yet another hit single, Roy kicked off his first big Australian tour on Wednesday, January 15, 1964, with the California sensations the Beach Boys in tow.

"They were really true performers, very much underrated, by the way," Roy said of the Beach Boys and their leader, Brian Wilson, whose voice he came to adore. "They were so much more than just surfing music, they were marvelous."

"I was fortunate enough to realize early in the game that it was a worldwide market and not just America," Roy told *Goldmine* magazine years later of his frequent tours abroad. "I didn't forget Canada, England, Australia or the Far East, and that has stood me in good stead."

After the tour, Roy met Claudette in Hawaii, and they enjoyed an eight-day holiday on Waikiki Beach before heading back home in mid-February for Roy to start working on material for his next single with Bill Dees.

"I was down on my luck then, eating over at my folks' house, when Roy called and asked me to come to Nashville," Dees remembered. "I headed there and brought a partly finished song called 'It's Over.' Roy came back from his trip with an idea for the chord changes and the melody in the middle, and we just whipped it out."

In early 1964, Fred Foster bought Sam Phillips's studio in downtown Nashville, at the Cumberland Lodge building, located at 319 7th Avenue North, and installed a studio on the third floor in the old Masonic hall with a view of the state capitol across the street.

With a large string section perched on a platform across from Roy and the background singers and the band situated in between, Foster led the assembled musicians through thirty-six takes of Roy and Bill Dees's new composition, "It's Over."

By now, with so many successes under their belts, Foster was willing to spend the time and money—"It was Roy's money anyway," he'd always insist when pressed by Wesley Rose—to achieve what he felt was the perfect result.

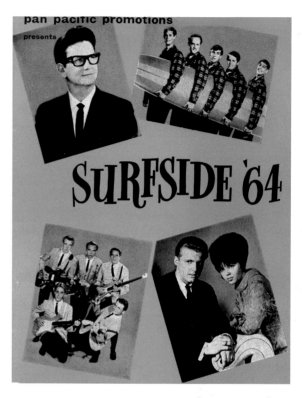

Opposite: British sheet music for "Pretty Paper," written by Willie Nelson. **Above**: Program from Roy Orbison's tour with the Beach Boys, 1964. **Below**: The *Roy Orbison Show,* October 1964.

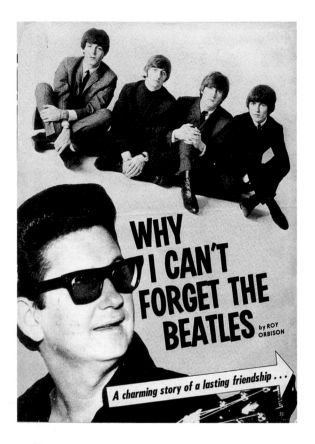

WHY I CAN'T FORGET THE BEATLES by ROY ORBISON

A charming story of a lasting friendship . . .

Above: Roy Orbison's piece about the Beatles 1963 tour from the March 1967 issue of *Teen Life*.
Opposite: John Lennon and Ringo Starr feed Roy cake on his 28th birthday, April 23, 1964.

Released in early April 1964, the song, which started soft and low and built to an emotional crescendo, was yet another song that would come to epitomize Roy's sound. "The drama-ballad king scores again with pathos and chorus and strings that build, build, build," *Billboard* wrote in its review.

Whereas "Falling," "Only the Lonely," and "Blue Angel" had showcased Roy's voice and, especially on the latter two, his falsetto, and "Running Scared" had experimented with drama, orchestration, and that remarkable full-voice crescendo, "It's Over" combined them all into one unmistakable package. The song entered the US charts on April 11 and the UK charts on May 2, quickly rising to the Top 10 in both countries. In fact, "It's Over" was the first song by an American artist to top the British charts since 1962, and with the demand for Roy high, a third British tour was announced.

On April 7, a couple of days after Roy's new house on Caudill Drive in Hendersonville— complete with indoor waterfall, state-of-the-art kitchen, steam room, and pool—was officially finished, Roy arrived in England with Claudette and rented a flat in Westminster, London, for the duration of his tour. The couple did some sightseeing, including a visit to the Imperial War Museum, and Roy bought a 1939 Mercedes-Benz 300. During his days off, he also visited his friends The Beatles on the set of their film *A Hard Day's Night*, on April 13, while John was filming the bubble bath scene. Ten days later, on Thursday, April 23, the same day The Beatles filmed the now-legendary "Can't Buy Me Love" segment for *A Hard Day's Night*, John and Ringo would join Roy, Claudette, and young Roy DeWayne at La Dolce Vita restaurant in London's swinging Soho area to celebrate the elder Roy's birthday.

Roy used two drummers for the tour, telling the press he liked "a big thumping beat," and made some radio and TV appearances, appearing again on *Saturday Club*, *Ready, Steady, Go!*, *Top of the Pops*, and *Thank Your Lucky Stars*, leaving an indelible impression on the millions of British teenagers for whom the shows were an essential part of life.

THE DRAMA-BALLAD KING SCORES AGAIN WITH PATHOS AND CHORUS —*BILLBOARD*

The tour was an enormous success, and Roy returned to the United States for an extensive string of performances in the south and the Midwest, again as part of a Grand Ole Opry tour headlined by Ray Price. After more dates on his own, he returned home to settle in to his new home.

Roy had personally helped plan many of the details of his $150,000 retreat, situated on Old Hickory Lake near Hendersonville, and was proud of the comfort and privacy it gave him and his family.

As you entered the property, the driveway curved past a garage, then the front door of the house, and then another garage. The two garages housed Roy's growing collection of cars.

There were almost no painted surfaces in the house, and everything was designed to be as maintenance free as possible. The staircases were covered with carpeting and leatherette, and the floors on the main level were made mostly of stone, while the ceilings and walls were made of neutral wood. The exterior, largely shingle, had the look of an oversize Swiss chalet.

The 8,000 square feet of living space included seven bedrooms, six baths, and a billiard room. Roy's private office contained assorted guitars propped against his desk and chairs, and his den housed his growing collection of trophies and awards. On the walls were the twelve gold records he had won, each representing sales of more than a million copies of a hit single. Five color televisions were scattered around the house. And although Roy didn't drink much, there were three bars to keep his many visitors entertained.

A stone chimney, located in the front room of the house, was the tallest point in the neighborhood.

Roy's personal bedroom was a two-level affair on the ground floor, anchored by a triple-size bed, featuring built-in remote controls for the room's lighting and Roy's television. It had no windows, owing to the irregular hours he kept.

A hanging stairway led to the upstairs area, where the children, and later Roy's parents, had their rooms. There was also a swimming pool in the living room, as well as a smaller wading pool, installed for Roy and Claudette's children. But

Roy Orbison at his new home on the lake in Hendersonville, TN.

perhaps the most remarkable part of the home was the waterfalls that ran down each side of the staircase, which Roy had installed for their "pretty sound" more than anything else.

A hundred-foot terrace finished in Crab Orchard stone with a fantastic view ran across the lake side of the house, and the walls on the side of the house facing the lake were made largely of glass but also featured a huge single slab of stone with a natural reddish pattern, which visitors almost always mentioned looked remarkably like the mushroom cloud of an atomic explosion.

As Roy and Claudette settled into their dream house, Monument had released *More of Roy Orbison's Greatest Hits*, and, like its predecessor, it was a smash. The album peaked at Number 19, staying on the *Billboard* charts for thirty weeks.

Meanwhile, even though he'd just discovered that his contract with Monument was due to expire during the next year, Roy was working on material for his next single. The song he came up with would be the one that would make him a superstar for the rest of his life.

Early one evening in late July, Roy and Bill Dees were settled in at Roy's palatial new home for a writing session when Claudette announced that she was headed for the store.

"Give me some money, honey," she said coyly to Roy.

"What do you need it for?" Roy asked her flirtatiously.

"A pretty woman don't need no money," Dees said, feeling like a third wheel and trying to cut the tension.

Catching himself, he asked Roy, "Hey, would that make a good song title?"

"No, but 'Pretty Woman' sure would," Roy replied, and he started fiddling with his guitar, recalling the guitar figure he'd been toying with all those months ago in the back of the tour bus in England as John Lennon, Paul McCartney, and George Harrison listened, while Dees slapped on the table between them to keep the rhythm.

By the time Claudette returned forty minutes later, Roy and Dees had finished the song.

Although they had written it quickly, the pair continued polishing it over the next few days. "Oh, Pretty Woman" borrowed elements from a previous Orbison-Melson composition called "Pretty Woman" that they'd written with Ray Rush, but the new song was so fresh and unique that the similarities practically ended with the titles.

"I just loved it," Fred Foster recalled of the song, when Roy and Dees presented it at their next session. "Except here he's talking about this pretty woman walking down the street, and then at the end he says, 'Well, you're not the only fish in the sea. Just go ahead and walk away

Various promo photos and ad for the release of "Oh, Pretty Woman" in 1964. **Above right:** Backstage during filming of the *Roy Orbison Show* in England, October 1964.

FLX 3135

PRETTY WOMAN

ROY ORBISON

ROY
ORBISON

Nee, het succes is R
niet naar het hoofd
stegen. 'Pretty Wom
en 'Pretty Paper' bra
ten hem bergen goud
.... fanmail maar g
verwaandheid. Toch
er een gezellig fees
mét vier zéér charma
fans best af en natuur
mocht MP's fotogr
dit feestelijke, kleurri
tafereeltje vastleggen

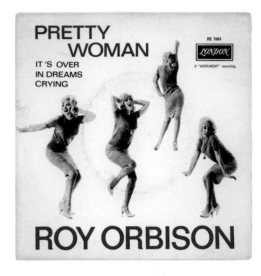

from me.' I said, 'Roy, the girl is either pretty or she isn't. Because she doesn't jump your bones, that doesn't make her any less pretty. You gotta correct that.' Roy said, 'Mercy, how did that get by?' And he came back with it corrected."

"Oh, Pretty Woman" was written on a Friday. The next day, August 1, 1964, Roy and Foster recorded it. The following Friday, with The Beatles topping the charts and set to begin a summer tour of the United State on August 19, Fred Foster rush released the song.

"It was the fastest thing I'd ever seen," Dees said later.

"Oh, Pretty Woman" went on to be the top-selling American record of 1964, and Roy received a Grammy nomination. But the sessions were like any other. After rehearsing in Foster's office, everyone piled into the studio, Roy armed with a Coke.

As the session dragged on, guitarist Jerry Kennedy made a suggestion that put the icing on the cake. "Why don't you put the guitars on one at a time?" he suggested.

Foster knew immediately that it would make an already great arrangement perfect.

"Oh, Pretty Woman" entered the US charts on August 29, at Number 51. By September 26, it was Number 1, Roy's first since "Running Scared," and stayed at the top of the charts for three weeks, also topping the charts in England, where he became the first American to have two consecutive Number 1 hits. Roy also became the first American to top the US and UK charts simultaneously since the Everlys had with "Cathy's Clown" in 1960. It was also a hit in the rest of Europe, Australia, Japan, Canada, and most other parts of the world.

Roy appeared on *Shindig!* and *The Ed Sullivan Show*, as Fred Foster tried to keep up with the intense demand for his latest smash.

"We had sold probably a million copies of 'Oh, Pretty Woman,'" he recalled of the aftermath of the *Ed Sullivan* appearance. "It was a perfect performance. On Monday, following that Sunday-evening show, I got an order for another hundred thousand. Tuesday, another hundred thousand. It went on a hundred thousand a day for another two or three weeks."

By late October, Roy found himself back in England for a slew of radio, concert, and television appearances,

Opposite: Roy surrounded by pretty women while doing press for his smash hit. **Above**: "Pretty Woman" EP art on London Records. **Below**: Roy on the *Ed Sullivan Show*, New York, October 11, 1964.

including the one-off *Roy Orbison Show*, in which he acted as host while also performing and introducing the other acts.

"Pretty Paper" was released in the United Kingdom in early November, backed with "Our Summer Song," a track taken from the album *Crying* from 1962. It entered the British charts on Saturday, November 21, 1964, and quickly reached the number 6 position, becoming a Christmas hit yet again.

Back in the United States in November, Roy hit the road again, with his dad, Orbie Lee, now acting as road manager, traveling in a Dodge motor home that slept eight that Roy had purchased to help make his seemingly never-ending life on the road more bearable.

Meanwhile, two compilation albums came out toward the end of 1964. One, *Early Orbison*, was released by Monument Records in the United States in October, featuring songs from the *Lonely and Blue* and *Crying* LPs, plus the B-side of "Uptown," "Pretty One." In the UK, London Records released another one that November, cleverly calling it *Oh, Pretty Woman*. It included well-known sides from 1962 to 1964. It rose to Number 5 on the English charts.

In all, "Oh, Pretty Woman" sold 7 million copies in 1964. Finally Roy was a worldwide superstar.

Roy's long tours and months away from home had taken a toll on his and Claudette's marriage. Their split, which shocked their family and friends, took place just as Roy's career was reaching its early zenith.

On Saturday, September 12, 1964, in Springfield, Tennessee, Roy's attorney, Ward Hudgins, whom Roy knew through his work for Acuff-Rose, petitioned for an annulment. It was finalized on Wednesday, October 14.

Claudette received custody of the couple's two boys and moved to Pasadena, Texas, where her parents lived. Roy never really got over their split and continued to visit her. Soon Claudette announced that she was pregnant and that she and Roy were expecting their third child in May.

Meanwhile, lonely and blue in his dream home in Hendersonville, Roy called Bill Dees and the pair started polishing up a couple of new songs. A recording session, Roy's first in five months, was arranged for Saturday, January 16, 1965.

Opposite: Roy Orbison backstage during filming of the *Roy Orbison Show* on the ITV network in England, October 1964. **Above**: (top) Roy getting ready to go on the road, at home, May 1961. (bottom) Roy and his younger brother, Sammy, waiting to board the tour bus in Nashville, TN.

Reeling from his split with Claudette, Roy found himself in the middle of another dispute. Despite Roy's success, Wesley Rose and Fred Foster began to clash more ferociously than ever over the choice of songs he was to record. The disagreements went back to Roy's "Uptown" session, especially when Roy and Foster set about recording songs for which Acuff-Rose didn't control the publishing, and Wesley Rose soon made it no secret that he wanted Roy off Monument when his contract expired on June 30, 1965.

"When he told me, he called it off with 'Pretty Woman,' the biggest single we ever had," Fred Foster remembered of the final conflict between him and Rose. "He comes to me, and he says, 'Under the contract you have four more songs to record with Roy, and I'm gonna tell you what you're gonna record, when you're gonna record, and when you're gonna release it.'"

Rose insisted that any new contract include a guarantee of $1 million, twenty prime-time television appearances a year for the life of the contract, and a film deal. Though Foster was more than prepared to pay the million dollars Rose demanded, he didn't own a movie studio and so couldn't guarantee a film deal. And after eighteen hit records in a row, the producer felt it was Rose's responsibility as Roy's manager, not his, to pick up the phone and book the twenty television shows, something he knew Rose could easily do.

As a result, when Roy headed back into the studio, Rose was in charge of the session. No one there, especially Roy, was happy with the situation. But he didn't have time to worry much about the state of his recording contract. A few days after the session, he flew to Australia. With a tour of Australia and New Zealand starting on Friday, January 22, 1965, and a return to the United States not planned till almost April, he had to get down to business.

Backed by his opening band, the Newbeats, during the tour and supported by Australia's own Rolf Harris, Roy also had another UK sensation along as a supporting act. This time it was England's newest hit makers, the Rolling Stones.

Above: Roy and Claudette at a diner, May 1961.
Opposite: Roy on ITV's *Thank Your Lucky Stars*, England, February 11, 1965. **Following pages**: Movie still from *The Fastest Guitar Alive*, 1967.

Chapter 4
CRYING

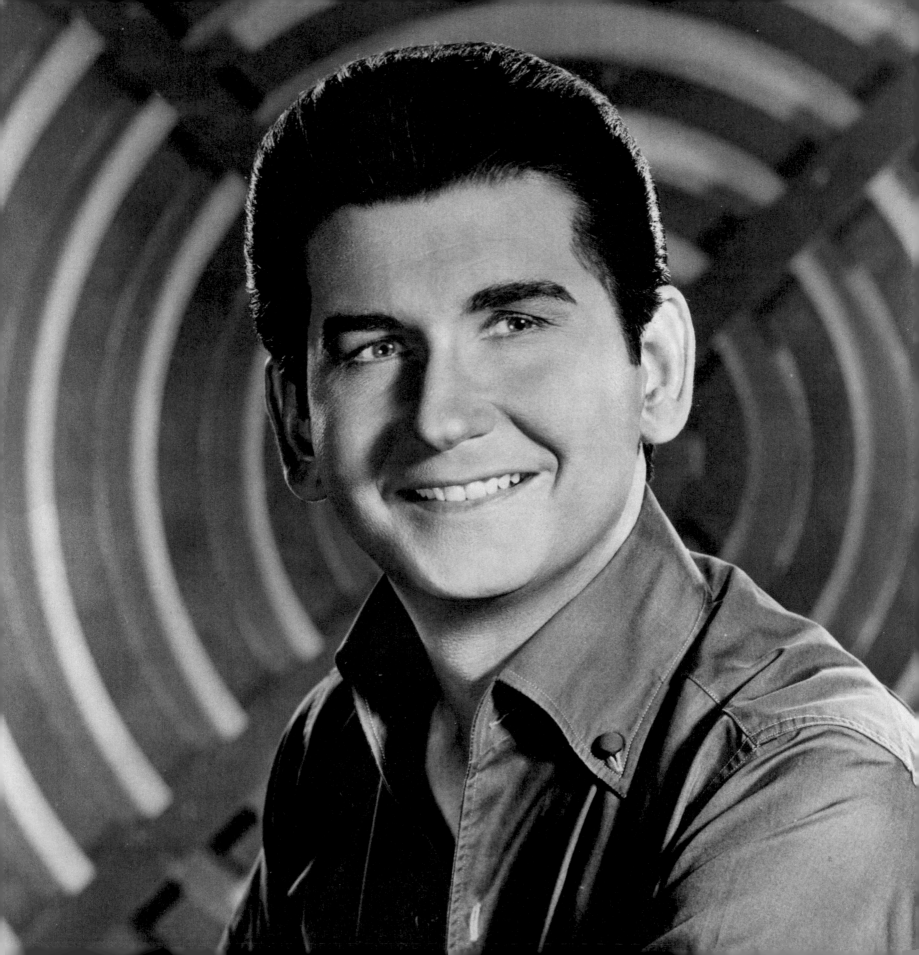

Roy recalled touring Australia

with the Rolling Stones with mixed emotions. "It was sort of a challenge," he said. "I felt that it wasn't the right coupling. It wasn't really a good, balanced show. But they were trying to express themselves in terms of rock and roll."

In fact, the Stones were doing exactly what Roy had been doing when he was at Sun Records; they were part of the younger generation, trying something new.

"Wow!" the Rolling Stones bassist, Bill Wyman, recalled about learning that the group would be touring with Roy. "We were quite bizarre in those days for the average American. But he'd toured with The Beatles before, so it was easy for him to accept us. We had a lot of laughs. He was top of the bill. It wasn't a problem for either of us. We went out with other people that were top of the bill, and we just wiped them off the stage. But there was a mixed audience. There were a lot of Orbison fans there. We'd never been there before."

Roy remembered years later how the Stones had taken inspiration from "Oh, Pretty Woman." "They liked 'Pretty Woman,' and that song had much the same feel," he recalled of the Stones's worldwide smash "(I Can't Get No) Satisfaction," which they'd soon write and record on a stopover in Los Angeles on the heels of the band's tour with Roy. "It had the same drum lick and guitar riff set up, and the drums by themselves. Anyway, they liked 'Pretty Woman' well enough to go back and write '(I Can't Get No) Satisfaction.'"

Roy and the Stones traveled Australia in armored vans, getting let off their chartered flights at the end of the runway only to end up in the back of the bulletproof vans, where the money would normally be carried. The hysteria that followed them around was such that Roy and the Stones resorted to using back-door entrances and service elevators at their hotels.

"We got to Melbourne," Roy remembered, "and there were two flagpoles, with a girl on each, way high up in the sky, hanging on these flagpoles. And they wanted to kiss me and Mick Jagger. If we didn't do it, they were gonna

Opposite: Promo shot for Roy's debut feature film role as Johnny in *The Fastest Guitar Alive,* 1967 (picture from September 1966). **Below**: Roy Orbison on tour in Australia with the Rolling Stones.

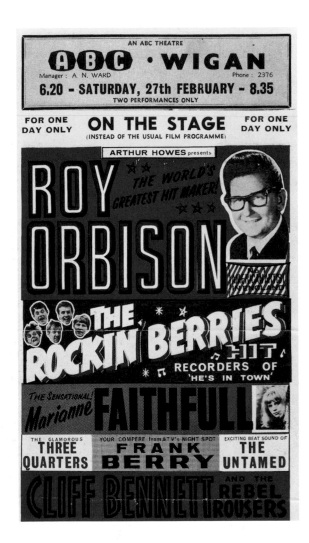

Above: Show flyer featuring Roy Orbison, the Rockin' Berries, Marianne Faithfull, Cliff Bennett, and more, 1965. **Opposite**: Roy Orbison and Marianne Faithfull in *Tuney Tunes* magazine, 1965.

stay there. So we had to go up. We gave them a kiss, and they came down. It was madness, but it was great fun."

Always the prankster in those days, Mick Jagger terrified the entire touring company, including Roy, when he announced on the intercom during one of their intercity flights that the plane they were on was going down, only to break up with laughter soon afterward.

More hijinks took place that Roy never forgot. "I remember the boys asking me to sing the worst song that I'd ever recorded," he said years later. "Mick Jagger said, 'I'll do the worst song I've recorded if you'll sing the worst song you've recorded.' I took him seriously, and I sang 'Ooby Dooby' on the show. Then they came on, and of course he didn't do whatever it was he was going to do. I called him everything under the sun, because for the longest time I wouldn't do the early material. I had done that for the first time onstage—'Ooby Dooby'—from '56 to '65. But at the end of the tour they gave me a silver cigarette case, and it says, 'To Ooby Dooby from the Rolling Stones in 1965.'"

While in Melbourne, Roy taped a TV special called *The Big Beat Show*, featuring all the performers on the tour and on which he acted as host, lip-synching "Only the Lonely," "Candy Man," and "Oh, Pretty Woman."

From there, Roy headed straight to England to begin a thirty-date UK tour with Marianne Faithfull, the Rockin' Berries, and Cliff Bennett and the Rebel Rousers, wrapping things up on Sunday, March 21 at the Empire Theatre in Liverpool.

When Roy appeared on *Top of the Pops* on Thursday, February 18, "Goodnight," the song he had cut at his last session at Wesley Rose's insistence, was already on the charts. It peaked at Number 21 in the United States on March 20 and Number 14 in England on March 13. The next day he appeared again on *Ready, Steady, Go!*, and on Saturday, February 27, on *Thank Your Lucky Stars* with Dusty Springfield, Johnny Rivers, and Tom Jones.

Roy also toured Holland, during which his dad and the heavily pregnant Claudette joined him, and he had his only ever concerts in Paris and Stockholm, both of which were recorded, before heading back to Hendersonville for some much-needed vacation. Claudette, meanwhile, headed back to Pasadena.

Roy's third son, Wesley K., was born on Thursday, May 13, at the Bayshore Hospital in Pasadena, Texas, nine months to the day that "Oh, Pretty Woman" had been written. Claudette's mom, Gerry, recalled that Roy and Claudette were together to welcome Wesley into the world and stayed with her at her house in Pasadena.

ROY ORBISON

MARIANNE FAITHFULL

Tuney Tunes

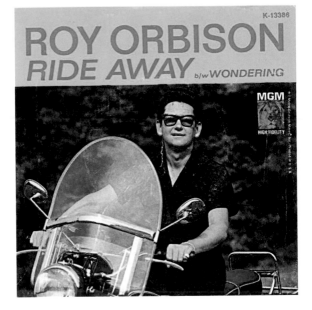

K-13386

ROY ORBISON
RIDE AWAY b/w WONDERING

MGM
HIGH FIDELITY

Roy and Claudette, of course, began to seriously discuss remarrying, but first Roy headed back to Nashville for what would be his final sessions with Fred Foster for many years. The single they recorded, "(Say) You're My Girl" backed with "Sleepy Hollow," proved to be a flop when it was released in late June, just as his Monument contract ended.

"MGM was a big company, and they painted a rosy picture for me and gave me a lot of money," Roy told *Rolling Stone* in 1988. Following the poor sales of "(Say) You're My Girl," orchestrated in no small part by Wesley Rose, and after a bidding war for Roy's services, Roy followed Rose's advice and chose MGM Records as his new home. That Acuff-Rose and MGM had strong ties going back years, when Wesley's father, Fred Rose, had served as the label's unofficial A&R man—the person who scouts for talent and then manages their choice of material, recording sessions, and releases—supervising sessions by Hank Williams, Bob Wills, and many other acts, was never disclosed to Roy.

"Obviously it was very painful when Roy left," Fred Foster recalled. "He sat in my office and wept, and I'm not talking about a tear or two, I'm talking about honest to God tears. He said, 'I hate to leave.'"

Under his new contract, MGM would distribute Roy in the United States and Canada, while London Decca would distribute his records in the rest of the world.

On July 3, *Billboard* reported:

Roy Orbison will be signing a $1 million 20-year contract with MGM records and Decca, according to informed sources here. Orbison also will be appearing in Metro-Goldwyn-Mayer films.

The deal calls for MGM to have the distribution rights to Orbison's disks in the U. S. and Canada, with Decca distributing his product throughout the rest of the world. . . .

Virtually all the major labels entered into the hot bidding for his talents. The Acuff-Rose organization has booked Orbison for a two-week tour of Ireland in July at the "biggest money any single pop act has ever received."

Then, on July 17, *Billboard* published a follow-up story from Nashville:

Roy Orbison reported to RCA Victor studios here last week to cut his first material for

MGM and British Decca under his new $1 million, 20-year contract. Orbison said he would cut 12 to 14 original tunes in a week-long series of sessions.

Orbison wrote some of the original material and wrote some of it with his composer partner, Bill Dees. Dees was co-author with Orbison on "Oh, Pretty Woman," which Orbison said was his top hit. Orbison was backed in the sessions by a chorale group and ten violins. He will leave later this week for two weeks of one-nighters in Ireland.

Money and a film deal weren't all that was included in the twenty-year contract Roy signed with MGM's president, Mort Nasatir. Sadly, the emphasis had shifted from quality to quantity. He was obligated to record no fewer than three albums and three singles every year, a total of at least forty-two new songs a year.

At roughly the same time that he signed his MGM contract, he also signed a new management and publishing deal with Acuff-Rose. In an article by Chris Hutchins called "My Films, Tour, Marriage by Roy Orbison," published by the British music paper *New Musical Express* during Roy's tour of Ireland, Roy gave an insight into his deal with MGM:

It's during my Irish tour that I am going to decide which film script to do first out of the several which have been put forward. Shooting on the first film begins in October and then I want to make three every two years under my new deal—which includes a record contract, of course—with MGM. I'm not out to collect any Academy Awards, but I think that I will be able to make some good pictures with the ideas that have so far come up.

MGM want me to film my own story in the near future but, obviously, I will make a picture or two before that so I get the hang of the movie business.

Roy also discussed his reconciliation with Claudette. "I haven't decided yet, but Claudette and I have been getting together and the possibility is by no means remote," he said when asked if the couple planned to remarry.

Roy's first MGM single, "Ride Away," with its B-side, "Wondering," was released in August. "Ride Away" reached only Number 25 in the United States and number 34 in the UK, but *Billboard*'s review of the single on August 14 was enthusiastic: "Making his debut on the MGM label, Orbison has a winner in a driving piece of material that moves from start to finish with a strong dance beat."

RIDE AWAY

By ROY ORBISON and BILL DEES
RECORDED BY ROY ORBISON FOR M.G.M. RECORDS

PUBLISHED BY
ACUFF-ROSE PUBLICATIONS, INC.
Sole Selling Agents:
ACUFF-ROSE SALES, INC.
2510 FRANKLIN ROAD
NASHVILLE 4, TENNESSEE

Opposite: Roy Orbison's first MGM single, "Ride Away," 1965. **Above**: Sheet music for "Ride Away." **Following pages**: British sheet music for "Wondering," and Roy's first MGM album, *There Is Only One Roy Orbison*.

Wondering

By ROY ORBISON & BILL DEES

Recorded by **ROY ORBISON**
on LONDON Records

ACUFF-ROSE MUSIC LTD.,
15, ST. GEORGE STREET, LONDON, W.1.

ACUFF-ROSE PUBLICATIONS INC. U.S.A.

2/6

Made in England

18 12233

there is only one
ROY ORBISON

MGM
HIGH FIDELITY

Above: Claudette with sons Roy DeWayne,
Anthony King, and newborn Wesley, summer 1965.
Opposite: (top) Sheet music for "Breakin' Up is
Breakin' My Heart." (bottom) Single art for a Coca-
Cola jingle featuring Roy Orbison, circa 1966.

"It should have been a hit," Bill Dees told the BBC's Spencer Leigh. "A lot of women have hooks out to get you, and 'Ride Away' is about escaping that. I like the idea, as it represents the spirit of all men wanting to be free."

A few weeks later, Monument Records released a song that had remained in the vaults, "Let the Good Times Roll," marking the beginning of a long feud between Roy's old and new labels. *Billboard* called the single a "rhythm-blues classic [that] gets the outstanding Orbison treatment which spells hitsville all the way!"

Meanwhile, MGM's *There Is Only One Roy Orbison* was released in August, peaking at Number 55 in the US album charts. It would be Roy's last charting album with original material in the United States until his late-1980s comeback. More encouraging, however, was his British chart placement. The album reached Number 10 there.

The Monument years will perhaps always be remembered as Roy's most glorious years as a recording artist. Moreover, Nashville was the place to be in 1960. But by 1965, it had become isolated for an artist like Roy. With The Beatles dominating the American charts, the Rolling Stones having just released "(I Can't Get No) Satisfaction," and Bob Dylan breaking all sorts of rules with "Like a Rolling Stone," the music world was changing fast.

"All artists—writers, painters, musicians—need a climate of freedom in which to work," Roy acknowledged at the time. "They need time to think and feel and plan. They need time to contemplate the direction their careers are going to take; they need a climate of freedom which

WITH THE BEATLES DOMINATING THE AMERICAN CHARTS, THE ROLLING STONES HAVING JUST RELEASED "(I CAN'T GET NO) SATISFACTION," AND BOB DYLAN BREAKING ALL SORTS OF RULES WITH "LIKE A ROLLING STONE," THE MUSIC WORLD WAS CHANGING FAST.

will allow them to expand, develop new ideas and concepts. This is exactly my kind of freedom my signing with MGM Records will allow me as an artist."

October 11 saw the release of MGM's second single, "Crawling Back," which peaked at Number 46 in the United States and was into and out of the charts in seven weeks. Nevertheless, the quality of Roy's singles was still strong, and he still enjoyed chart success in the United Kingdom.

At about that time Roy also recorded several Coca-Cola advertisements as part of Coke's $10 million promotional campaign in which popular singers all over the United States and Europe contributed modified versions of their hits with Coke's jingle, "Things Go Better with Coke." Designed for radio broadcast by William Backer of Coca-Cola, Roy and Bill Dees adapted his music to form the basis of eleven different commercials. Roy was thrilled at the chance to promote his favorite soft drink.

Around this time, Roy's MGM recordings, such as "Crawling Back" and "Breakin' Up Is Breakin' My Heart," seemed to reflect his personal life even more than his Monument hits had. "Men are too macho to think that they would ever crawl back to a woman," Bill Dees told Spencer Leigh.

. . . Roy put himself at risk in "Crawling Back" for what he thought was the truth. That is definitely our song, but it's in his heart because he was taking Claudette back at the time. Her heart and personality came out through the split, and he realized her worth more and wanted her back. "Breakin' Up Is Breakin' My Heart" is also very real, true to life stuff. Actually when he and Claudette split up, 'It's Over' was like a slap in the face. I could hardly see how he could go on stage and sing it."

Roy would later say that he couldn't eat, couldn't sleep, and certainly couldn't write a song when he was heartbroken. He needed to let some time go by so he could internalize what had happened.

Roy and Claudette had been seen together as far back as March 1965, during Roy's European tour, and the couple finally remarried in Nashville in December, after an application for marriage was filed with the State of Tennessee on Monday, December 20, 1965.

The Orbison Way, Roy's next MGM album, continued the nice-and-easy style of Roy's first MGM LP. Meanwhile, MGM's brass was already arranging sessions for another album. In perhaps a desperate move to catch the eye of record buyers, it was to be called *The Classic Roy Orbison*; in fact, it turned out to be the rockingest and most experimental album of Roy's career, reaching Number 12 on the UK charts.

Meanwhile, Roy arrived in London on Friday, March 18, 1966, to appear on *Sunday Night at the London Palladium* and for his tour with the Walker Brothers and Lulu, scheduled to start on Friday, March 25, as well as the usual round of radio and television appearances.

During the Palladium show, Roy performed "Oh, Pretty Woman," "In Dreams," "It's Over," and his new single, "Twinkle Toes." Surviving footage from that performance in brilliant color, which served as a test for the eventual conversion of British television to color, is as clear as if it had been filmed yesterday.

In the meantime, England's *Record Mirror* published an article that gave fans a nice inside look at the private Roy Orbison and his enjoyment of motorcycles, on Saturday, March 26: "Roy's stable includes a Harley Davidson, a 400 Honda and a BMW," the article stated. "It's a relief from frustration and the desire for thrills is satisfied," Roy was quoted as saying. "You get a good thrill and atmosphere, the good wind and the sun and it's an outdoor sport. I'm completely taken with it."

But in the midst of the thirty-one-date Orbison–Walker Brothers tour, Roy's fifth of England, another motorcycle outing, on Sunday, March 27, provided more thrills than Roy had bargained for: "American singer Roy Orbison took a tumble in front of 15,000 spectators," reported Syndication International. "Roy, a keen motorcyclist, had been watching a scrambling event at Hawkstone Park, Shropshire, when rider Dave Bickers offered to loan him his 250 c.c. Czech machine for a trial run. But after covering only 100 yards of the track, Roy fell off in the high wind. Gallantly, he remounted and rode back to the pits unhurt."

But Roy was hardly unhurt. He had hit a sand pit and broken his ankle, forcing him to finish the tour perched on a stool and sporting a cast. Upon hearing the news, Claudette immediately flew to England

Opposite: A regal-looking Claudette follows Roy, cane in hand, while recovering from a broken foot in England. **Above**: A Walker Brothers tour program, 1966. **Below**: April 23, 1966 show flyer for the Walker Brothers/Roy Orbison tour.

to be with him, helping to ease the pain. Though Roy always blamed the fall on the foot controls on the borrowed British race bike being reversed, the fall also served as an opportunity to let the world know that he and Claudette were back together.

Roy turned thirty during the tour, and at the Odeon in Hammersmith, on the evening of April 23, his fan club surprised him.

"I know there were a lot of you in the audience at the Odeon, Hammersmith in anticipation of Roy's birthday, and with lots of scheming we managed to keep our plans secret for presenting Roy with a birthday present from the club," Margaret Finch, the president of Roy's UK fan club, wrote in the *Official International Roy Orbison Fan Club Magazine* in May 1966. "I had previously asked Claudette if there was anything special that might interest Roy, and one of my suggestions was a sheepskin coat. Claudette immediately jumped at the idea and said that this would be marvelous and it was something that they had both wanted."

It seemed that everybody in the theater knew about the surprise but Roy. Along with Finch, her vice president, Mick Perry, and Ron Heymans of the Dutch fan club, presented Roy with a cake and presents in the midst of the show, complete with a crowd-sung "Happy Birthday."

After the show, Finch presented Roy and Claudette with the twin sheepskin coats, which they immediately put on and wore to Roy's birthday party, held at La Dolce Vita restaurant in Soho, a favorite of Roy's, where he'd often party with his old touring buddies The Beatles when they all found themselves in London at the same time.

Finally, on May 1, before leaving England for more promotional appearances and recording sessions, Roy performed at the annual NME Poll Winners concert at Wembley, alongside The Beatles, the Rolling Stones, the Walker Brothers, the Shadows, the Yardbirds, Cliff Richard, Herman's Hermits, Sounds Incorporated, Dusty Springfield, and the Who.

After traveling to California to appear on ABC's *Shivaree* TV show, Roy returned to Nashville, and the recording studio, to finish his LP *The Classic Roy Orbison*, after which he headed back to Los Angeles to tape appearances for ABC's *Where the Action Is*, as well as Dick Clark's *American Bandstand* for the second time. During a short interview after Roy had performed "Oh, Pretty Woman," Roy told Clark that he'd be back in Hollywood that autumn to begin filming *The Fastest Guitar Alive*.

Above: Roy and Claudette celebrate Roy's birthday at La Dolce Vita restaurant in London, England, with a guitar-themed cake after his Hammersmith Odeon appearance, April 23, 1966. Birthday cake and twin coats were a present from the British Fan Club. Fred Foster can be seen between Roy and Claudette in the background.

Sunday, June 5, 1966, was a beautiful spring day in Tennessee, and Roy and Claudette made the most of it. Along with 50,000 other fans, they took in the National Hot Rod Association Springnationals at the Bristol International Dragway, where Jimmy Nix won the Top Fuel category at a speed of 213 MPH at "the finest, fastest, and largest springtime drag racing event ever staged," according to *National Dragster* magazine.

Roy and Claudette had spent the weekend in Bristol and headed home on Highway 11 West, with Roy riding his Harley and Claudette on her Honda motorcycle. On the way, Claudette's bike had a flat tire, so the pair spent the night in Knoxville, about 185 miles away from their home in Hendersonville. The next day, June 6, they continued home. By 6:45 p.m., they entered Gallatin. Riding a few blocks apart, with Roy in the lead, he stopped at a light at the intersection of South Water and Maple Streets in Gallatin. When the light turned green, he made a left but quickly realized he'd lost track of Claudette. He stopped, turned around, and saw an ambulance at the intersection of South Water Street and Coles Ferry Road. When he got there, the scene was mayhem.

A pickup truck had run a stop sign and pulled out in front of Claudette. She'd run into the side of the truck at full speed. The thirty-year-old driver, Kenneth Herald, was uninjured in the crash and said he had not seen the motorcycle when he pulled onto the main highway from the side street.

Claudette was taken to Sumner County Memorial Hospital on Hartsville Pike in Gallatin, barely five minutes away, but nothing could be done to save her. She was pronounced dead two hours later, at 9 p.m.

Herald was initially charged with manslaughter, and bail was posted at $750, but the charges were later dropped.

Roy headed home to tell their children so they wouldn't hear it first on the radio. "Momma's not coming home," he told his oldest boy, R.D.

"Did Momma go to Heaven on a Honda?" young Tony finally asked.

Wesley was just a baby.

Services were held on Wednesday, June 8, at 10 a.m. at the Hendersonville chapel of Phillips-Robinson Funeral Home at Hadley Avenue and Old Hickory Boulevard. When the service was over, a small group of family and close friends headed to Woodlawn Memorial Park in South Nashville for the burial. Claudette's parents came up to Hendersonville from Houston. Roy's friend Bobby Blackburn was also there, as was Wesley Rose.

PRETTY LITTLE PET, CLAUDETTE

NEVER MAKE ME FRET, CLAUDETTE

'CAUSE SHE'S THE GREATEST LITTLE GIRL THAT I'VE EVER MET

I GET THE BEST LOVING THAT I'LL EVER GET

"I remember my mind just going numb, and it seemed it was all a dream," Claudette's brother, Bill Frady, recalled. "I just couldn't bring my mind to accept the fact that my sister was gone. She was so much a part of my life."

Frady helped carry Claudette's bronze-colored casket to the grave site. As he stood there, while the preacher spoke, he tuned him out, saying his final good-byes to Claudette silently to himself. The funeral ended, and everyone slowly drifted back to their cars and limos, but Frady stayed there until he was alone, not wanting to leave his sister for the last time, reliving their lives together in his mind.

Roy, in shock, retreated to his home. Alone now, but with three young boys who needed him, he knew he had to get back to work.

A few weeks later, he was interviewed by *Disc* magazine and seemed to be trying to make sense of the tragedy and to gain some perspective. "I don't think this terrible shock has put me off motorbikes," Roy said. "I try to think along the lines that people have accidents in automobiles, in airplanes, just as much as on motorbikes. At least I'd like to feel this way about it. I don't know yet that I really do. It was such a tremendous shock to me that I'm still numb. I think it is probably a little early to say how I feel.

"My thinking, you see, just isn't connecting at the moment," he went on. "In a month's time I'm starting my first movie, *The Fastest Guitar Alive*. I'll enjoy the work. In fact I aim to do a whole lot of work for the next few months. It'll help."

"I was supposed to be with him on that trip when Claudette was killed, but my bike was in the shop so I didn't get to go," Bill Dees later recalled to Spencer Leigh of the BBC. "After all those things, Roy couldn't settle. He was in and out of things, and it was like being with a high pressure cooker. He had a hard time getting over these hurdles, and I like to think I helped him. He felt he should keep on working, but he was vulnerable and delicate. He didn't like to let anyone down."

Roy did indeed stay busy. He kept working and recording, building model airplanes, riding motorcycles, and collecting old cars. In June, Monument released the single "Lana" from Roy's *Crying* LP, and in July MGM issued "Too Soon to Know."

"I didn't want to go into the studio and record something new, so I just said 'release whatever you think is best,'" Roy told *NME*. Nevertheless, he was criticized in the press for releasing the single so soon after the crash. "That was 'Too Soon to Know.' Every song I do from now on could be subject to misinterpretation."

The single peaked at Number 68 in the US charts, while in the United Kingdom it entered the Top 10, peaking at Number 3.

Opposite: Original painting of Claudette Orbison, artist unknown. **Above**: Roy on one of his BMW motorcycles during a promo shoot for his MGM single "Ride Away," July 1965.

Top: Roy Orbison with his Excalibur SSK.
Below: Outtake from the *Cry Softly Lonely One* album cover, 1967. **Opposite**: Roy Orbison sans glasses as Johnny in *The Fastest Guitar Alive*, wielding the gun/guitar for which the movie is named.
Following pages: Roy Orbison's debut feature film role as Johnny in *The Fastest Guitar Alive*. MGM Pictures, 1967.

Meanwhile, Roy worked on songs for *The Fastest Guitar Alive*. "We tried to make them more or less timeless," Roy told *Movie Go Round* at the time.

In the meantime, Orbie Lee and Nadine had moved to Hendersonville from Texas to watch over the kids, and by late July, Roy was back in Los Angeles appearing on Dick Clark's *Where the Action Is*, performing two hits from his Monument period, "Mean Woman Blues" and "Dream Baby." After recording the soundtrack album and an album of songs by Don Gibson, Roy began shooting in Culver City, California, in September. Elvis and Colonel Tom Parker sent a telegram to MGM in Hollywood wishing him the best of luck.

The film premiered on July 19, 1967. Intended as a serious film, it ended up a comedy and stiffed at the box office.

"We had a seven-picture contract," Roy told Glenn A. Baker in 1980. "I was gonna make seven motion pictures for MGM, but they were getting into financial trouble at the time. I didn't know it, but they weren't doing well. So I made this first movie, and it was intended to be a serious film. And what happened, before I got to Hollywood, *Cat Ballou* had won the Academy Award in April, so they figured they would follow suit and have a funny western. It's got to make a little money, they figured. But they figured wrong."

On Wednesday, October 26, 1966, Roy went into the studio and cut one of the strongest songs from the MGM period, "Communication Breakdown." Released in November 1966, it reached only Number 60 in the US charts. Although he was in peak form, his upcoming tours of the United Kingdom and later Australia would do big business, and he would still enjoy regular chart success in both countries, his hits in his home country had dried up.

Meanwhile, he ordered a white 1967 Excalibur SSK for $7,915 from Excalibur Motors in Houston, Texas. The gorgeous car would show up on the cover of the upcoming "Cry Softly Lonely One" single and LP.

"As many of you will know I have a wonderful home over Lake Hickory in Hendersonville, which is not far from Nashville," Roy wrote in "A Letter to You from Roy Orbison" in the United Kingdom's *Record Mirror*. "I keep several of my 16 cars at home, but the others are at a garage in the town.

I haven't done a great many concerts since my six-week British tour, but have been concentrating on song writing and recording," he continued, adding that he did most of his writing in the afternoons and recording at night, prefacing the rock star lifestyle that so many of his peers would soon adopt.

Incidentally we have two or three tracks which everybody seems to like and from which a new single will be chosen very shortly. I am also putting the finishing touches on another LP.

When I am not recording I often visit friends' homes in the area or go and watch a movie. Very occasionally I go to a nightclub. Some evenings I just swim in the pool, which is built into the lounge of the house, and then relax watching some good color television. There is always plenty to occupy my mind, but it is not an exhausting life like touring is. However I have an American college tour to do next month [October] and then a Canadian concert tour in November."

He then signed off, noting that production on his next film had been shelved until the spring.

By now the relationship between Roy and MGM had soured. "The first few things for MGM were hit records, so I knew that everything wasn't terribly amiss," Roy told *Rolling Stone* in 1988. "But the transition wasn't really that smooth. I think the records were okay, maybe, through '68 or so. But I was having to record a lot, plus I'd had some personal problems. My first wife was killed in '66. I'm a bit hazy, but I think the company was sold. So on one hand you had a company that wasn't really viable, and then on the other you had me, with things happening around me and to me. I mean, it was a dark period for me."

Roy never did incorporate his MGM material into his live set in a way that would showcase the remarkable work he was churning out at a breakneck speed.

"The movie will help sales of this LP, but the album also contains a sleeper that packs powerful emotion—"There Won't Be Many Coming Home," *Billboard* wrote of Roy's soundtrack for *The Fastest Guitar Alive*. But the song wasn't featured in the film, and the soundtrack failed to make a mark on the charts. In association with MGM, Roy had started his own movie company, Kelton, but *The Fastest Guitar Alive* proved to be his one and only appearance in a major motion picture.

Roy toured Canada following the release of *The Fastest Guitar Alive*, his last with his band known as the Candy Men, but a tour of England and Ireland was postponed when he developed kidney stones. In the meantime, he was buying up real estate around Hendersonville and had accumulated twenty vintage cars from the 1920s and '30s.

"The most interesting to me is the '27 Bentley racing car with short chassis," he told *Late Night Extra*.

On Wednesday, July 24, 1968, after a performance at the Batley Variety Club, Roy was ca-joled into a night out at a discotheque in Leeds. There he met Barbara Anne Marie Well-höner Jakobs, the daughter of a wealthy West German industrialist who had been appointed as his country's consul to Panama. Born in 1951 in Bielefeld, Germany, Barbara didn't know who Roy was. But as soon as he spied her across the floor of the disco, Roy wanted to meet her.

"I'd been living in England since I was 11, though I was born in Germany," Barbara later told the *Sunday Times*.

In 1968, when I was 17, I travelled from London to Leeds to visit a friend of mine, Patricia, who had started architectural college. We went to this really glitzy discotheque, and we heard that a singer named Roy Orbison was going to come later.

When Roy saw me he decided he wanted to meet me, so somebody came up and asked me if I would meet him. I ignored them, but then somebody else came to ask me, and I went to say hello. We started talking then, and for 20 years we never really stopped.

"I was doing a tour of England in 1968, and I never go any-where after the show really, except back to the hotel," Roy recalled in 1981. "This was a variety show, and there were other acts on the show: a ventriloquist and comedian and a female singer. They all said, 'Let's go to a discotheque.' And I said, 'Thank you, no thanks.' And the next thing I knew, one had one arm and one had the other and I was off to the discotheque. And so in this dark place, with loud music, I met Barbara and she said she'd never heard of me, and I didn't believe that. Then she told me a lot of things, and I didn't believe her. And I told her quite a few things; she proba-bly didn't believe me. But anyway, she said, 'That's a terrible-looking jacket you have on.' And I said, 'Thank you very much.' It was a Levi's jacket, but I said, 'I just borrowed this so I wouldn't catch cold. It belongs to my friend there.' And I said, 'Come to the show tomorrow night, and I'll show you my finest suit.'"

Opposite: Roy Orbison and Barbara Anne Marie Wellhöner Jakobs in Australia, 1970.
Above: Newlyweds. Roy plays photographer while Barbara models, London, April 1, 1969.

Barbara went to see Roy the following night. It was a nightclub show that was essentially a glorified dress rehearsal for Roy's upcoming performance on *Talk of the Town*, and he wore a tuxedo. Not used to wearing a bow tie onstage, he felt uncomfortable. But the outfit did the trick. "You know, if you were trying to impress me, you did all right," Barbara told him afterward.

The *London Evening Standard* was equally entranced and described Roy's *Talk of the Town* performances as "hypnotic."

Roy's tour was a huge smash. On September 14, 1968, after a week of performances at the Birmingham Theatre, he and his band were set to wrap things up before flying back to the United States. After soundcheck, as the audience filed in, he sat in his dressing room and chatted with his bassist, Terry Widlake. He opened his wallet and showed off pictures of his young boys. Then he showed Widlake pictures of his home, with its glass walls, waterfalls, and magnificent stone fireplace.

"That's beautiful," Widlake remarked. "You know, if something ever happened in the fireplace, the water would put it out."

"Aww," Roy said with a shrug, "the house is virtually fireproof."

In a cruel twist of fate, later that night, back in his hotel room, Roy picked up the phone to hear Bobby Blackburn's frantic voice. His house had burned to the ground, and two of his young sons were gone.

When Claudette's brother, Bill Frady, got a call that something terrible had happened, he jumped into his new Pontiac GTO and headed for Hendersonville. When he arrived the following morning, he was shocked. Not a wall was left standing, as though a bulldozer had flattened everything, only the remnants of the chimney reaching into the morning sky. The only things he recognized were the stairways that had led to the boys' rooms.

Walking around the property, Frady came upon a charred Coca-Cola bottle, the only object he could find that even hinted that people had once lived in the smoldering ruins.

Above: Roy's parents, Nadine and Orbie Lee, with Roy's son Wesley at Roy's house. **Below**: Roy's sons Anthony King and Wesley, spring 1968. **Opposite**: (top) A newspaper clipping shares the details of the tragedy. (bottom) Roy DeWayne and Anthony King outside their Hendersonville, TN home, spring 1968.

Orbie Lee and Nadine had been on the main floor of Roy's sprawling home, watching TV, while the boys were playing downstairs. Suddenly Wesley appeared, saying excitedly to Orbie Lee, "Hot! Hot!"

"Grab a pan and fill it with water," Orbie Lee told Nadine, and he headed downstairs. When he opened the bedroom door, the room was filled with smoke. He threw the pan of water Nadine brought him where he thought the bed was and headed back upstairs. Meanwhile, the house was filling with smoke. Fast.

Orbie Lee yelled to Nadine through the thickening smoke, "We'd better get outside!"

But by the time they got to the front door and Orbie Lee tried to open it, the fire had created such a vacuum that the door wouldn't budge.

Nadine was by his side, holding Wesley on her hip with one hand and holding on to Orbie with the other. Roy D. and Tony were holding on tight to Orbie's leg.

Orbie tried the door again, but it still wouldn't budge. He gave it everything he had, and the door opened a few inches. The awful sound they heard was, as Orbie Lee later described it, "as loud and ferocious as a jet airplane engine." Suddenly the door flew open and sucked Orbie Lee, Nadine, and Wesley outside with a force so great that they went flying through the air, landing in the yard about twenty feet from the door.

Roy D. and Tony, meanwhile, were ripped from the hold they'd had on Orbie's leg and sucked back into the house. With the home engulfed in flames, Orbie Lee was never able to make it back inside to save the grandchildren he loved so dearly.

Johnny Cash and his wife, June Carter, canceled their tour dates as soon as they got the news. The pair chartered a jet home, but there was nothing to be done. Roy sent word that he was unable to face anybody, so they just stayed home, waiting to hear about funeral arrangements, looking out the window now and again at the now-vacant lot and blackened chimney where Roy's magnificent home had stood.

"I couldn't even approach Roy at the funeral," Cash recalled in his memoir.

For the first time in my life I was at a total loss of words, gestures, anything. And it was a week or more before I found it in myself to call him. Then I just told him that I loved him. He said he'd be all right, but I couldn't imagine how he could be.

I didn't see him for a long time after that. He'd moved in with his parents, who lived across the road, and they'd put a "No Visitors" sign on the door. I asked his father about him from time to time, but the answer was always the same: He was there in the house, but he stayed shut up in his bedroom.

Eventually I had to act. I crossed the road, told his father I had to see him, and went to his room. And there he was: So pale that he could have been dead himself, just sitting in bed with his shades on, facing a large-screen television with the sound turned all the way down. He didn't get up from the bed when I came in. I don't know if he was crying because I couldn't see his eyes. I don't know if he even looked at me. He didn't speak.

TWO FEARED DEAD IN FIRE

HENDERSONVILLE, Tenn. (AP)— Two small sons of singer Roy Orbison were missing and presumed dead Saturday night after fire destroyed the country music star's lakeside home near here.

Hendersonville fire authorities identified the missing children as Roy Duane Orbison, 11, and Tony Orbison, 6.

No bodies had been found late Saturday.

A third son, 3-year-old Wesley, escaped without injury.

Firefighters said flames raced throughout the house, then were followed by an explosion in the basement which shook the burning residence.

Orbison, whose wife was killed in a motorcycle accident in 1966, was reportedly on his way home after engagements in England.

The children were being cared for in Orbison's absence by their grandparents, Mr. and Mrs. Orbie Orbison and a housekeeper.

Gallatin, Tenn., Fire Chief George Thompson quoted the grandfather as saying he was trying to get the three children out of the house when the fire broke out about 6:30 p.m.

"He had gotten the kids almost to the front door when an explosion erupted in the basement," youngsters got out, but we believe the other two were trapped inside."

The grandparents escaped without injury.

Above: Roy is escorted by a TWA employee after rushing back to the United States upon learning that two of his sons died in a fire, New York, 1968.
Opposite: Roy during his first visit to England, possibly at the Westbury Hotel, London, 1962.

I was still at a loss for words that seemed anywhere close to adequate, so I said what I could: That I loved him and that I wouldn't know how to handle it if I lost my own son that way. "I don't know how to handle it, either," he said, and that was all. I left.

The next time I saw him, he'd emerged from his room and decided to build a new house on the lot adjacent to the old one. I walked up to the construction site one day and was happy to find him almost his old self. We talked about the new house, and then he told me that he'd like June and me to have the old lot. Sure, I said. We worked it out and I bought it from him, and then I told him that I'd never build on it or sell it to anyone else, even though it was the most valuable land in the neighborhood. I'd plant a vineyard and an orchard there, and their first fruits each year would always be his. He liked that; I think he was glad that strangers wouldn't live where his children died.

Cash had moved next door to Roy in early 1968, into a house built by the same builders as Roy's and featuring some of the same characteristics. The two were as close as two musicians who traveled the world constantly could be, and the Cashes had become godparents to Roy's children. In a strange twist of fate, many years later, in 2007, Johnny's house also burned to the ground.

"About three or four months after Roy's house burned, he called and asked if I could come by his hotel," recalled Roy's buddy Harold Bradley, his guitarist on his early '60s Monument sessions. "He didn't have a home. I went over there, knocked on the door, and he opened it. Inside it was absolutely dark, with food wrappers all over the room. He evidently had not been out of the place in a week. He wanted to talk about getting some guitars. I think that was his way of regaining his sanity."

I SAID WHAT I COULD: THAT I LOVED HIM AND THAT I WOULDN'T KNOW HOW TO HANDLE IT IF I LOST MY OWN SON THAT WAY. — JOHNNY CASH

Chapter 5
THE WILDERNESS YEARS

"I remember going on a worldwide tour after . . . after both things happened. Sort of as therapy, but also to keep doing what I had been doing," Roy told *Rolling Stone* in 1988.

If you're trying to be true to yourself, and you would normally tour and write and function that way, if something traumatic happens to you, I've never seen the sense in dropping all that. Because it's not necessarily a personal thing, you know? It happens directly to you, but it's not directed *at* you, necessarily. In my case I went ahead and did what I normally did, insofar as I could, and then let love and time and things like that take care of everything. I guess I'm talking about faith, probably. And if you feel really singled out, I think you can make a lot of mistakes. I don't know of anyone who hasn't lost someone. . . .

It may be a mystery to you at the time, and is. But if the faith is there, you ask yourself, "What is it all about?" But not every day, every minute.

I feel that that's what went on with me. It was a long, long time ago, but I'm trying to reach back and really give you what went on as opposed to what I would like to have had happen. It was a devastating blow, but not debilitating. I wasn't totally incapacitated by events. And I think that's stood me in good stead. You don't come out unscathed, but you don't come out murdered, you know? And of course, I remarried in '69, Barbara and I, and we started our life together. . . . I don't know whether she knows this, but she was a source of inspiration and faith too. So I have to give her credit.

Previous pages: Roy with Rolls Royce in England, May 1970. **Opposite** and **Right**: Roy and Barbara, London, April 1970.

BARBARA WAS A SIGNIFICANT SOURCE OF STRENGTH FOR ROY IN THE AFTERMATH OF ROY D. AND TONY'S DEATHS.

Indeed, Barbara was a significant source of strength for Roy in the aftermath of Roy D. and Tony's deaths. They'd talk daily, and she'd take him out of his pain and misery. It created an unbreakable bond between the two of them.

Roy proposed to Barbara over the phone, and in November he flew to Germany to meet her parents and formally ask for their daughter's hand. They returned to Tennessee in December so Barbara could meet Roy's parents. A wedding was planned for March 1969.

Under Roy's contract with MGM, he still owed the struggling label three albums each year, and the frantic pace was taking its toll. Still, in the aftermath of the tragedy in Hendersonville, Roy and Bill Dees began work on new material and Roy was back in the studio on Tuesday, January 21, 1969, to record three new songs: "My Friend," "Child Woman, Woman Child," both by Orbison-Dees, and "Sweet Memories" by Mickey Newbury. From that session, "My Friend" would become the next single.

On Friday, January 24, Roy was in the studio again, recording four new songs, "If I Had a Woman like You," "Tennessee Owns My Soul," "Laurie," and "Loose Lip Lucy," and four days later, he was recording again, this time "Judy, Judy, Judy" and "The Defector." "Southbound Jericho Parkway," written by Bobby Bond, was put to tape on January 30, and by the end of the month they had also cut "Give Up" and "Leaving Makes the Rain Come Down."

Those January 1969 sessions resulted in some of Roy's strongest material while at MGM. The songs were contemporary and mostly upbeat, and they sounded fresh and new. For all that was going on in his private life, he sounded as though he were in top shape. Still, MGM decided to shelve the material, and Wesley Rose hatched the idea for Roy to record an album's worth of music by Hank Williams, whose music Acuff-Rose controlled.

Roy went on tour shortly after the sessions, playing across Canada to make up for concerts he'd canceled in October 1968. Local newspapers reported that Roy had grossed $10,000 in Winnipeg alone and that the entire tour had netted him roughly $90,000, tremendous sums in 1969. Meanwhile, Bob Dylan was in Nashville recording his *Nashville Skyline* album and hanging out with Johnny Cash. While there, Dylan stopped by Roy's house and knocked on the door, but Roy wasn't in.

"What I try to do is knock a bit of the tops off of the mountains and fill in a bit of the valleys, and it works well," Roy told Brian Matthew on *Round Midnight* in 1980. "My new family helped a lot and the career helped a lot," he told Radio Trent that same year. "Then, about six months later, I really realized the full impact of what I'd gone through, and that set me back a little bit. But I wrote some great songs during that time."

"When the first record came along, there was a lot of money involved, but I didn't stop doing what I normally do," Roy said on *Tomorrow with Tom Snyder*. "In other words, I didn't go crazy, I didn't dress differently, I wouldn't be any different to you, and I've been taught by my parents that that shouldn't change anything, after all you're just another person. So I didn't get the big head, didn't throw wild parties. So when something traumatic happens to you, I try to maintain a steady balance. Time takes care of a lot of things. You just don't go off the deep end, you accept it, live with it, the same way with the high praise that people have given me. I think you have to let a little time go by to see how great something is or what it really means to your existence."

Roy married Barbara on Tuesday, March 25, 1969, in Madison, Tennessee. Bill Dees was his best man, and Ira North, the minister of the Madison Church of Christ, who had officiated at the burial of Roy's children, solemnized the ceremony. Wesley Rose, Orbie Lee, Nadine, and Wesley, who was nearly four at the time, also attended.

Before meeting Roy, Barbara had been going to college. "Now I'm giving that up," she told the press. "Now I'm going to travel with Roy." The couple left for Germany after the wedding, and Roy formally presented his bride at a press reception in London on Tuesday, April 1.

Playing a black 1969 Gibson Les Paul Custom, known by musicians as a Black Beauty, featuring deluxe fingerboard inlays, gold-plated parts, and dual Humbucker pickups, Roy set off on a two-month tour of Ireland, Scotland, and England, including a two-week residency at the Batley Variety Club, where he recorded a planned live album, to be called *Roy Orbison Live in England*; however, the album featured the Monument hits that made up Roy's usual setlist, which MGM was loath to release. And since Wesley Rose had neglected, in Roy's contract, to require MGM to release live albums—the way Colonel Tom Parker had for Elvis, to great success—there was nothing that could be done.

When Roy returned from England, he hit the road again and then headed straight back into the studio for a series of sessions in July, bringing with him two songs by Sammy King, a young songwriter from Leeds, England, whom Roy had met while on tour there.

"After Tonight" and "Penny Arcade," by King, were recorded during a two-day session on July 17 and July 18, and "Penny Arcade" was chosen to be Roy's next single. Roy found himself with a monster hit in continental Europe, the United Kingdom, and Australia. The single sold

more than 100,000 copies in Australia alone, becoming the best-selling single there that year. It reached the Number 1 and became Roy's first gold disc there since "Oh, Pretty Woman."

In September, Roy was recognized by the Nashville Country Music Hall of Fame when his star was added to the Walk of Fame there. Although he never considered himself a country and western artist, he took the honor in stride.

Then, on Saturday, September 27, Roy was in downtown Nashville, appearing on *The Johnny Cash Show*, which was filmed at the Ryman Auditorium, the home of the Grand Ole Opry. He performed an outstanding version of "Crying," as well as "Oh, Pretty Woman," with Cash.

"I wonder if you remember the advice you gave me many years ago," Roy chided his old friend during one part of the show. "You said, 'If you change your name and lower your voice, you might make it.'" Cash laughed, clearly embarrassed.

For the rest of the year, Roy kept up a busy schedule, alternating between live appearances and long days in the recording studio.

In 1969, the Las Vegas developer Kirk Kerkorian bought the near-bankrupt MGM Corporation, including its movie studios and record company, and, along with it, Roy's recording contract. He then hired twenty-five-year-old Mike Curb to helm the struggling MGM Records.

Roy met Curb, considered a "boy wonder" in the music business, in January 1970 while on his way to Australia for a couple of weeks of shows, immediately hitting it off with the fledgling label executive. Curb loved Roy and his music, and Roy was taken with Curb's enthusiasm and encyclopedic knowledge of his career, including the recording dates and stories behind some of his best-known songs. Finally, Roy thought, he might get the support he needed from MGM.

Rejuvenated by the meeting and by starting a new life with Barbara, Roy's hopes were high as he headed for Australia. Sporting a new haircut, recommended by Barbara, and a white jumpsuit, Roy looked fantastic when he appeared on Australian television in January 1970.

With "Penny Arcade" still topping the charts there, Roy enjoyed wall-to-wall press coverage and appeared all over radio and TV during the tour.

Opposite: Roy on Australian TV, January 1970.
Above: Roy Orbison with some members of his new band, The Art Movement: Billy Dean, Roger Bryan, Keith Headley, Terry Widlake, Bob Monday, and John Switters, Australia, January 1970.

Roy Orbison

PENNY ARCADE

TENNESSEE OWNS
MY SOUL

LONDON

Left: Roy and Barbara, 1970. **Above**: "Penny Arcade" UK London single. **Below**: Roy with Tommy Leonetti on Australia TV, January 1970. **Opposite**: Roy in Australia, January 1970.

On their way back to Nashville, Roy and Barbara stopped again in Los Angeles for a couple of weeks, to meet with Mike Curb.

Not afraid to buck tradition and have Roy record music outside of the Acuff-Rose stable, Roy and Curb collaborated on "It Takes All Kinds of People," which appeared in the movie *The Moonshine War*, and "So Young," with Roger Christian, which was featured in Michelangelo Antonioni's *Zabriskie Point*.

"They wanted a song written for the movie so it could be an Academy Award proposition," Roy told Glenn A. Baker later. "So me and Mike Curb and another fella, we wrote the song and recorded it. And it was for the film. I saw the film before I wrote the song. So then they were to just let it come in at the end of the film. And I got to England and people wanted to know what was going on, and I said, 'Well, I've done this song for *Zabriskie Point*.' Everybody went down to see the film and said, 'You are not singing in the film.' And I couldn't believe it. So I called and they said, 'Well, we've missed the first three or four'—whatever it was—'prints of the film.'"

Early prints of the film did not feature Roy's song, though that was rectified later.

"So Young" added depth to the closing scenes of *Zabriskie Point*, though it did not appear on the soundtrack album, which features music from various artists popular at the time, including Pink Floyd, the Youngbloods, Jerry Garcia, Patti Page, and the Grateful Dead.

Also while on the West Coast, Roy, Barbara, Mike Curb, and a few MGM executives trekked east to Las Vegas to see Elvis Presley at the International Hotel there. During the show Elvis graciously introduced his old friend to the audience.

"There's a fella in the audience who started out at about the same time I did, I'd like you to give a hand to Roy Orbison," he said before launching into his final number. Then the King sang his last number and went backstage and into his waiting car, leaving Roy to sign autographs for the hungry fans in the audience.

Back in Nashville, on Wednesday, April 1, 1970, Roy appeared on *The Johnny Cash Show* again, singing "So Young" and a medley of "Only the Lonely" and "Oh, Pretty Woman."

After a short run of shows in Canada, Roy and Barbara paid a short visit to Barbara's parents in Bielefeld, Germany, before heading to the United Kingdom on Wednesday, April 22, 1970. There they were met by Roy's parents, Orbie Lee and Nadine, and young Wesley and celebrated Roy's birthday. While in England, Roy announced that he and Barbara were expecting their first child in October.

"I'm really over the top," he told reporters.

The British tour was an unprecedented success, with record-breaking attendance at every concert, but by summertime, Roy was back in Nashville, just as MGM released the clutch of Hank Williams songs he had recorded the previous year as *Hank Williams the Orbison Way*.

The reviews were favorable, but the heavily orchestrated and rushed recordings stiffed with the public. The fact that Decca had quit paying Roy and there was no US distribution didn't help. Meanwhile, Sun Records continued repackaging his Sun catalog, much to his dismay, and he continued his grueling schedule on the road, performing at the 3rd Annual WMAK Nashville Music Festival, held at Centennial Park that August.

"In 1970, I rode for fifteen hours in the back of a U-Haul to open for Roy Orbison," Bruce Springsteen, who supported Roy at the festival with his band Steel Mill, would recall almost twenty years later. "We drove all the way down there in a truck from New Jersey. We played at about one in the afternoon, and Roy Orbison was the star, and he came on at night. I remember he came out, and he had his hair swept back and the dark glasses on. I'd never seen him before, and the thing that shocked me the most about him is that he was so still. And the voice: he always had that big voice, that big operatic voice. And he had a feeling about him where it seemed that if you went up to him and tried to touch him, your hand would go through him. He seemed that he'd fallen from another planet. And he had purity when he sang. He did something nobody else did. And he always had that loneliness."

"I went backstage after Bruce's show," Roy, who remembered the occasion, too, said later. "He was onstage for about four hours. We had to wait a couple of hours just for him to cool off. Or for us to cool off, I guess. Then we had a good chat; his honesty and openness struck me. I always say about Bruce, 'He says what he means and means what he says.'"

Opposite: (top) Roy in Australia, 1970. (bottom) Roy playing at Festival Hall, Melbourne, Australia, October 3, 1972. **Above**: Roy playing at Festival Hall, Melbourne, October 3, 1972.

. . . THE THING THAT SHOCKED ME THE MOST ABOUT HIM IS THAT HE WAS SO STILL. AND THE VOICE: HE ALWAYS HAD THAT BIG VOICE, THAT BIG OPERATIC VOICE. —BRUCE SPRINGSTEEN

Above: Roy Orbison performs for guests at the home of his best friend and neighbor, Johnny Cash, 1970.

Roy and Barbara had a bet: Roy was sure the baby they were expecting would be a boy, but Barbara insisted it would be a girl. On Sunday, October 18, 1970, Roy won the bet when Barbara gave birth to their first child at what is now Saint Thomas Hospital in Nashville.

"I sure did win the bet," Roy told the press, who'd assembled at the hospital. "It was a real bet of $1,000, which she still owes me. I had things going for me there on my side because I come from a family of three boys and I had three boys previously, so I was sure it would be a boy."

The birth announcement the couple issued read, "Announcing . . . A New Star in his first personal appearance, at Hendersonville, Tennessee, on October 18, 1970 at 4:00 o'clock PM. A sweet and innocent 7-pound, 10-ounce dream baby named Roy Kelton Orbison Jr."

Busy with a new baby at home, Roy still had work to worry about. On Wednesday, December 23, he appeared on Johnny Cash's Christmas special. At the star-crowded party, filmed in Johnny's living room, were Johnny and June, Johnny's brother Tommy, Johnny's parents, other members of the Carter Family, the Everly Brothers, Carl Perkins, and Roy, who played a gorgeous solo rendition of "Pretty Paper."

After spending the holidays at home and squeezing in a recording session, Roy headed off again for Australia, with a repertoire that included Neil Diamond's "Sweet Caroline," Tony Joe White's "Polk Salad Annie," Kenny Rogers's "But You Know I Love You," and Paul Simon's "Bridge over Troubled Water." His busy schedule in Australia included a taping for a TV special in Adelaide on Sunday, March 14, which was shown a week later, before he headed off to spend April, May, and June in Ireland and the United Kingdom, during which he celebrated his thirty-fifth birthday and appeared on the BBC's venerable *Top of the Pops*.

But in the midst of the tour, Roy developed a throat infection. "Last night, I missed my first appearance in sixteen years," he told reporters. "I just couldn't go on. Tonight I felt even worse and had to have penicillin to help me stand up."

Roy was back in the United States in June and back in the studio on Thursday, July 22, 1971, after polishing up a few more tunes with Joe Melson, with whom he'd started working again. "(Love Me like You Did It) Last Night" was the best of the bunch but hardly a typical Roy Orbison song. Fast paced, contemporary, and catchy, it failed to make the charts when it was released in August. While his contemporaries, including Elvis, Johnny Cash, Bob Dylan, and even the Rolling Stones, were enjoying enormous success, Roy was struggling commercially, especially in the United States, although his live audiences remained faithful, particularly in the United Kingdom, continental Europe, and Australia. But in his personal life, he was in great shape, and he was convinced that good things were headed his way.

"I'm doing as well now as in the early days, and in spite of the change in attitudes, I personally believe that the next five years will be even better," Roy said at a press conference in 1971. "But I never look too far ahead. I am talking to you now as Roy Orbison the person rather than the performer or pop star, whatever you care to call me. I suppose, in fact, there are two people and the public never sees one side of me; that is the case with most people in my position."

"I remember very well all the good times that I had in my life, before those events, and I could draw on those," he said of his darkest days, after Claudette's death and after his sons perished in the fire at his home. "But it was not easy. Now I am very happy. My wife, Barbara, goes on most tours, and we live only a couple of blocks away from my old house.

"I have to admit that I have probably missed certain things in life because I am withdrawn from the normal working existence that most people have," he continued. "But I have been very happy with the money, the fame, and the success. Now it's nice not to have to ride around in armored cars, fight off fans, and buy fresh shirts and suits after every performance."

It was true; Roy was wealthy beyond his wildest dreams. He had built a marvelous new home for Barbara and their growing family to live in and didn't hesitate when he wanted a new car, motorcycle, or boat, or if he wanted to indulge in the latest technology. When the local hobby shop closed down, he bought out the contents and had them moved, lock, stock, and barrel, to his workshop. At the same time, while he remained a huge worldwide star, he didn't have to worry about being mobbed in the same way that his old friend Elvis did.

"It's hard for an artist to evaluate his fan club, so I couldn't be critical about the fan club," Roy told the BBC's Brian Matthew in 1973 of the legions of fans who belonged to the official

> I'M DOING AS WELL NOW AS IN THE EARLY DAYS, AND IN SPITE OF THE CHANGE IN ATTITUDES, I PERSONALLY BELIEVE THAT THE NEXT FIVE YEARS WILL BE EVEN BETTER.
>
> —ROY ORBISON

Roy Orbison fan clubs that had cropped up throughout the world. "I'll just say that an artist should be very grateful that someone takes that interest in you. They are important 'cause you know work is being done on your behalf. What I mean to say about it is that you have the population working for you, it's not a paid enterprise, and these people do it because they like what you do and there is no reward for it. I think it's a very commendable thing that they do for you."

Roy's Monument music was being rereleased while he and Joe Melson continued to collaborate on new music. While there was no MGM album in 1971, Roy was busy in the studio, recording a trilogy of albums that would stretch over the next few years, beginning with *Roy Orbison Sings* in 1972.

Roy began a British tour on Wednesday, May 17, 1972, at the venerable Royal Albert Hall, which lasted for seven months, almost earning him an entry in the *Guinness Book of World Records*, taking in fourteen countries across four continents, including the Netherlands, Denmark, Spain, Italy, Switzerland, Belgium, and the Far East, where his Chinese audiences remarkably knew every word to every song.

The tour then proceeded to Australia, where Roy was as big a star as ever. On Tuesday, October 3, he played two shows at the Festival Hall in Melbourne. Televised by HSV-7 on Monday, December 4, 1972, it was later released on DVD as *Live from Australia* and stands as a great historical document of Roy in the early 1970s.

"We did two concerts at the Melbourne Festival Hall," Alan James, one of Roy's guitarists at the time, recalled later. "One was televised with a full orchestra; we had violins and horns, which was nice. And we had this violinist named Martha and we ended up calling her, for the rest of the tour, 'Weeping Martha' because she was so into Roy Orbison's lyrics that she would be playing away and weeping and crying. I would turn around, and her eyes would be full of tears."

Roy stayed on in the Far East after the Australia shows, eventually ending up in New York, where the final show of the tour took place at Madison Square Garden on Friday, December 29, 1972.

"It is very hard work, but I love music so much, so much a part of my life, or is my life, that I'm pretty much like an actor who would act pretty much anywhere, anytime for the fun of it," Roy said on the show *Playback* on Radio Cleveland in 1973.

Although it's very hard, it's very rewarding. I mean, you can travel day and night and one good show makes up for everything. One successful show is worth it all. Pretty

Above and **Opposite**: Roy in London, April 1970.

much like the cliché there's no business like this business. And I don't particularly like to be in a situation where I don't get to eat or don't get to sleep or I don't get to see anybody, I don't get to see my friends or family or anything like that. So as I've become more successful I've been able to alter that slightly. I work very hard but at the same time I generally bring my family with me on tour. I wouldn't come just for the money, or probably just for the stardom or just for any one thing. It's very many things. People

realize that I do give them my best when I'm onstage. And that I don't go through the motions of singing the song or singing at the song, I try to sing it for the first time, every time, and I think the audience realizes this, and whether they are young or old, I think they know that I'm there, always on time, and that I'm going to do the best that I can do. And for the most part, I think that's the type of person that would come to see my show, someone that I can communicate with. And as an artist I just want to sing for people that want to hear me. That might sound like a strange statement, but those are the people I like to sing to—all the people who really want to hear me. If someone comes along out of curiosity, if they have no better place to go and all that, then that's okay, but I'm not singing to them. I sing to the people who want to hear me, and they seem to feed back to me, a warmth and a feeling, and the better I do, the more they appreciate it.

"This is undoubtedly one of the best efforts that Roy Orbison has come up with in years," *Billboard* wrote of Roy's *Memphis* album, the second in his trilogy, released that fall. "He's in-voice, the arrangements are more up to level of the Orbison of olden days."

Regardless, he was making moves toward being seen as more contemporary, rather than a thing of the past. He and Barbara had a plan, and they were on their way.

Roy's Madison Square Garden show at the end of his 1972 world tour was a tremendous success. As much as he disliked package shows, this one, called the Rock & Roll Revival, was one of a kind.

More than 20,000 people screamed for Roy when he was introduced by his friend and neighbor Johnny Cash. While his new *All-Time Greatest Hits of Roy Orbison* LP was getting excellent reviews and selling like hotcakes all over the world, the Madison Square Garden appearance marked the end of a 164-day world tour, during which he had played 350 shows. Exhausted, after the show he and Barbara headed home to Tennessee.

"I still ride a big Harley Davidson and get a big thrill out of it," he said at a press conference while there. "I don't have a super fast car. I have a big car that will do about 140 MPH. I like the car but I'm sort of [taking it] easy now, a little more easy now than I did."

After a well-deserved rest, he headed back into the studio. Between January and June 1973, he recorded more than thirty songs. "Blue Rain," released as his next single in the United States, is among his best recordings.

Between recording sessions, he played some US shows. On Saturday, April 14, he appeared at the Los Angeles Forum in front of 18,000 screaming fans, and those fans would make "Blue Rain" Roy's first-ever country hit record.

"I never had a record in the country charts until right now," Roy told the BBC's Brian Matthew when interviewed for the show *My Top Twelve* in 1973.

"Since '62 and '63, I've been doing England, Australia, America, Europe every year ever since then, and I have had a hit in one part or the other of the world at all times, even up to today," he continued, acknowledging how his career had developed over the years. "I would say that the career is more international as opposed to out of England or America or Australia or Canada or Germany or wherever."

In reality, he was waiting for his contract with MGM to expire and was concentrating on touring. The last straw was the last of the trilogy of LPs he'd recently recorded, which turned out to be his final MGM album. *Milestones* was released in the United States on September 24, 1973, and featured a unique collection of songs, including tunes penned by the Bee Gees, Otis Redding, and Neil Diamond alongside "Blue Rain." In fact, the *Milestones* sessions included many songs that Roy had recorded just to fulfill his deal with the company, while still trying to negotiate to leave the label diplomatically, although, out of frustration with his label, he had

Opposite: Roy Orbison on stage, circa 1972.
Above: Roy in New York, mid 1970s.

hired just about every musician in town for the sessions, spending $85,000 cutting "Blue Rain" alone. After Kirk Kerkorian had sold off MGM to Polydor in 1972 and Mike Curb had moved on as well, leaving him without the support at the top echelons of MGM that he'd always enjoyed, he was ready to move on. On July 1, 1973, his contract expired. He would never again commit to a long-term contract.

With *Milestones* unnoticed by the American record-buying public, Roy began a four-week British tour on Sunday, September 16, 1973.

"I've got a magnificent wife, Barbara, and a new baby boy who will be three this month," Roy told Brian Matthew on his BBC 2 radio show *My Top Twelve*. "My other boy, Wesley, is eight years old and going to school," adding that they were all "healthy and happy and everything is marvelous."

After the final date of the UK tour, Roy, Barbara, and Roy Jr. returned home to Nashville for a few days of rest and to visit Wesley, who lived across the street with Orbie Lee and Nadine, before Roy hit the road in the United States for dates put together by promoter Richard Nader, who would become famous for his Rock & Roll Revival shows. Then, on Monday, November 26, Roy's brother Grady Lee was killed when his car hit a utility pole eleven miles south east of Gallatin, Tennessee, very close to where Claudette had been killed.

Services for Grady Lee took place on Wednesday, November 28, at Phillips-Robinson Funeral Home in Hendersonville, with burial in Woodlawn Memorial Park. He was buried next to Claudette and the boys.

In early 1974, Roy recorded a special for NBC called *Best of the Midnight Special* in Burbank, California. *The Midnight Special* was a weekly music television show noted for featuring popular acts performing live, which was unique in an era when most performers lip-synched to prerecorded music. Roy hosted the show on that occasion and performed three songs with his band, including "Only the Lonely," "Oh, Pretty Woman," and "Dream Baby." It aired on Friday, February 15, just as he began yet another Australian tour, but not before signing a multi-million-dollar, one-year contract with Mercury Records, which reportedly put him on the same terms as Elvis.

Roy had signed the contract with Mercury, headed by Jerry Kennedy, who had played on "Mean Woman Blues," "Goodnight," and "Oh, Pretty Woman" and had known Roy for years, while sitting on his bed in Nashville.

Opposite and **Above**: Roy and Barbara with their son, Roy Kelton Orbison, Jr.

Van-O-Rama auto show, Cincinnati Gardens, OH,
April 23, 1976.

Above: (top) Barbara, Roy, and Roy Jr. shortly before Alex was born, spring 1975. (bottom) Album art for "I'm Still in Love With You" on Mercury Records, 1975. **Opposite**: (top) Roy Jr. receives a guitar from his father on stage as a fifth birthday gift, Queens Theatre, Essex, England, October 18, 1975. (bottom) Australian tour program, 1975.

While Down Under, Roy scouted for land for a health ranch hideaway camp for himself and some of his famous friends. "They had one piece, and when I asked them how big it was, they said it was just a bit bigger than Belgium," he told the press there. "But I don't think I want to buy a whole country."

Roy said he planned to work only about four months a year from now on and that he wanted to spend about three or four months every year at the ranch. "I need somewhere to rest and get away from it all with my family and my friends," he said. "Friends like Johnny Cash, Elvis, Tom Jones, Ringo Starr, George Harrison, and Sammy Davis Jr. I know they would love it."

Meanwhile, after returning to Nashville in June 1974, he met up with Harrison and Starr's erstwhile bandmate Paul McCartney.

"Paul was over for a recording session," Roy later told the BBC. "We got together, and we sang songs for each other. We sure did enjoy each other."

In spite of a very successful touring year and recording dates for Mercury that seemed to bode well for the future, 1974 saw the closure of the US and Australian fan clubs. It was a surprising move, especially the Australia one, considering Roy's huge recent success there. But Roy and Barbara had big plans for the future that did not necessarily include the things that had made Roy successful in the past.

After the UK tour, Roy and Barbara headed for Germany, where they spent Christmas with Barbara's family, after a quick stop in the Netherlands, where Roy appeared on the *TopPop* show, lip-synching "Sweet Mamma Blue," his latest Mercury single.

"We spent Christmas here in Bielefeld, and before that we were in Bavaria, skiing," Roy told Germany's *Radiothek* in January 1975. "Marvelous. We'd just done a television special for the BBC in England and a German firm has the world rights to that film—to that television show—and I leave here to go to Canada, then after Canada to Australia and Japan, then back to America, then to England in August, and then probably after the English tour I might do a couple of things in Germany and Holland and Belgium."

More important, the couple got some truly good news when they discovered that Barbara was expecting a second baby the following May. After a string of US dates and before Roy went back out on the road in late May, he became a father again on May 25, 1975, when Alexander Orbie Lee Orbison was born at 3:24 a.m. at Vanderbilt Hospital in Nashville.

On September 15, Roy's Mercury album *I'm Still in Love with You* was released. Featuring the Johnny Ace classic "Pledging My Love," which his friend Elvis would cut less than a year later using Roy's version as his template, the album failed to give Roy's career the boost he and

Barbara had hoped it would. In fact, in a twist of irony, after leaving MGM, which was owned by Polydor, due to the myriad problems there, Mercury was bought by PolyGram, which Polydor had morphed into by that time, thus subjecting Roy to more of the same, most notably distribution problems.

Meanwhile, Roy's stock was never higher with the ascendant crop of singer-songwriters making their own mark on the charts. At the front of the pack was Bruce Springsteen, who had pledged his devotion to Roy in early interviews and whose song "Thunder Road," from his new chart-topping album *Born to Run*, name checked Roy. With Springsteen soon gracing the covers of both *Time* and *Newsweek* magazines and never missing a chance to mention his hero, Roy set off on yet another tour of the United Kingdom. The reviews were uniformly raves.

"While many of his contemporaries have disappeared into obscurity, he's still on top of the bill," one reviewer wrote. "He is a true 'American success story' of a star who started off as an amateur—doing free gigs—and went on to become an international favorite."

In the midst of the tour, on October 18, Roy Kelton Orbison Jr. celebrated his fifth birthday and joined his father on tour to celebrate. Roy even interrupted his concert that night to ask his fans to join in and help sing "Happy Birthday" to his son, who wore a western outfit and hat, "like me in *The Fastest Guitar Alive*," Roy said.

The Big O and Little O shared the stage for the first time, and a cake and presents were brought out to celebrate, including a talking teddy bear and a miniature guitar.

At the same show, Roy was given a gold disc for the multimillion seller *The All-Time Greatest Hits of Roy Orbison* LP before playing an instrumental version of "Ooby Dooby" on a brand-new custom-made guitar he had been presented with that night, followed by "Oh, Pretty Woman" to close the proceedings.

After another record-breaking barnstorming tour of Australia and New Zealand and a short tour of the United States—during which he wore a light blue jumpsuit decorated with sequins—Roy's return to Monument Records was released in 1976. Foster's label had expanded beyond anyone's imagination in the years since Roy's departure, releasing music by the likes of Dolly Parton, Kris Kristofferson, Larry Gatlin, and Ronnie Hawkins, and Roy hoped to reap the benefit of the expansion.

"I didn't write any of the songs, and I only had a few days to do the album," he told *Rolling Stone* in 1988. It was true, but the record sounded like classic Orbison, while also marking him as one of the great artists of the era.

... LADIES AND GENTLEMEN ... ONE OF THE FINEST SINGERS OF ALL TIME. ROY ORBISON!

—ELVIS PRESLEY

Opposite: Roy Orbison concert program, 1977.

Three singles, "Belinda," "I'm a Southern Man," and "Drifting Away" also marked a short-lived reunion with Bill Dees, who wrote most of the single "Drifting Away" while sitting on the boat deck at Roy's house in Hendersonville. One of the best songs Roy recorded during the 1970s, it was a standout track that complimented a uniformly strong album that showcased Roy's always remarkable voice alongside the sorts of backing, arrangements, and songs he could have recorded in his heyday.

"There's a couple people in the audience I'd like you to meet," Elvis Presley said from the stage of the Las Vegas Hilton on Saturday, December 4, during his 9 p.m. show. "They're some of the finest singers in the world, so that's why. That's one of the reasons I have to be good. I'm being judged not only by you, and everybody onstage, but also by them.

"There's a song, 'Please Release Me, Let Me Go,'" the King continued, gesturing into the crowd. "No one ever sung it like Engelbert Humperdinck. And next to him, ladies and gentlemen, is one of the finest singers of all time. Roy Orbison!"

After the show, Elvis and Roy hugged and chatted backstage. The pair had reconnected recently when Presley had flown Roy to Graceland on his private plane, the Lisa Marie, named for his young daughter, but the pair took the opportunity to reminisce about touring and their Sun pals, like the ever-colorful Jerry Lee Lewis. Roy was surprised to find that his friend looked overweight, but contrary to the tabloid reports, he thought Elvis looked good. He came away with the sense that Elvis had a strong faith, but later, when he recalled the meeting, he'd feel angry that there had been no one close enough to Elvis who loved him enough to call him out for what he was doing to himself.

It was the last time Roy would see his friend.

The year 1976 was a good one for Roy. "I received eighteen gold albums and one platinum album just since January of this year," he said in an interview. "Platinum is a million seller, and a million dollars' worth of albums is a gold album.

"I've always been active," he continued, a master of understatement considering the grueling schedule he kept. "I've been touring six or seven months out of the year ever since 1960. It's just a matter of covering the world. We do a tour of England every year, a tour of the States every year, a tour of Australia every year, a tour of Canada every year. It gets very hectic to be in person where you need to be when you are covering that much ground."

So it was that he began 1977 with a six-week tour of Britain. On BBC's *Open House* he

ROY ORBISON

gave his fans a clue to his next Monument release, saying that he was hard at work writing new material, reading books about history, and enjoying his motorcycle collection and palatial home. When asked if he missed his home while on the road, he said, "I don't think about it much the first two or three weeks, but eventually it creeps in and I get a bit homesick."

Although Roy tended to stay away from performing his latest releases, "Drifting Away" crept into his set, and by the time he and his band played at the Old Waldorf club in San Francisco on Saturday, May 28, 1977, it was obvious that some kind of renewal in his music was taking place.

"Bette Midler was there, the Eagles were there, it was incredible the amount of megastars that would come to see Roy," guitarist Alan James recalls.

James was right. Like Springsteen, young artists were making it plain how important Roy was to them. Creedence Clearwater Revival had covered "Ooby Dooby," and Linda Ronstadt would soon score a global smash with "Blue Bayou," which earned her Grammy nominations for Record of the Year and Best Pop Vocal Performance by a Female Artist.

Every time Roy and Barbara were in Los Angeles, they'd meet more artists who'd tell them how much Roy meant to them and how he'd inspired them to dig deep inside themselves as performers and, especially, songwriters. And that glow affected everyone in Roy's orbit.

One night, Roy was at a party at Emmylou Harris's house in Studio City, California, with Fred Foster. Don McLean and Linda Ronstadt were also there, and at one point Ronstadt cornered Foster. "I want you to tell me once and for all what kind of recording technique you're using to get those high notes," she demanded.

"I don't understand what you're sayin'," Foster protested.

"Well, you know, you gotta be messin' with the tape speed or something," Ronstadt shot back.

"Nope, he's hittin' those notes," Foster retorted in defense of Roy's awesome singing talents.

At that point, Harris, who'd had a hit single with Ronstadt with "The Sweetest Gift" the previous year, picked up her Gibson acoustic, handed it to Roy, and asked him to sing "Crying." Seated there in the middle of the small room, armed only with an acoustic guitar, he blew the crowd away.

In August, Roy was on tour in California with a new band, the Price Brothers, getting ready to kick off another tour, this time in San Diego on Wednesday, August 17, 1977. Resting in his hotel the day before, he got the tragic news: Elvis Presley was dead. He was only forty-two.

The King of Rock and Roll, one of Roy's oldest and dearest friends, no matter how far apart their careers had taken them, had collapsed in his bathroom. Rushed to Baptist Memorial Hospital in Memphis, he had been pronounced dead on arrival, the result of a massive heart attack.

There had been indications of his declining health for some time, and earlier that year he had canceled several performances in Louisiana and had returned to Memphis suffering from what his doctors termed "exhaustion," but the blow to Roy was indescribable. He considered canceling his San Diego performance, as well as one the following day at the Santa Monica Civic Auditorium, but he soldiered on, albeit numbly.

"In December of last year I went to a concert and spent about an hour and a half with him," Roy told the reporters who cornered him in the aftermath of Presley's death. "He was in good spirits. He wasn't overweight, he was hefty but not overweight. He was very lucid. We talked about the old times and recent times and he was in great shape. He gave me a big hug and I gave him a big hug and we talked about from '56 onward, and we were mainly talking about people who sang with feeling, as we were taught to do at Sun Records. It's a great personal loss to me and an even greater personal loss to all the people who loved him through his music."

In fact, it was a crushing blow to Roy, and the strain was noticeable. He'd always felt close to Elvis, even a little protective. But what most sickened him in the aftermath of Elvis's death were the hangers-on who seemed to come in a never-ending stream across his television screen, telling stories about him that Roy felt broke the musicians' code of keeping what should remain out of the public eye behind closed doors. Finally, back in Hendersonville one night, word broke that some of Elvis's "Memphis Mafia" were attempting to steal the King's body. Roy

Opposite: Roy and Barbara at 3DB radio station in Melbourne, Australia, 1970. **Above**: Roy with Benny Mardones (center) at *Rolling Stone* magazine headquarters in New York, early 1981. **Following pages**: Roy and band prepare for a TV appearance on the *Midnight Special* show at NBC in New York, May 1980.

figured they'd head east and announced, gun in hand, that he was going to head them off.

Calmed down by worried family and friends there, Roy sat back down and stewed. He couldn't believe Elvis was gone. He couldn't believe what a sad and tragic end his friend had faced.

In late 1977, Roy landed a series of television appearances, as the expected Elvis tributes filled the airwaves. In Nashville in October, he was part of the taping of Johnny Cash's Christmas television special filmed at the Grand Ole Opry, which would air on November 30. Along with Cash, Jerry Lee Lewis, Carl Perkins, Roy Clark, and June Carter Cash, he sang "This Train," dedicated to Elvis, and "Two by Two," as well as "Oh, Pretty Woman," sporting glasses so dark you couldn't see his eyes.

Then, on December 19, 1977, during a football game between the Nebraska Cornhuskers and the North Carolina Tar Heels broadcast on ABC, Roy was part of a half-time tribute to Elvis, singing bits of "Don't Be Cruel" and "Hound Dog," followed by fireworks. Running up the stairs to the stage at the Liberty Bowl, he felt a pain in his chest, but he didn't think much of it.

On what would have been Elvis's forty-third birthday, Larry Gatlin introduced Roy as "Elvis's very good friend" on *Nashville Remembers Elvis*. Roy sang "Crying" and "Running Scared," which Roy knew were Elvis's favorite songs of his.

After the show, Roy received a telegram from Don McLean, whose hit "American Pie" owed a lot to the way Roy had always eschewed conventional song structure in service of the bigger story he was trying to tell. "What a beautiful performance of a beautiful song," the telegram said. McLean would go on to record "Crying," scoring a worldwide hit with his version, only adding to Roy's growing income from cover versions by younger artists of the many songs he'd written.

By the end of 1977, work on Roy's next Monument album was wrapping up. Roy and his new band, the Price Brothers—Dan, Ron, Chris, Regi, and Erick—had fifteen songs nearly complete for the follow-up to *Regeneration*, written mostly by the Price brothers but also including a new version of "Best Friend," written by Roy and Bill Dees and originally released on the *Fastest Guitar Alive* soundtrack album.

Opposite: Carl Perkins, Roy Orbison, Johnny Cash, and Jerry Lee Lewis perform a tribute to Elvis Presley on the *Johnny Cash Christmas Special,* 1977.
Above: Roy in London, April 1970.

Before Christmas, Roy and Barbara decided to take a vacation to Hawaii. Roy intended on putting his vocal tracks for the new album down as soon as he returned.

He hadn't been feeling well for a while—ever since Elvis's death, in fact. But he thought a little holiday in Hawaii would do the trick. Almost as soon as he and Barbara landed, however, he began having chest pains. They went to the hospital, but the staff there couldn't find anything. They headed back to Nashville, which at the time had one of the top heart centers in the world. On the way home from the airport Roy pulled over at a pay phone. As he hung out the window of his car to make the call, the doctor he spoke with told him to come in right away. He was checked over thoroughly that Saturday night, and by Tuesday his team of doctors had determined that he needed open-heart surgery, which was scheduled for the next day, Wednesday, January 18, 1978, and would include three coronary bypasses.

"Leave me a nice scar up top, because I wear open-neck shirts," he told the assembled doctors. They looked at him as though he were crazy.

"We're trying to save your life, we are not worried about scars," his surgeon told Roy.

"Well, I am, make sure it's right," Roy shot back.

After his surgery, in therapy, Roy's fellow patients were jealous about his scar, because the doctors had indeed acceded to his request.

By the second day after his surgery, Roy thought he was going to die. The following day, the pain was so great that he wished he had died. But by the third day, he was more comfortable. He took a nap and woke up feeling like a seventeen-year-old. With his blood flow increased by 60 percent, he felt like a new man. His perspective about everything—who his friends were, what the music business was all about—had been repaired along with his clogged heart.

Roy's doctors implored him to exercise and to quit smoking and drinking. "One thing that will put you in the grave is to worry about things and carry the stress that has brought you to this point," Roy's doctor told him once he was back on his feet. "So if there's anything bothering you, upsetting you, or disturbing you, either move it or go around it."

LEAVE ME A NICE SCAR UP TOP, BECAUSE I WEAR OPEN-NECK SHIRTS. — ROY ORBISON

Knowing the unbearable stress that he'd felt after Elvis's death and seemed to always carry around with him, Roy knew the doctor was right. He promised he would.

While recovering from the surgery, Roy received a call from Earl Owensby, an independent filmmaker from Charlotte, North Carolina, about a film he was working on. Owensby wanted Roy to record the soundtrack for *Living Legend*, the story of a rock and roll singer who had fallen into the pitfalls of stardom. Owensby's girlfriend at the time was Ginger Alden, who Roy knew had been Elvis's girlfriend at the time of his death, and she was going to star in the movie. Impressed with Owensby's drive, touched by the story and the connection with Elvis, however slight, Roy wanted to get back to work without having to face life on the road and agreed to do it. He and Barbara flew to Charlotte to meet Owensby.

The music for the soundtrack was recorded in Charlotte, at the Arthur Smith Studios on Monroe Road, as Roy had just sold his Nashville studio, U.S. Recording, to Ronnie Milsap. For the project, he chose to record some of the new songs he had been writing with Chris Price, as well as some of the Price Brothers' own compositions. A total of ten songs was recorded in North Carolina before the actual shooting began.

Living Legend was released regionally around the Carolinas and was nominated for Motion Picture of the Year by the Academy of Country Music, though it lost out to Willie Nelson's *Electric Horseman*. Only about a hundred copies of the soundtrack were pressed and given away at the time of the film's regional release, making it one of the rarest Roy Orbison releases ever.

Soon, within ninety days of his open-heart surgery, Roy was back on the road and back smoking cigarettes. With Fred Foster having moved on to other projects in Roy's absence, his next Monument album was shelved indefinitely. Eventually, unhappy with his second Monument album under his new deal, he would buy back the rights to it and he and Foster would part company, amicably, once again.

But with Linda Ronstadt now enjoying a worldwide hit with Roy's "Blue Bayou," his commercial stock was higher than it had been in some time. He signed a one-album deal with Elektra/Asylum Records. Soon after joining the label, he hired attorney David Braun and turned over his bookings to the revered William Morris Agency in Los Angeles, leaving Acuff-Rose Artists Co. after a twenty-year association. Though he would still be associated with Acuff-Rose as his publisher and management company, the move was the beginning of a new chapter in his life as an artist and performer.

In January 1979, Roy was back in the studio, this time at Wishbone Studios in Muscle Shoals, Alabama. Recording was finished by February 15. The reviews of the heavily disco-

Above: Sheet music featuring Linda Ronstadt for her cover of "Blue Bayou."

Above: (top) Soundtrack album art from the movie *Roadie*, which includes Roy Orbison and Hank Williams Jr.'s recording of "The Eyes of Texas Are Upon You," 1980. (botoom) Single artwork for Roy's Grammy-winning duet with Emmylou Harris, "That Lovin' You Feelin' Again," also found on the *Roadie* soundtrack.

influenced album were brutal, with *Rolling Stone*'s Dave Marsh being particularly harsh, though they all remarked on the power and durability of Roy's voice. Roy was crushed.

Meanwhile, *The Best of Roy Orbison* compilation album was such a huge success in England that another compilation LP, called *20 Golden Greats*, was released in Australia and New Zealand in January 1979, and Roy was soon heard on television singing "Oh, Pretty Woman" on behalf of Tone Soap and spoofed by the comedian John Belushi on NBCs *Saturday Night Live*, as well as by the legendary British comedian Benny Hill. A die-hard fan of comedy, Roy was thrilled.

After turning down the producers of the film *More American Graffiti*, who wanted to use his songs in their sequel to *American Graffiti*—"if you're not going to have Elvis or the Beatles in your film, then you're not going to have my music," Roy told them—he appeared in the film *Roadie*, alongside Meat Loaf, Asleep at the Wheel, Alice Cooper, Hank Williams Jr., and Blondie.

Roy's part in the movie would be shot in Austin, Texas, in March 1980, but before the shooting began, he headed out on a Canadian tour in January and February, during which two of his guitars and a guitar strap were stolen while in Vancouver, followed by eight consecutive sold-out dates with the Eagles in Los Angeles and San Francisco, where he performed in front of stadiums packed with a new, young audience for him to wow. In fact, one review, paying tribute to Roy, said simply, "You don't often find an opening act that has had more hits than the headliner."

After the string of Eagles concerts, Roy flew to Austin, Texas, to film his cameo in *Roadie* at the Soap Creek Saloon, performing "The Eyes of Texas" with Hank Williams Jr. for the occasion. Then he was on to Germany, on Thursday, March 13, for his own television special to be broadcast live to the entire European continent on the fifteenth. He returned to the United States to tape the *Pink Lady* television show for NBC on Monday, March 17. And although he was suffering from laryngitis, two days later he flew to London for a monthlong tour of the United Kingdom, Germany, and the Netherlands. Two days after the tour was completed, he celebrated his forty-fourth birthday.

Although Roy kept up a grueling schedule, he found touring rewarding. It allowed him to stay in close touch with his fans, while also earning him tremendous sums when sales of his new records were virtually nonexistent. Though Linda Ronstadt's cover of "Blue Bayou" and Don McLean's recording of "Crying" had helped, both selling millions of copies, it was on the road that Roy felt at home, and it was there where he continued to earn the most money.

Back in the United States, Roy again appeared on the *Midnight Special* show, filmed at the NBC studios in Burbank, California. Along with his appearances with the Eagles and with "Blue Bayou" and "Crying" storming the charts, his performances of "Oh, Pretty Woman," "Only the Lonely," "Crying," "Running Scared," "Hound Dog Man," and "Blue Bayou," introduced by host Wolfman Jack, helped establish Roy with a new generation of record buyers and concertgoers.

"For me, each tour is the first tour, each night is the first night, perhaps that's why I am still around after all these years," Roy told reporters while on tour. When asked about his recording plans, he was blunt: "Well, I'll probably start working on a recording deal when I get a chance. I just haven't had a chance lately. I've been so busy with dates. But when I stop touring for a month or so, which will be pretty soon, we'll work out some kind of recording deal, and maybe even record. It doesn't leave a lot of time for writing, though."

Meanwhile, his music had crossed over to the country charts. "That Lovin' You Feelin' Again," recorded with Emmylou Harris, won the Grammy for Best Country Performance by a Duo or Group with Vocal at ceremonies held at Radio City Music Hall in New York on Wednesday, February 25, 1981.

In the 1980s, the record industry had been taken over by attorneys, agents, and public relations teams. They made the business arrangements and deals for artists deemed "hot." Frustrated, Roy just couldn't seem to make it into that exclusive club. But he and Barbara were slowly sowing the seeds that would lead to a career resurgence unlike anything else the music industry had ever seen.

Meanwhile, with bills to pay, he stayed on the road, touring the United States and Canada in early 1981. The dates, which included an appearance on an episode of *Second City Television*, the Canadian sketch comedy show, which aired on Friday, July 17, 1981, marked a notable uptick in his North American schedule relative to previous years. He and Barbara were setting out to reestablish his preeminence, one appearance and market at a time.

BMI, the music publishing organization, also honored Roy around that time, presenting him with two Certificates of Achievement in 1981, this time for radio airplay of "That Lovin' You Feelin' Again" and Don McLean's "Crying."

The following year, while Roy was away in England on yet another tour, featuring a performance at London's Wembley Arena that was aired on the BBC and Capital Radio, one of the world's hottest bands, Van Halen, from Pasadena, California, released the album *Diver Down*.

FOR ME, EACH TOUR IS THE FIRST TOUR, EACH NIGHT IS THE FIRST NIGHT, PERHAPS THAT'S WHY I AM STILL AROUND AFTER ALL THESE YEARS.

— ROY ORBISON

A version of Roy's "Oh, Pretty Woman" was included on the album and was also released as a single, quickly reaching Number 1 on the Mainstream Rock Charts and Number Twelve on the Billboard Hot 100. A music video made it onto heavy rotation on MTV. As a result, the young people of the nascent MTV Generation, who didn't know who Roy Orbison was, fell in love with Roy's most famous song, the grandaddy that had gone on to inspire guitar riffs by The Beatles, the Rolling Stones, and later Stevie Ray Vaughn, Guns N' Roses, and Van Halen's own Eddie Van Halen.

More cover versions followed, including "Crawling Back" by Frank Ifield, a punk rock version of "Only the Lonely" by Laurie and the Sighs, "In Dreams" by Marty Wilde, "Running Scared" by the Fools, and "Uptown" by Robert Gordon, though none had the impact that Van Halen's did.

After celebrating his birthday at home in Hendersonville, Roy headed behind the Iron Curtain, where he lived out a dream, performing in June, headlining the first night of the eighteenth annual Golden Orpheus international song contest in Sunny Beach, Bulgaria. The concert was viewed by nearly 200 million people on television and Roy was the first American ever to perform there.

After that Eastern European adventure, Roy began yet another British tour, his last there for three years owing to his busy schedule in the United States, Canada, and Australia. It ran until early July, and then he returned to the United States for a tour of the South, during which he appeared on the *Austin City Limits* TV show, which he taped on Thursday, August 5, 1982, giving fans a great chance to catch him on national television.

Seizing his newfound momentum, on Monday, August 16, and Tuesday, August 17, 1982, Roy filmed a Sasson jeans commercial in Los Angeles. The Sasson clip featured a new studio recording of Roy singing a revamped version of "Oh, Pretty Woman" as "Sasson Woman," recorded in Nashville, and the commercial was on national TV about two weeks later.

Roy was back on the road in September and October. As his never-ending tour continued and his popularity in the United States grew, he finally chose to cut his ties with Wesley Rose.

"Legendary singer Roy Orbison is suing his manager, Wesley Rose, for $50 million, half of which is apparently punitive damages," England's *New Musical Express* reported. "Rose is one of the most respected businessmen in Nashville and operates the publishing company Acuff-Rose. Orbison claims one contract he signed was obtained when the singer was 'severely depressed'—possibly referring to a period when his first wife, Claudette, died in a road accident, [and] two of his children in a fire."

Opposite: Roy Orbison's music has appeared in many countries and has been covered by countless artists. Notice one of Roy's rarest singles, "Mama" b/w "San Fernando" released only in Germany in 1963. **Above**: Roy Orbison in a cameo appearance on the ABC sitcom *Just Our Luck,* November 1, 1983.

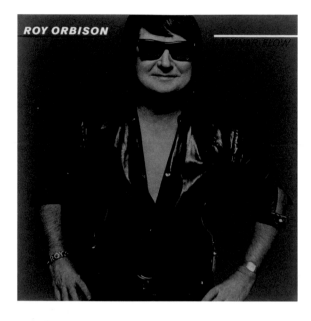

In the lawsuit, Roy claimed that Wesley Rose had mismanaged his career, booking him halfway down the bill on unsuitable tours with country and western artists all through the 1960s, forcing him to record and release two country albums unnecessarily and obligating him to release songs during the late 1960s and early '70s that weren't up to his normally high standards.

The lawsuit became a drawn-out affair, lasting until 1985, and proved to be very costly for Roy. But he and Barbara knew that breaking free from Rose's control was essential to taking the next steps along the way toward putting him back at the top of the heap in the entertainment industry.

Roy and Barbara knew they had their work cut out for them. Roy needed to repair his reputation in the United States and began by hitting the road, this time with gusto. And so yet another US tour began on Wednesday, February 2, 1983, with Roy performing in Atlanta, New Orleans, and Fort Worth, Dallas, and Amarillo, Texas, before leaving for a five-week tour of Australia.

After a short vacation in Mexico with Barbara in early April, Roy and his band flew to Las Vegas for a series of shows at the Sahara from April 19 to 24 that proved so popular that he was booked for twelve consecutive nights the following September. He continued with a US and Canadian tour in May and June, during which time he taped an episode of the short-lived sitcom *Just Our Luck* in Los Angeles.

Wrapping up the tour in Texas, on Saturday, November 5, 1983, Roy performed at Gilley's in Pasadena, and the show was recorded by Westwood One for radio broadcast across more than three hundred stations in the US and Canada.

With another Canadian tour due to start in January 1984, he found himself fighting bronchitis. He was forced to cancel an appearance on NBC's *Great Moments of Rock*, on which he was to sing duets with Tom Petty and Linda Ronstadt. Against doctor's orders, he set out on the road, only to end up hospitalized for two weeks with acute bronchitis during the tour, forcing him to cancel several dates. He returned home from Canada to relax before taking off on another extensive US and Canada tour.

In the summer of 1984, Roy was contacted by the songwriter Will Jennings. Jennings had been asked by the director Nicolas Roeg to contribute some songs to his forthcoming film *Insignificance*. Jennings hoped that Roy would perform his songs and maybe even collaborate

Above Sleeve for the 1979 album, *Laminar Flow*.
Opposite: Roy Orbison promo photo for the album.

with him. Taken with the young songwriter and impressed by his recent success with the song "Up Where We Belong," performed by Joe Cocker and Jennifer Warnes, Roy invited him down to Nashville. Jennings was thrilled but nervous to meet Roy.

Will Jennings, born in Texas in 1944, became a prolific and highly successful songwriter. Legend has it that he got his big break while playing his "last gig" in Nashville. A starving songwriter, ready to pack it in and go back to Texas, he was trying to auction his PA system when a member of the audience who worked for BMI approached him with an offer. His songs eventually appeared on numerous motion picture soundtracks and were recorded by innumerable popular singers over the years, including Steve Winwood, Joe Cocker, and Eric Clapton. He received a Golden Globe for his work on Clapton's "Tears in Heaven," as well as "Up Where We Belong." He also received a Grammy and an Academy Award for "My Heart Will Go On" in the film *Titanic*.

Jennings showed up at Roy's home in Hendersonville with a draft of a song called "When Your Heart Runs Out of Time." In no time, he and Roy had revamped the song, renaming it "Wild Hearts Run Out of Time." Within a week the song was recorded and Jennings was on his way to London with the master to present to Roeg.

Although Roeg liked the song, only a snippet was featured in his film. Roy and Jennings were disappointed but had become friends in the process, finding common ground in their Texas oil field upbringings, and vowed to continue writing together.

Through Will Jennings, who was also writing songs with Jimmy Buffett at the time, Roy was soon invited to be a special guest on Buffett's *Last Mango in Paris* album. Jennings would also connect Roy with J. D. Souther and Rodney Crowell, spurring fruitful collaborations over the next few years.

Roy was writing again and getting the itch to get back into the studio. Although he never minded doing his older hits, he felt he needed new material to compete in the marketplace and to appeal to a new, younger audience. Writing new material with a new generation of songwriters would be key to launching his return.

Closer to home, Roy's father, Orbie Lee, passed away in Hendersonville from a heart attack on December 5, 1984. The man who had instilled in Roy a love of music—who had encouraged Roy's career at every turn—and who had given him an unshakable work ethic was gone. The loss was incalculable. When Roy appeared on Dutch radio in December, it was obvious that he took the loss hard.

"I guess why you don't hear much of me is because I haven't done much recording lately," he said. "I did do a single record for a film called *Insignificance*. The song is called 'Wild Hearts.' That should be out in February. And I'm supposed to sign with a new record company in February. We don't know who yet—there are three or four companies that would like to have me, and they say they would, and they want to talk to me—so I just now quit playing on the road long enough to talk to them."

On Monday, December 31, Roy flew to New Orleans for a special New Year's Eve show.

ZTT, a British record label founded in 1983 by *New Musical Express* journalist Paul Morley, famed record producer Trevor Horn, and record company executive Jill Sinclair, signed Roy in February and released the soundtrack of *Insignificance*. Although much of the album was filled with music by composers such as Stanley Myers and Hans Zimmer, Roy's "Wild Hearts Run Out of Time" was a standout and was issued as a single in May 1985.

Roy's music video for "Coming Home"—his first since his video for "Walk On," shot in 1968, but unseen for more than forty years—was shot in May in Nashville, on a hot day in a little pool hall on Elliston Place. Tony Curtis and Gary Busey, who both appeared in the film, made cameo appearances, as did Will Jennings, and Roy is shown driving around in a pickup truck, and singing the song while the pool hall's patrons are seen playing pool.

Seeking to take advantage of his newfound momentum, he and Barbara planned tours of Canada and England for that summer. The upcoming British tour would unofficially be called his 25th Anniversary Tour.

"Success only means being able to take care of my family," Roy said in 1987. "Continuous success means that you can build for the future. As an artist, the most important thing about commercial success is that what I'm doing is reaching a lot of people. I don't quite know how to feel when so many people compliment me and use words like legend or inspiration, things like that. But there again, these were just gifts that I was given, and I like to—if I receive the gifts—to pass them along."

Opposite: Roy Orbison at home in Malibu, CA, 1987. **Above**: Album artwork for what would ultimately be a posthumous release, *King of Hearts*, 1992. **Following pages**: Roy Orbison in concert at the Front Row Theatre, Highland Heights, OH, May 15, 1987.

Chapter 6
A CAREER REVIVAL
AND THE TRAVELING WILBURYS

From the outside, things didn't look so great for Roy as he embarked on

his 1985 UK tour. His lawsuit against Acuff-Rose was still pending, and the law firm representing him was suing him for unpaid legal bills. "A little bit of everything's gone wrong," he told the BBC. "Not looking after business would be the main thing. You have to be very clever to keep on top of all that. I would rather write songs and sing them and tour instead of counting figures."

But behind the scenes, Roy and Barbara had begun to work real magic.

Roy had signed with a new booking agent, Triad Artists, based in Los Angeles, and hired

Opposite: Roy Orbison as photographed by Sheila Rock, 1987. **Above**: Roy Orbison, his band, and Roy Orbison Jr. backstage the night George Harrison, Tom Petty, and Jeff Lynne asked Roy to join the Traveling Wilburys, 1988.

a new manager, Jim Mervis, a New York lawyer whom he knew from his MGM days. Roy had met Mervis in 1984 while discussing a possible autobiography and film project. Not lost on Roy and Barbara was the fact that Jim's wife, Stephanie Bennett, had a book and film company, Delilah Films, that they saw as crucial to Roy's future.

Meanwhile, ZTT recorded the opening night of Roy's tour at the Royal Albert Hall for possible release as a live album at Christmas.

Even more important, though, while on tour in England Roy met with Jeff Lynne. The frontman, principal songwriter, and producer of England's Electric Light Orchestra, Lynne and Roy had met briefly in Nashville a few months before and had hatched a plan to work together. Jeff was helping to produce a new Everly Brothers album with Dave Edmunds, and Roy had been impressed with what he'd heard. Lynne's sound was contemporary and full of hooks, but it also paid tribute to the music he'd grown up with as a kid in Birmingham, England, not least of which was Roy's.

The meeting, and the friendship that would come from it, would prove to be a turning point in Roy's life.

Above: At home in his purple writing studio, late 1970s. **Opposite**: Album art for the *Class of '55*, by supergroup Carl Perkins, Jerry Lee Lewis, Roy Orbison, and Johnny Cash, released in 1986.

After the UK tour, Roy and Barbara flew to Miami for a recording session with Larry Gatlin and Barry Gibb. The pair had asked Roy to sing with Gatlin, who was working on a new Gibb-produced album called *Smile*.

Born in Seminole, Texas, Gatlin was a Nashville fixture and had been with Monument Records. He counted Roy and Barbara among his closest friends.

In Miami, Gatlin and Gibb presented Roy with a song they had written called "Indian Summer," which they recorded at Middle Ear, the studio Gibb and his brothers, the Bee Gees, had called home since 1980. The session was a tremendous success, and Roy and Barbara left Miami feeling great.

In September 1985, Roy, Barbara, Alex, and Roy Jr. moved to Malibu, California, while Wesley and Nadine stayed on in Hendersonville. Roy needed a change, and there was a lot of music being made in California in the 1980s. He and Barbara had agreed that it was the place to be. Roy sold his house and the house he had built across the street from where the fire that had killed his young sons had taken place, and Wesley and Nadine moved into a beautiful apartment in the Williamsburg Apartments complex, right off Walton Ferry Road in Hendersonville.

The Orbisons moved to the famous gated community called Malibu Colony before decamping to 3415 Sweetwater Mesa Road in Malibu and finally settling for good back in Malibu Colony, which was right on Malibu's storied beachfront. Roy loved their place by the water, which featured a small music studio on the upper level.

Eventually the family would settle into a beautiful ranch home overlooking the ocean at 3915 Sierks Way, a short but beautiful drive along the Pacific Coast Highway north of Los Angeles.

But Roy had hardly any time to enjoy his new home and growing family. In between tour dates and the move to California, he headed to Memphis to meet up with his old Sun labelmates Carl Perkins, Johnny Cash, and Jerry Lee Lewis for a project that would be known as the *Class of '55—Memphis Rock & Roll Homecoming*.

After a press conference on Monday, September 16, at the Peabody Hotel announcing the project that would reunite the Sun alums and a jam session at Sun Records for the assembled press, recording sessions started the following day, lasting five days at both Sun Records and American Studios in Memphis, where, on Thursday, September 19, after complaining of a sore throat earlier in the week, Roy laid down a new song, "Coming Home," that he'd written with Will Jennings and J. D. Souther.

Although things were awkward at first, especially given all the press trailing the old friends, as the week progressed everyone involved got into the spirit of the occasion, which was in large part a tribute to their mutual friend Elvis Presley.

"Elvis is with us in spirit," Roy told Dick Clark's film crew when asked about the group's collective history. "I wish he were here personally. We were very, very fond of each other and sent messages to each other through busy careers and everything. When I started a movie, he sent a telegram. If he opened a show somewhere, like in Vegas, I'd send a telegram. [He was] a wonderful fella. He came to the studios, we sat around many evenings at the studio, and sometimes we'd play and sing. So it's like he's not gone, and that's very, very good."

Class of '55 was released in May 1986 by Mercury Records. The album would be nominated for Best Country Performance by a Duo or Group, but it was the special interview disc that would go on to win a Grammy for Best Spoken Word or Non-Musical Album, earning the four performers, plus producer Chips Moman and Sam Phillips and Ricky Nelson, who did backup vocals, awards. *Class of '55* turned out to be Nelson's last recording session and the only Grammy Award of his career. He died on December 31, 1985.

Meanwhile, with *Class of '55* completed, Roy traveled to Illinois in September to take part in the first Farm Aid concerts, followed by more dates in the United States and Canada. Farm Aid, which was born at Live Aid on July 13, 1985, when Bob Dylan asked, "Wouldn't it be great if we did something for our own farmers right here in America?" Inspired, Willie Nelson, Neil Young, and John Mellencamp put together the show in aid of America's farmers in just six weeks. The show, held on Sunday, September 22, 1985, in Champaign, Illinois, before a crowd of 80,000 people, raised more than $7 million.

On Wednesday, November 13, Roy was in New York, attending a celebration for Bob Dylan hosted by Dylan's record label, honoring his career and presenting him with a plaque in recognition of selling more than 35 million records worldwide.

Roy's new publicist, Sarah McMullen, was frustrated. She knew that Roy was a star who deserved coverage, but call after call to her music industry contacts went unanswered. When she did get them on the phone, she inevitably had to explain that Roy was not the dark, tragic person they thought he was. In fact, she told each of them, he was a world-class performer whose songwriting had broken every rule imaginable and had become the template for a generation of artists who had followed.

Time and again she met with Roy and Barbara, and she could sense their shared frustration. Little did she know that her phone would soon be ringing off the hook.

Will Jennings picked up his phone one day to hear Roy's voice, and his friend sounded as though he were next door. In fact, he was nearby in Malibu and wanted to work on some new songs.

Roy soon began driving over to Jennings's Agoura Hills home every week to write. Driving a different car every time—one day a Corvette, the next a classic Mercedes convertible—the two would almost always end up at the local car wash together, where employees and customers alike would pester Roy for autographs. Then they'd sneak over to Lupe's on Thousand Oaks Boulevard for Mexican food or to the nearby mall for guitar strings and picks at Instrumental Music. Back at Jennings's house, they'd work on songs, talk about music, Texas, the oil fields, and even ideas for films. As they both recalled from their days growing up in Texas, they'd spent their time "drinking coffee and telling lies."

Roy also spent time in a studio in Sherman Oaks, California, in January 1986, this time to record new versions of his greatest hits for an upcoming double LP release. With the old Monument hits unavailable after the label's recent bankruptcy and thus no record sales revenue being generated for Roy, he decided to rerecord the songs he played each night to make them available to the fans who continued to pack his shows.

During the sessions on Thursday, January 23, 1986, the first Rock and Roll Hall of Fame induction ceremony took place at the Waldorf Astoria in New York. Ten performers, including Elvis, Chuck Berry, Buddy Holly, Jerry Lee Lewis, Little Richard, Fats Domino, James Brown, Sam Cook, Ray Charles, and the Everly Brothers made the cut.

"I must be around twelve or thirteen on that list," Roy thought to himself at the time.

Meanwhile, the album Roy had recorded was released on Silver Eagle Records. Called *The Great Roy Orbison*, it was produced and arranged by Jennings's friend Mike Utley, marking the beginning of a long and fruitful relationship with Roy.

Opposite: Roy photographed for *Rolling Stone* magazine, at home in Malibu, CA, 1988.
Above: Roy with a sampling of his car collection at his Hendersonville, TN, home before his move to California.

As the 1980s dawned, Barbara Orbison was struggling with alcohol dependency. She found relief in the twelve-step program Alcoholics Anonymous, as well as the fellowship and support it afforded her. Never much of a drinker, Roy joined to support his wife and partner but found he also loved the friendship he found in the meetings, especially in their adopted hometown of Los Angeles.

Roy's childhood friend Bobby Blackburn had moved to California at about the same time as Roy and Barbara. After Roy discovered that Bobby was having his own struggles with alcohol, the pair became as inseparable as they'd been as kids. Roy helped Bobby with his steps and encouraged him to go to AA meetings regularly. But though it was no surprise to Bobby that Roy had tried drugs and would occasionally drink more than he should, he never seemed to need such mental supports. In fact, the only thing he had ever seen Roy indulge in was cigarettes and his beloved Coca-Cola. Still, Roy became his rock, joining Bobby at meetings in downtown LA, where afterward they'd take long walks to talk about their experiences. But although Roy could enjoy the anonymity the meetings afforded him, once they were out on the streets he was constantly recognized, and Bobby found himself shocked at the teenagers and college students who would shout out to Roy or even introduce themselves, especially the young girls who asked for kisses, clearly in awe of the man he'd known practically his whole life.

Around that time, Silver Eagle released *Roy Orbison Live in Texas*. Recorded at Rockefellers in Houston in 1986, the home video was released just as Roy hit the road for yet another string of dates across the United States that stretched from May until August of that year.

Though Roy's concerts that time around leaned on his greatest hits, he was still delivering show-stopping performances. "Although Roy Orbison's show at Wolf Trap Tuesday night was exactly the same one he's been performing for years, his songs are so good, his passion so grand and his voice so stunning that it hardly matters," a local Vienna, Virginia, newspaper said after Roy's show there in June. "Like a perfect performance by a gymnast, Orbison's incredible operatic feats on big ballads like 'Running Scared' and 'Crying' brought the crowd to their feet in near disbelief."

Roy was getting into shape and working on new material, preparing for the burst of activity that he and Barbara were sure was coming soon. It came sooner than either of them could have expected.

Below: Barbara and Roy, circa 1986. Roy holds his 1969 José Ramirez Flamenco Guitar. **Opposite**: (above) T Bone Burnett, Roy Orbison, and David Lynch at the Ocean Way studio in Hollywood to rerecord "In Dreams" for the upcoming Virgin LP and single, April 20, 1987. (below) Artwork for the new Virgin single, "In Dreams."

In the summer of 1986, Roy got a call from David Lynch, asking for permission to use his song "In Dreams" in a film he was working on. The director had been hard at work on what would be his breakout film, *Blue Velvet*, and had been thinking about using Roy's song "Crying" in a pivotal scene featuring stars Dennis Hopper, Isabella Rossellini, and Dean Stockwell. He'd gone out and purchased one of Roy's many greatest-hits compilations, but had never gotten past "In Dreams." It was perfect for the scene, and Lynch knew it. With Monument bankrupt and nobody else to ask, he called Roy directly. With the problems that had plagued *Living Legend* and *Roadie* fresh in his mind, Roy declined. "In Dreams" simply meant too much to him.

But Lynch wouldn't give up, telling Roy how much his music meant to him and how perfect the song was for the scene. "It's make or break, really," he told his hero. Finally Roy relented.

When Roy saw the final product, however, he was upset. "In Dreams" was so personal, and Roy felt that Lynch had missed its meaning. But with just about everyone in Los Angeles talking about *Blue Velvet*, Roy figured that maybe he was missing something, and he and Barbara saw the film again.

Featuring Roy's original Monument recording of "In Dreams," the scene where Dean Stockwell, playing a drug dealer and owner of a rather unusual bordello, lip-synchs to the song, using a lamp as a microphone, was striking. Seeing it again, Roy understood where Lynch was coming from and changed his mind.

The eerie scene became one of the most memorable moments of the film, its surreal, nightmarish, dreamlike feel making a huge impact on moviegoers. And with Lynch's unconventional use of Roy's music placed front and center and the film a huge critical success, eventually earning Lynch his second Academy Award nomination for Best Director, Roy's phone was suddenly ringing off the hook.

In the midst of the success of *Blue Velvet*, Roy was inducted into the Rock and Roll Hall of Fame on Wednesday, January 21, 1987. The second annual ceremony took place again at the Waldorf Astoria in New York, with Roy's class also featuring Eddie Cochran, Bo Diddley, Bill Haley, B. B. King, Ricky Nelson, Carl Perkins, Big Joe Turner, Muddy Waters, and Jackie Wilson.

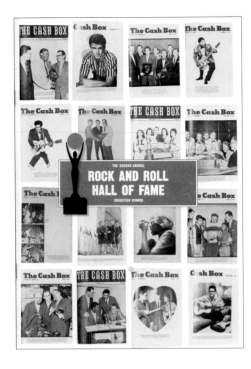

Above: Rock and Roll Hall of Fame ceremony program, 1987. **Opposite**: Roy Orbison, Bruce Springsteen, and others on stage at the Rock and Roll Hall of Fame ceremony when Roy was inducted, New York, January 21, 1987.

At first Roy was reluctant to get involved. He didn't know how dedicated or serious the founders of the Hall, which included *Rolling Stone* founder Jann Wenner, were. But once he arrived in the Waldorf's magnificent ballroom and saw the huge pictures of his fellow inductees, he knew it would be a dramatic evening, as well as a bit overwhelming.

He was right.

When it was time for Roy to be honored, he was introduced by his longtime fan and superstar in his own right, Bruce Springsteen. They'd of course met in 1970 at the Nashville Music Festival, but since then Springsteen had grown in stature, while never losing his admiration for Roy. All those years later, the feeling was mutual.

"In 1970, I rode for fifteen hours in the back of a U-haul truck to open for Roy Orbison at the Nashville Music Fair," Springsteen said from the stage, with Roy waiting in the wings to accept his honor.

It was a summer night and I was twenty years old, and Orbison came out in dark glasses, a dark suit and he played some dark music. In 1974, just prior to going into the studio to record my album *Born to Run*, I was looking at Duane Eddy for his guitar sound and I was listening to a collection of Phil Spector records and Orbison's *All-Time Greatest Hits*. I'd lay in bed at night with just the lights of my stereo on, and I'd hear "Crying," "Love Hurts," "Running Scared," "Only the Lonely," and "It's Over" filling my room. Some rock and roll reinforces friendship and community. But for me, Roy's ballads were always best when you were alone and in the dark. Roy scrapped the idea that you needed a verse-chorus-verse-chorus-bridge-verse-chorus to have a hit. His arrangements were complex and operatic. They had rhythm and movement, and they addressed the underside of pop romance. They were scary. Orbison's voice was unearthly. He had the ability, like all great rock and rollers, to sound like he'd dropped in from another planet and yet get the stuff that was right to the heart of what you were livin' in today, and that was how he opened up your vision. He made a little town in New Jersey feel as big as the sound of his records.

I always remember laying in bed and right at the end of "It's Over," when he hits that note where it sounds like the world is going to end, I'd be laying there promising myself that I was never going to go outside again and never going to talk to another woman [Springsteen went on, recalling later that his speech was payback for all Roy had given him]. Right about that time, my needle would slip back to the first cut

and I'd hear [the opening riff] to "Oh, Pretty Woman"—"I don't believe you/You are not the truth/No one could look as good as you"—and that was when I understood. I carry his records with me when I go on tour today, and I'll always remember what he means to me and what he meant to me when I was young and afraid to love. In 1975, when I went into the studio to record *Born to Run*, I wanted to make a record with words like Bob Dylan, that sounded like Phil Spector's production, but most of all I wanted to sing like Roy Orbison. Now everybody knows that nobody sings like Roy Orbison. So thanks for the inspiration.

Springsteen wrapped up his speech with a hearty "Grrrrrrrr . . . mercy!" Roy took the stage. "Thank you very much," he said as he approached the microphone. "You know, I've spent thirty years trying to be cool, and now I'm nervous and I have to go back to the rest room

again." The crowd laughed, but then he turned more serious. "What a wonderful thing to honor rock and roll and let these people honor rock and roll," he said. "I think it's fantastic."

He talked about how, in 1954, he had been converted to the "rock and roll backbeat" when he was playing a New Year's Eve dance. He closed his speech by saying "I think all of us who are in the business sing for many reasons. One of them is to belong. And I feel very honored and I feel like tonight, since the induction in the Hall of Fame, I feel that I do truly belong."

As the night ended, the assembled stars played "Oh, Pretty Woman," featuring Roy and Springsteen on vocals. Roy was back in the spotlight.

"The induction sort of validated my whole career," he said the following year. "It was a super night, and it was sort of a coming together of the past career and what we were doing at the time, but also brought me together with all these people."

The occasion also brought Roy to the attention of Jeff Ayeroff and Jordan Harris of Virgin Records, who signed Roy to a record deal.

Originally a British record label, Virgin was cofounded by the British entrepreneur Richard Branson and Nik Powell in 1972. Branson and Powell had initially run a small record shop called Virgin Records and Tapes in London, specializing particularly in German "krautrock" imports, before turning their booming business into a full-fledged record label. Notorious for having signed the Sex Pistols, who had already been forced to leave both EMI and A&M, Virgin became a New Wave outpost. After several false starts licensing its bands to various American labels, Virgin Records opened its American division, Virgin Records America, in 1987.

Jeff Ayeroff, a lifelong fan of Roy's music, had run into Danny Goldberg, who was now managing Roy. When Goldberg told him of his association with Roy, Ayeroff jumped at the chance to sign one of his heroes. Roy was tentative at first. He hadn't made a record for a major label in a long time. But he and Barbara got a good feeling about Ayeroff, who made it clear that he believed in Roy and wasn't doing the fifty-year-old rocker any favors by signing him.

"Roy was unique, and I thought he could be part of this era, too," Ayeroff said at the time of the signing. "There is something timeless about his voice and his music. When I saw *Blue Velvet*, I started thinking the movie made Roy's music current again. I have absolute respect for David Lynch, and if he sees the same in Roy's music, I knew I was on the right track."

"Roy looked so good and he felt so comfortable hanging out with his fellow musicians and artists," Roy's publicist Sarah McMullen recalled later. "He was absolutely thrilled, and he really felt good about the Virgin team. It was all about trust with Roy. But he heard creative ideas being exchanged, and Jeff Ayeroff had specific plans for him."

> ROY WAS UNIQUE, AND I THOUGHT HE COULD BE PART OF THIS ERA, TOO. THERE IS SOMETHING TIMELESS ABOUT HIS VOICE AND HIS MUSIC.
>
> — JEFF AYEROFF

Opposite: Roy at Graceland.

One of the first projects was to make a music video for "In Dreams." Barbara called David Lynch for permission to use parts of *Blue Velvet* for the video, but Lynch unexpectedly offered to direct the video. Along with Lynch and producer T Bone Burnett, who was fast becoming a first-call producer in LA, Roy rerecorded the song on Monday, April 20, three days before his fifty-first birthday, at Ocean Way Recording on Sunset Boulevard in Los Angeles. The single was released in late May.

It was Roy's first Virgin release. The AP report said, "Roy Orbison, whose hit songs include 'Only The Lonely' and 'Pretty Woman,' is re-recording his 24-year-old 'In Dreams,' which was revived last year in the movie *Blue Velvet*."

The video, which used very little footage of Roy in favor of footage from Lynch's film, was quickly finished and was soon in heavy rotation on both MTV and its sister channel, VH1.

Roy also turned over the 1986 rerecordings of his hits to Virgin, which remixed them and released them as *In Dreams: The Greatest Hits* in late May 1987, featuring the brand-new version of "In Dreams" as its centerpiece.

Roy then hit the road for a US tour that lasted the rest of the year, including a reunion with his old classmates after a concert near Wink, Texas, as well as an appearance on NBCs *Saturday Night Live*, hosted by Dennis Hopper. Whenever he had days off, he used them to write and record.

Bono, the magnetic frontman of the Irish rock band U2, couldn't sleep. In the midst of a grueling tour in support of the band's *Joshua Tree* album, he lay on his bed in the suite of his London hotel room and listened to the soundtrack of *Blue Velvet* over and over. When he woke up in the morning, he had a song in his head.

Convinced that it was one of Roy's, he scanned the back of the *Blue Velvet* CD but couldn't find it. When he caught up with his bandmates at Wembley Arena that night, he played them the song. After a fantastic performance in front of a sold-out hall that night—Tuesday, June 2, 1987—he started fiddling with the song, much to the chagrin of The Edge, Adam Clayton, and Larry Mullen Jr. "Doesn't this sound like a Roy Orbison song?" he asked the other members of U2. Then there was a knock on the door.

"I've got Roy and Barbara Orbison out here," said the security guy. "They want to say hello. Is that okay?"

Everyone looked at Bono. The coincidence was just too much.

"I really liked the show," Roy told the band in his quiet, seemingly shy voice after he and

LET'S START A BAND WITH ROY ORBISON.
—GEORGE HARRISON

Opposite: Roy playing harmonica during one of the unused shots from the Traveling Wilburys's video "Handle with Care."

Barbara were ushered in. "I can't tell you why I liked it, but I really liked it. You wouldn't have a song? Or maybe we could write a song together, 'cause I'm just kinda into what you are doing."

No one could quite believe their ears. There and then Bono played Roy "She's a Mystery to Me." Roy loved it and promised he'd stay in touch.

Roy had been in England to play some of his new songs for his team at Virgin Records and to meet with Jeff Lynne to plan recording sessions for what would be his first album of new material for Virgin Records. Lynne was in the midst of sessions for a comeback album by another of his heroes, former Beatle George Harrison. Working with a band consisting of Harrison, his former bandmate Ringo Starr, Elton John, and Eric Clapton, Lynne was having the time of his life. At night, he and Harrison would have dinner and talk about the music they were making, as well as dream up projects they might hatch one day.

"I'm producing Roy Orbison," Lynne told Harrison one night.

"Let's start a band with Roy Orbison," Harrison shot back with a confidence that only someone of his stature could muster. "We can call it the Trembling Wilburys."

Back in sunny California, Roy kept up writing with Will Jennings, also finding help from the famed guitarist Steve Cropper, as well as the recent transplant to LA, former Sex Pistol Steve Jones.

"I invited Steve to my house," Roy remembered later. "He roared up to the front gate on his Harley with his Gibson guitar. We had some coffee, then got straight down to work on a beat ballad. Very tender, quite the opposite from what his rough image would lead you to expect."

Roy found Jones a joy to work with. "He doesn't hold anything back," he said. "In a song he's looking for naked emotion, getting to the very heart of a song, and that's what I'm after, too. Like me, he enjoys losing himself in the music."

Jerry Lynn Williams was another songwriter Roy teamed up with around that time. Williams was a sought-after songwriter. Three of his compositions, including the hit "Forever Man," had appeared on Eric Clapton's 1984 comeback effort *Behind the Sun*. He had also contributed songs to Bonnie Raitt's Grammy-winning album *Nick of Time* and collaborated with the brothers Stevie Ray and Jimmie Vaughan on "Tick Tock," a song later played at the former's funeral after he died in 1990 in a helicopter crash that also killed Roy's agent, Bobby Brooks. Roy and Williams wrote "After the Love Has Gone," a beautiful song that remained unreleased until 1992.

Above: Roy in Malibu, CA, 1988.

Opposite: Promotional photo, 1987.

By now the songs were coming fast and furious. Tom Kelly and Billy Steinberg, a successful songwriting team who had penned Madonna's "Like a Virgin," wrote "I Drove All Night" for Roy. He both loved the song and the energy the young pair brought to their meetings.

Roy's old friend and collaborator Bill Dees also made contact with him around that time. Barbara and Roy invited Dees to Malibu, and, inspired by their rekindled friendship, the pair knocked out ten new songs in no time.

Elvis Costello, the New Wave sensation who had recently worked with Elvis Presley's TCB band on his *King of America* album and was secretly working with former Beatle Paul McCartney on new material, had meanwhile written a song called "The Comedians" for Roy.

"I had Roy Orbison in mind when I wrote the song, but I had no idea that I would ever meet him or that he would ever get to sing it," Costello recalled later. When Costello's friend T Bone Burnett inquired whether Costello had a song for sessions he was producing for Roy, Costello knew that he had a rare opportunity to have the song sung by the voice for which it was intended. With a "Bolero" rhythm borrowed from "Running Scared" and modulations perfect for Roy's stunning range, the song instantly became one of Roy's favorites among his new material.

The sessions for Roy's Virgin album began in earnest at Ocean Way Recording on Tuesday, July 28, 1987. In short order, Roy and company recorded "(All I Can Do Is) Dream You" by Billy Burnette and David Malloy, and Roy and Bill Dees's "You're the One." A few days later, on Monday, August 3, "The Comedians" was recorded.

After recording "The Comedians," Roy headed out on tour, something he never seemed to tire of. With dates beginning on Friday, August 14, and running until Friday, September 4, at venues from Saratoga, California, to Hyannis, Massachusetts, including an appearance at the Bumbershoot Festival at the KeyArena in Seattle, Washington, before 10,000 people, the shows were uniformly well received. Roy's voice had aged like a fine wine and featured a power and maturity, with greater range, a deep timbre, and a remarkable and spine-tingling control of his fabled vibrato. Roy felt energized and could hardly believe it was all coming together for him, one more time.

In late August, while Roy was on tour, he also became involved in a movie project, rerecording "Crying" for a film called *Hiding Out*. Pete Anderson, who often worked with Dwight Yoakam, produced the session, together with Don and David Was.

When Don Was came to write out the chart for the musicians assembled to rerecord one

of Roy's most famous songs, he was shocked. There was virtually no discernable structure to the song, which seemed to defy the rules of modern composition while at the same time being an almost perfect song.

k.d. lang duetted on the track with Roy.

Born in Edmonton, Alberta, Canada, k.d. lang was fascinated by Patsy Cline from an early age. She began performing and recording in 1983, when she was twenty-two years old, and in 1985 earned Canada's Juno Award for Most Promising Female Vocalist of the Year, her first of many Junos, including Country Female Vocalist of the Year in 1987 and Best Female Vocalist in 1989.

"Where Roy's vocal prowess and ability came from was his soul, and that is the number one basic ingredient—fundamental ingredient—to being a great singer," she recalled later. "And so it was effortless, because you could tell that he had done a lot of the internalization of what being a great vocalist was, consciously or unconsciously. And it was effortless for him, but it wasn't without effort.

"It's so hard to explain to you what Roy's energy was like, because he would fill a room with his energy and his presence but not say a word, being that he was so grounded and so strong and so gentle and quiet."

"I've always given my best," Roy told reporters after the sessions. "I work hard on my records and stage appearances to make sure that everything is just right. I can't afford anything substandard. There will always be room for a good song. And to that I would add a good song well sung."

"Crying," featured in *Hiding Out*, proved to be just that. Owing more to Don McLean's arrangement than Roy's original, the duet worked perfectly, and a video featuring Roy and k.d. was soon being played around the globe, just as another song, "Life Fades Away," which was featured in the Robert Downey Jr. film *Less than Zero*, was being released.

Though *Hiding Out* and *Less than Zero* were hardly *Blue Velvet*, both helped to deliver Roy's

Above: Roy receives a BMI award from Frances Preston for more than a million plays on "Crying," 1988. **Opposite**: A rare color photo from rehearsal for "A Black & White Night" concert, (left to right) Ron Tutt, Roy Orbison, Bruce Springsteen, Elvis Costello, and Glen D. Hardin, Los Angeles, CA, September 29, 1987.

music to a new audience.

Despite the fact that *Roy Orbison Live in Texas* from 1986 had only just been released, Roy was unhappy with the results, and he longed for a television special that would capture the energy and excitement of his live shows and present him in a way he felt his fans deserved.

After Barbara and T Bone Burnett approached Cinemax, the network gave the green light for a cable TV special for its *Cinemax Sessions* series. *Cinemax Sessions* had been created by

Stephanie Bennett of Delilah Films, who was also Jim Mervis's wife. She had recently produced Chuck Berry's film *Hail! Hail! Rock 'n' Roll*, in which Roy appears, so Roy and Barbara knew they were in good hands.

Filmed at the Cocoanut Grove nightclub in Los Angeles's Ambassador Hotel, the stunning film, which was shot in stark black and white, would go on to be one of the best-loved live performance videos ever released.

Roy Orbison and Friends: A Black and White Night, as it would be called, showed Roy in peak form, surrounded by friends such as Bruce Springsteen, Jackson Browne, J. D. Souther, Tom Waits, Elvis Costello, Bonnie Raitt, and others whom he had inspired to take up music as a profession. Backed by Elvis Presley's TCB band, Roy played hit after hit, as well as two new songs, including Costello's "The Comedians," to the star-studded crowd.

"He was almost not there," Springsteen said of the remarkable performance Roy gave that night. "You couldn't see his eyes, his mouth barely moved, and yet you were hearing this sound that was coming straight from his center to yours."

Filmed on Wednesday, September 30, 1987, *A Black and White Night* was a tribute to Roy's more than thirty-year contribution to rock and roll, while at the same time placing him firmly in the mainstream.

With his Cinemax special in the can, Roy continued to tour throughout the rest of 1987, and an appearance at London's Mean Fiddler was recorded by Virgin Records for possible future release.

Meanwhile, on November 2, 1987, George Harrison released his album *Cloud Nine*, his first in five years. Recorded at Harrison's house, Friar Park, Henley-on-Thames, in England, with producer and friend Jeff Lynne behind the board, it would go on to be a worldwide smash.

"I spent a lot of time getting to know Jeff, and I thought he'd be ideal to work with and as it happened it turned out very good, and he's an excellent record producer and also a song-

writer and a performer himself," Harrison told Australian television in 1988. "I've always had help from my friends as musicians, but the main input that helped me this time was in the production side, because it's a bit tiring doing everything yourself. So the input I've been missing during the last few albums I got with Jeff Lynne.

"Another reason I like Jeff is because there are certain things I don't like about pop music, and Jeff and I fitted together well. We both have a dislike for certain clattery sounds and stuff like that. I wanted to try and get it so it wasn't so much of a computer record that didn't have any human feel to it. We tried to get it so it had a feel so it was a bit more like you'd do it in the late '60s or early '70s."

After the release of *Cloud Nine*, Harrison and Lynne flew out to Los Angeles to do some promotion for the record.

"We had met in England when we were over there doing some shows with Bob Dylan," Tom Petty said later. "Jeff had come along with George Harrison, and they would come night after night and we were having a great time. Then we came back to LA, and on Thanksgiving Day, I'd just been playing this *Cloud Nine* record that Jeff had produced, over and over, and I thought it was fantastic. I was driving down to buy a baseball mitt at the drugstore, and I stopped at the red light and I looked over and there was Jeff Lynne in the car next to me. So I waved him down, and we were both kinda stunned and we exchanged phone numbers. And it turned out Jeff just lived a little ways up the road from where I was living.

"A lot of mystical things went on around that time," he continued. "I think it was Christmas Eve, or the day before, I was out and I went into a restaurant and I ran into Jeff and George in the restaurant. George had just asked Jeff for my phone number when I walked into the room. So there were a lot of strange coincidences."

Roy was back in the United States soon after his short European visit to start promoting his new single, "Crying" with k.d. lang. The promotional campaign included an appearance on the *Top of the Pops* TV show, now in the United States, and what would become an acclaimed performance on *The Tonight Show*, on Monday, December 7. In New York in early January to promote *A Black and White Night*, Roy appeared on Wednesday, January 6, on *Late Night with David Letterman*. Roy did a fantastic version of "Mean Woman Blues" with bandleader Paul Shaffer's group. Even though it was one of his earliest hits, to the millions of viewers, Roy sounded fresh and full of energy.

After a short break, on Sunday, February 21, Roy returned to New York to film a cameo appearance in the movie *She's Having a Baby*. While there, he called his longtime friend

Bobby Blackburn, who was by then living in Bakersfield, California, and had just suffered a stroke.

"Roy was magnificent, he called me three or four times a day for the next three weeks," Blackburn recalled later.

"I'm here in the hotel room reading the ticker on the Times Square building," Roy told Blackburn during the call. "It says 'Hard Rock Cafe Tribute to Roy Orbison: Sold Out.' I'm having lunch today with Billy Joel and Christie Brinkley."

On Monday, April 4, 1988, Jeff Lynne called Tom Petty in to sessions for Roy's new album. Humbled at meeting one of his childhood heroes, Petty was still able to get down to business when Lynne told him they needed another song. In no time, they'd written "You Got It."

That same day, after returning to England for a break from promoting *Cloud Nine*, George Harrison was now back in Los Angeles. With a new single set for imminent release, he needed a song quickly for the European extended play version of the third single off *Cloud Nine*, "This Is Love," due for release in June.

"I was asked by my record company to give them an extra song to put on a twelve-inch extended single for Germany and Great Britain," Harrison said later in 1988. "I didn't have any extra tunes recorded at the time, so I just thought, 'Well, I'll go in tomorrow, I'll go into a studio somewhere, and I'll just write one and do it then.'"

That night at dinner, Harrison was joined by Lynne and Roy. "Do you feel like coming along?" Harrison asked.

"If you do something, give me a call," Roy told Harrison as they parted that night, and Harrison drove over to Petty's house to pick up one of the guitars he'd left there, so he'd have it for the session the next day.

When Harrison told Petty what he and Lynne were up to, Petty replied, "Oh, I was wondering what I was gonna do tomorrow."

But on such short notice, Harrison figured he'd have trouble finding an available studio. He called his old friend Bob Dylan, who he knew had a studio in a converted garage, and Dylan said, "Sure. Come on over."

Harrison headed over to Dylan's house in the morning and cobbled together a tune while sitting in his garden. Soon joined by Roy, Jeff Lynne, Tom Petty, and Dylan, the former Beatle challenged his friends: "Okay, come on, I've got all these great writers, let's have some lyrics."

"Well, what's it called?" Dylan asked.

Opposite: Limited edition Traveling Wilburys guitar.
Above: The Traveling Wilburys album art.

Having noticed a cardboard box in Dylan's garage earlier, Harrison replied, "Handle with Care."

Everyone loved it, and soon the lyrics were finished. The five musicians wandered into Dylan's garage, and, sitting in a circle with five guitars, they played the song twice to an electronic drum track. By the end of the day, the song was done.

After some finishing touches by Harrison and Lynne, Harrison played the results for his old friend Mo Austin, the head of Warner Bros. Records.

"This is too good to bury on the back of a single!" Austin exclaimed after hearing "Handle with Care." "How about if you record nine more and make an album?"

"We had this fictitious group that we thought we might have one day called the Trembling Wilburys," Jeff Lynne remembered in 2007. "It's just what you do in the studio at about four o'clock in the morning."

"Last year, when Jeff Lynne and I were doing *Cloud Nine*," George Harrison said in 1988, "I don't know, we probably had too many drinks and were just talking about something and this came out, the Trembling Wilburys, suddenly, and then it turned into the Traveling Wilburys, and that was it, it was forgotten about, really."

"I thought, 'Ah, let's just stick a bit in it for Roy,'" he told VH1 of "Handle with Care." "And so everybody was there, and I thought, 'Well, I'm not just going to sing it myself. I've got Roy Orbison standing there.' And then, as it progressed, when we were doing the vocals, I just thought, 'I might as well just see if—you know, to push it a bit—if I could get Tom and Bob to sing the bridge.'"

As they were doing their vocals, Harrison turned to Lynne and said, "Hey, Jeff, this is it, the Traveling Wilburys!"

"It was wonderful, just a wonderful time, and completely accidental, really," Tom Petty said in the press kit for his album *Full Moon Fever*, which featured Roy, Lynne, and Harrison and would be a worldwide chart topper. "We couldn't have ever planned it or handpicked who would be the Wilburys."

The lyrics for "Handle with Care," however, were more than a quick scribble. They were a witty, autobiographical nod to both Harrison's and Roy's past. And giving listeners exactly what they wanted to hear from the former Beatle and one of the true architects of rock and roll was nothing short of magical.

Opposite: Traveling Wilburys fan illustration. **Above**: (top) "End of the Line" single art. (bottom) The Traveling Wilburys—(left to right) Tom Petty, Jeff Lynne, Bob Dylan, Roy Orbison, George Harrison—at Dave Stewart's home in Encino, CA, May 1988.

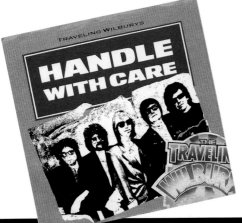

Encouraged by Austin and Virgin's Jeff Ayeroff, perhaps only George Harrison could have pulled those five stars together. He'd created the rock charity concert with the Concert for Bangladesh in 1971; now he'd created the only supergroup worthy of that moniker. Each was a star in his own right, but it was George who created the Wilbury environment in which they could indulge in an ego-free collaboration. Everybody sang, everybody wrote, everybody produced, and they all had great fun doing so.

On the other hand, it was Roy who gave the project a wider dimension. Though all five were good friends, who admired and respected one another, Roy was somebody the others all idolized. Of course they revered Bob Dylan. But Dylan was closer to being a contemporary. It was Roy who gave the Wilburys that special glow from rock and roll's early, formative years.

With that in mind, and Dylan on board, Harrison, Lynne, and Petty headed off to see Roy perform at the Celebrity Theatre in Anaheim on Saturday, April 9, to ask him if he wanted to join their band.

After Roy's show, which was another triumph, the trio trooped backstage. When they found Roy, Harrison got down on his knees and bowed his head. "Hey, Roy, we're gonna have a group," he told him once he'd gotten up. "Will you be in it?"

"Yeah, sure will," Roy replied.

On the way home from Anaheim, the limousine full of some of rock's biggest stars couldn't believe what had just happened.

"Roy Orbison is in our band!"

"I don't think we ever got over it," Petty recalled later.

In the midst of sessions for Roy's album in April, at the studio in Heartbreakers guitarist Mike Campbell's garage, which yielded "You Got It," "California Blue," and "A Love So Beautiful," but with Dylan set to hit the road soon, the Wilburys assembled in May at musician Dave Stewart's home in Encino, California, where they had decided to record the rest of the Traveling Wilburys album.

"We were at Dave Stewart's house, and it was a nice environment because you could kinda sit outside; it was warm and the doors were always open," Tom Petty said later.

Above: (top) "Handle with Care" single art. (below) and **Opposite**: The Traveling Wilburys: Bob Dylan, Jeff Lynne, Tom Petty, Roy Orbison, and George Harrison.

Dave Stewart of Eurythmics, who had worked with Tom Petty and Bob Dylan, had a little guesthouse at the back of his house. Though it was hardly a studio—it was a kitchen and a room with a console in it, plus a little vocal booth—engineer Don Smith made the best of his surroundings. Tom Petty's long-serving roadie Alan "Bugs" Weidel, who handled everything from instruments to recording equipment, was also there as the group's utility man.

On the first day, Bob Dylan presented the song "Last Night." As he was strumming the guitar, he said, "Why don't we do one like that?" Everyone pitched in, and soon the song was finished.

But inspiration was there in abundance. Right in the middle of getting the sounds to record "Last Night," Dylan started playing yet another song. It soon became "Congratulations."

Though they were all old hands, Roy's fellow Wilburys were in awe of his gifts. When he sang his parts, they would stand around with their mouths open. They marveled that Roy's incredible, intense voice seemed always to be done with the least amount of effort.

"It's just totally effortless for him," Harrison said to Lynne at one point, clearly in amazement.

Still, the sessions were joyous. "Every time it came to Roy, he always got the 'trembling Wilbury' line," Lynne recalled of recording the ending of the song "Dirty World." "It was the funniest thing—Roy, the big voice, 'trembling Wilbury'—and we all collapsed every time. No matter how we rearranged it, he always ended up with 'trembling Wilbury.'"

"There is a song, which we wrote specifically for Roy, which is very much like an old kind of Roy Orbison song," George said of "Not Alone Anymore," which Jeff Lynne reworked one night especially for Roy after everyone had called it a day. "But the album is not like we tried to set out to do something. We didn't want it to be folks going out and buying an album of mine, or ELO, or Tom Petty, Bob Dylan, or Roy Orbison. We tried to combine everything, and it's worked very well."

"One night I broke in, into the studio to try this alternative chord pattern, because that was one particular one I couldn't stand the way it was, and just as an alternative I put this telecaster on and tried these other chords and pulled out the other stuff," Lynne recalled of the

Above and **Opposite**: Roy Orbison as photographed by Glen Erler for *Mystery Girl*. Los Angeles, CA, November 1988.

song in *The True Story of the Traveling Wilburys*. "Then everybody else arrived, they heard this new thing: Same tune but different chords. And they loved it.

"One of the most amazing things ever about the Wilburys was this wholes–a part thing of Roy and Bob Dylan," he added. "The best singer and the best lyricist, and they are both in the same group."

"Those 10 tracks was all we did," Tom Petty said later in the *Full Moon Fever* press kit. "And we did it pretty fast, really. We'd all sit on the floor in a circle and write the songs, then we'd go cut the track and we'd have dinner and work on the lyrics over dinner. Then we'd go do the vocals, and bang!"

"It's the first band that I can think of that has five rhythm guitar players," Harrison quipped while promoting the album. "We added touches here and there, but we tried to keep it more or less like it was when we wrote it and did it. It's polished off a bit but not too much."

After his parts for the Wilburys' album were done, Roy left town for some concerts before flying over to Harrison's house in England to put the finishing touches on the Traveling Wilburys album, as well as what would become *Mystery Girl*.

But soon, on Monday, June 27, Roy was at Eleven Eleven Sound in Nashville with engineer Lynn Peterzell, recording a Will Jennings and Richard Kerr song called "In the Real World," as well as another called "Heartbreak Radio," a Troy Seals and Frankie Miller composition.

After a return to Harrison's Friar Park, Roy continued sessions for his album in Los Angeles at Rumbo Recorders in Canoga Park, California, in between dates on the road.

"Mr. Orbison knows how to freeze time, so that every element of a song gleams as if magnified, and he would insert into tunes sections where the instruments would fall away to expose his voice," Peter Watrous wrote in the *New York Times* of his show there. "The audience, standing up and singing along, was ecstatic."

Roy was back home in early September, and on Thursday, September 15, U2's Bono was in Los Angeles as well for a scheduled appearance at Amnesty International's Human Rights Now! concert at the Los Angeles Memorial Coliseum six days later. At Rumbo Recorders, Bono and Roy finally laid down "She's a Mystery to Me," the song Bono had dreamed all those months before.

Hoping to please Roy, Bono, who was producing the session, jumped up when Roy arrived. "What would you like? Mexican dancing girls? What is it?" he asked.

"Well, have you got any Coca-Cola?" Roy replied.

Above: Album art for *Mystery Girl*, a body of work that is best described as Roy's final opus.
Opposite: Roy Orbison in a haunting photo by Sheila Rock, 1987.

Standing next to Roy when he recorded his vocal for "She's a Mystery to Me," Bono was shocked. It seemed as though Roy hardly opened his mouth. Was he saving up for the next take?

When they headed into the control room to hear what they'd done, it was one of the finest vocals Bono had ever heard. It was like the voice of an angel.

The song was tailor made for Roy and was exactly the type of song he needed. He had finally broken away from his own past, revitalized, original, and modern.

"He was very contemporary, very current, and he thought of himself that way," Tom Petty recalled. "I think the album proves that."

By October, with recording complete, sessions had moved to A&M Studios on La Brea Avenue in Hollywood for mixing. Built by Charlie Chaplin in 1917, it had been taken over by Herb Alpert and Jerry Moss in 1966, when they had founded the A&M label. Thousands of sessions had since taken place there, including by John Lennon, the Doors, the Police, Bruce Springsteen, even the session for the "We Are the World" single. Now Roy was there, too.

Meanwhile, the first Traveling Wilburys video was shot in Los Angeles in early October. Filmed at an old brewery near Union Station at 650 S. Avenue 21, the day of shooting proved to be a marvelous time for all involved. The British director David Leland was behind the camera, and the stylist Roger K. Burton, who had worked on *Quadrophenia*, *Chariots of Fire*, and other films, as well as music videos by Mick Jagger, UB40, Paul McCartney, David Bowie, and the Eurythmics, made sure everyone looked sharp and fit. Roy sported a long black coat with fringe, black pants, red shoes, and his ever-present diamond-encrusted Maltese cross, which he had bought in England many years before. He also sported a ponytail, which he wore in honor of the Founding Fathers, from the books he loved so much, and which he'd dared friend Johnny Cash to join him in growing the last time they'd seen each other. For the video Roy played a beautiful acoustic Gibson guitar, rather than his black Gibson 335 electric.

MR. ORBISON KNOWS HOW TO FREEZE TIME, SO THAT EVERY ELEMENT OF A SONG GLEAMS AS IF MAGNIFIED.

—PETER WATROUS, *THE NEW YORK TIMES*

The video ranks among the best rock videos of all time.

"We tried to do something different, like a nice film, where we're just playing, with nice shots of guitars, and heads, and feet and stuff," Jeff Lynne said later. "And it worked. It's a nice video, and I'm really pleased with it, because it's got a lot of quality photography, as opposed to gimmicks and fireworks and all that."

"Handle with Care" began airing on MTV in late October, at about the same time as it was released as a single. The LP, *The Traveling Wilburys, Vol. 1*, was released on October 25.

"Now we see what happens, and after that who knows," George Harrison told MTV. "Maybe we'll all just go back to being whoever we were before the Wilburys, or maybe we'll do something else. We just have to wait and see."

Fans scouring the album's liner notes were tickled to find that their heroes had adopted new names for the project. Harrison was Nelson Wilbury, Lynne was Otis, Dylan was Lucky, Petty was Charlie T. Jr, and Roy was Lefty, an obvious nod to his childhood hero, Lefty Frizzell.

Michael Palin of Monty Python wrote the liner notes. Harrison, who had self-financed the troupe's film *Monty Python's Life of Brian* after other investors had backed out, was thrilled to discover that Roy was a fan, too.

"I didn't expect him to know all the words to Monty Python's 'Sit on My Face and Tell Me That You Love Me,' which he did," George recalled. "He knew all those things. He did. He was hysterical, really."

"Roy's laughter was really infectious," Jeff Lynne added. "You couldn't help but just join in. Roy loved Monty Python. He knew all the sketches, and he could do them by himself, which he did. The one day we'd driven to the Union Station in downtown LA to do the film of 'Handle with Care,' in the car on the way there Roy was doing the sketches on his own and laughing his socks off and giggling."

"I'm so honored to have known Roy, really, 'cause I loved him so much," Tom Petty said, recalling Roy fondly years later. "He was just a lovely fella. You know, he has this image of dark and lonely, but he wasn't. Never seemed that way to me. He seemed like a very happy person, and just full of life and really living every day. And he loved the Wilburys. But I remember Roy's laugh the most, I think. He had this beautiful laugh."

Above: Roy Orbison at a press conference in Antwerp, Belgium, after his appearance at the Diamond Awards Festival, November 19, 1988.
Opposite: Roy performing at the Diamond Awards Festival, November 19, 1988. This appearance was filmed and televised, and later segments were used for the official "You Got It" video.

Plans for a Wilburys tour were hatched but batted down by Harrison, and there were plans for a movie, too.

"Everything is fitting together so nicely of late," Roy told *Music Express*. "Life is going real good for me now. I've got a lot of songs in me that I haven't written yet, a lot of records that I haven't made yet and a lot of tours I haven't done. I'm just looking forward to each day knowing that Roy Orbison is making music again."

On November 11, with the Wilburys' album and single climbing the charts, Roy jotted down his proposed running order for his upcoming Virgin release. The list, which was included as part of the American Master Series dedicated to Roy Orbison in November 2006 at the Rock and Roll Hall of Fame in Cleveland, read as follows:

You Got It
In the Real World
Dream You
A Love So Beautiful
California Blue
She's a Mystery to Me
Windsurfer
The Only One
Careless Heart
The Comedians

By November 15, all the mixes were compiled on two master tapes, and on the seventeenth the album master tracks were put onto two tape reels, each containing one side of the LP. The new album sounded, as the journalist Nick Kent described it after hearing an early promo, like "genuinely luxurious contemporary 'pop,' combining accessibility and a depth of feeling, highlighted principally by Orbison's singing—technically probably the best of his career."

On Thursday, November 17, with the master tapes for the new album finished, Roy was on his way to Europe with promo copies in

Above: Roy with Chris Isaak. **Right**: Roy during his last UK performance, at the Mean Fiddler, London, November 10, 1987. **Below**: Roy in his tour bus in Boston, MA, December 3, 1988. **Opposite**: Roy performing his last concert, Front Row Theatre, Highland Heights, OH, December 4, 1988.

hand for the press there. His track list had been altered slightly, and the running order was now "You Got It," "In the Real World," "Dream You" (single remix with intro), "Dream You" (album mix without intro), "A Love So Beautiful," "California Blue," "She's a Mystery to Me," "The Comedians," "The Only One," "Windsurfer," and "Careless Heart."

During his visit to Europe, Roy looked great, as he and Barbara and his band made one appearance after another. After visits to Belgium and Paris Roy and Barbara landed in London on Sunday, November 27, for several long days of interviews to promote the Traveling Wilburys release. Roy was in high spirits.

On Tuesday, November 29, *BAM Magazine*'s Martin Ashton noticed that Roy was noticeably relaxed and talkative and was surprised when Barbara cut their interview short, saying she wanted to get Roy to a doctor that afternoon to get some antibiotics. She was worried because he had to fly home the next day.

By the time Roy was interviewed by the Swedish journalist Kristina Adolfsson, he had a blinding headache. "I don't understand it, it just won't go away," he told her. "I've taken a couple of pills, but they haven't helped. It just keeps throbbing away."

Barbara put Roy on a plane back to the United States from Heathrow Airport on Wednesday, November 30. She headed to Germany to see her family and do some promotion and negotiations, while Roy went off to finish up a couple of concert dates on the East Coast and in the Midwest. The Traveling Wilburys were on top of the charts, and Roy was hotter than he'd been in twenty-five years.

"By the end of the evening, he was really wiped out," the owner of Boston's Channel club said after Roy's remarkable show there a few days later.

After wrapping up his commitments with one more show in Cleveland, Roy headed down to Tennessee on his tour bus to spend a few days in Hendersonville with his mother, Nadine, his son Wesley, and his brother, Sammy, before leaving again for London to film two more Traveling Wilburys videos on December 12.

"All right, I'm going home," Roy told his band as he got off the bus. "I'll see you in January. We'll get back together, learn some new songs, and have a ball."

Above, **Opposite** and **Following pages**: Rare images of Roy performing his last concert, Front Row Theatre, Highland Heights, OH, December 4, 1988.

On Tuesday, December 6, he spent time flying model airplanes with his bus driver and friend Benny Birchfield. He had had a passion for model airplanes since the 1940s, and that day at Sanders Ferry Park, they had a blast. Afterward, they had dinner at Birchfield's home.

"We ate supper about 5:30, and he was going to spend the night with his mother," Birchfield's wife, country music star Jean Shepard, recalled later. "He went over there, and close to eleven o'clock Sammy Orbison, his brother, called and said, 'Benny, can you get over here? Roy's passed out in the bathroom and he is not breathing.'"

Paramedics were already there when Birchfield arrived. They worked on Roy for thirty minutes before taking him to the hospital. Doctors were unable to revive him, and he was pronounced dead in the emergency room at six minutes before midnight on Tuesday, December 6. The cause of death was a massive heart attack. The registrar listed on Roy's death certificate was Naomi Jones, who had also been the registrar on Claudette's death certificate twenty-two years earlier.

Roy's death was sudden and shocking, but earlier that day, Roy had visited with his only surviving son from his first marriage, Wesley, and had closed the distance that had grown between them. They had said they loved each other, as usual, and at Wesley's request Roy had played one of his new songs, "Windsurfer," and told him how much fun the new band was.

"He'd had heart problems for some time," Barbara told reporters later. "We had all expressed our concern that he was working too hard, but Roy was a strong-willed person. He loved the fact that he'd been given a second chance for success and told us several times he wasn't going to let it slip away from him. For Roy, that meant working harder and longer than anyone had a right to expect of him. He was driven."

I THINK, MAYBE, IF I MADE SOME FORM OF
A CONTRIBUTION THAT BROUGHT A LITTLE
HAPPINESS TO SOMEONE OR HELD A FEW THINGS
TOGETHER, THAT WOULD BE GREAT. —ROY ORBISON, 1987

Chapter 7
SAYING GOOD-BYE

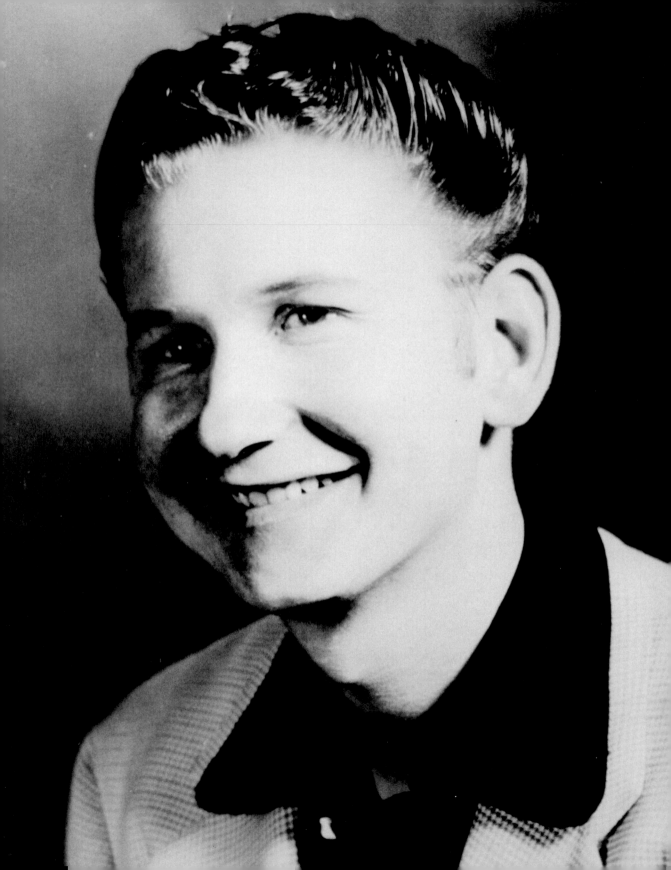

The mood on the set

of the Traveling Wilburys video for the group's upcoming single "End of the Line" was uncharacteristically somber. It was set in a railroad freight car on the outskirts of Los Angeles on Saturday, December 10, 1988, just four days after the soul of the group, Lefty Wilbury, known to the world as Roy Orbison, had died.

But Roy had loved the Wilburys dearly, and the collective decision to go ahead with the shoot was made all the more poignant when it was decided to highlight the sections of the song that Roy had sung by dimming the lights on the set and shooting a rocking chair with a Gibson guitar perched atop it.

"It was very odd to not have Roy there, because we had become a group," bandmate Tom Petty said of the video, which premiered to much acclaim on MTV the following month. "I think he was there in the sense that we could feel him there. It was a little sad, because his funeral was about a day before the video, but we tried to go on and hope that we did him justice. It turned out to be a curious song for the next single, you know, the 'End of the Line.' But you write these songs, and it's funny how events come down and later on when you hear the song, it can mean so much more than it did when you were writing it."

"I was in England, and I just got a phone call saying—and it didn't even say who it was—it just said, 'Mr. Orbison is dead.' And hung up," Jeff Lynne recalled in 2007. "And still, to this day, I don't know who it was."

"I've always felt that if anybody was ever prepared to leave, Roy was," Petty said of his friend. "He was a very deep man, and he'd lived a lot, and he was a very wise man. But mostly I just miss him, just to hang around with him. I think Roy went out on top, and I'm sure he knew that. I think the last conversation I had with him was a couple of days before he died, on the phone, and he was just so thrilled that the Wilburys had gone platinum. And he was going 'Ain't it great? It's great.'"

Opposite: Sun Records promo photograph of a young Roy Orbison, 1956. **Above**: Roy on the cover of the January 26, 1989 issue of *Rolling Stone* magazine following his untimely death, on December 10, 1988.

Barbara Orbison was in Germany when she got the news. The shock was almost too much to bear. She and Roy had been through so much together since meeting so long before in a nightclub. They'd worked so hard together to get Roy back on top. To have it all disappear in an instant was unfathomable. Crushed, she headed back to the United States immediately.

Perhaps fittingly of the man who never let up and who had worked so hard to reclaim his mantle as one of the greats of rock and roll, Roy's next single was in production at Precision Lacquer in Hollywood when word began to trickle out in the press that he had died.

As the news spread around the world and pictures from Roy's career graced every newspaper and his music filled the airwaves, his body was taken to the Phillips-Robinson Funeral Home in Nashville before being flown to Santa Monica on Friday, December 9, for burial. While Barbara planned a "Celebration of Life" at a secret spot in Los Angeles restricted to friends and family, another memorial, planned by Roy's old friend Jean Shepard, was held in Nashville at the College Heights Baptist Church at 2100 Nashville Pike, between Hendersonville and Gallatin, at three in the afternoon on Sunday, December 11.

"Good friends are hard to come by, and Roy was a good friend," Shepard told the *Tennessean* of the event, which was also originally intended only for friends and family. But after an outpouring of grief within the tight-knit music community, Shepard relented. Fans were not turned away.

"It would be okay, I'm sure. Roy belonged to the people," she said.

Roy had attended the church and knew the minister, Brother Larry Gilmore, who gave a touching speech. The mourners included Roy's band, who brought Roy's tour bus, his brother Sammy and his oldest son, Wesley, and some of the legendary Nashville musicians and personalities who had played with Roy.

Nobody could believe Roy was gone. "He'd really been working hard," bass player Michael Joyce told the press. "The crowds had been getting wilder and wilder. The crowd in Boston [the week before] was shouting 'Roy, Roy, Roy' before he went onstage. There was a real momentum building."

The humble remembrance on Nashville Pike was a long way from the glamorous, private celebration that took place in Los Angeles on Tuesday, December 13, at the Wiltern Theatre. Kris Kristofferson, Graham Nash, T Bone Burnett, Johnny Rivers, Tom Waits, Tom Petty, and Jeff Lynne attended, and Bonnie Raitt, J. D. Souther, and the Stray Cats performed. Will Jennings, his friend with whom he'd written so many songs, recited Lord Byron's "So, We'll Go No More A-Roving."

Opposite: Claudette and Roy Orbison at home in Hendersonville, TN, May 1961.

"Roy Orbison was one of the genuinely nicest persons I've ever known," Kristofferson said. "He had one of the most beautiful voices in the history of recorded music. He could easily have had an opera star's ego, but he was one of the humblest, kindest, sweetest human beings to grace this planet; a brave, beautiful blessing of a man."

As Roy Orbison Jr. later wrote in the liner notes for the career-spanning boxed set *The Soul of Rock and Roll*, "There is only one Roy Orbison. And there are many. Blue-haired Rockabillys, Japanese leather rockers, All-American college girls whose favorite movie is 'Pretty Woman,' Elvis-lovers, country music fans, 15-year-old Goths who paint their fingernails black, Pavarotti and classical music buffs, Ramones punk rockers, Johnny Cash disciples, and good old-fashioned Roy Orbison diehards who have stood by him from the beginning. They all see a different Roy Orbison. They all see their own Roy Orbison."

Roy was buried in an unmarked grave at the Pierce Brothers Westwood Village Memorial Park Cemetery on Wilshire Boulevard in the Westwood area of Los Angeles on Thursday, December 15, with a few friends and family members present. Barbara's father read the Lord's Prayer in German as a torrential rain, uncharacteristic for Southern California, poured down.

The fourth annual Rock and Roll Hall of Fame ceremony was held in New York on Wednesday, January 18, and it was dedicated to Roy. During the all-star jam session that wrapped up the proceedings, Bruce Springsteen led everyone in a heartfelt rendition of "Crying." Though there was hardly a dry eye in the house, it was hardly the last we'd hear from Roy.

On Saturday, January 21, 1989, *Billboard* published a review of "You Got It," which had just been released. "It's hard to believe he's left us, but this fine selection from the artist's forthcoming *Mystery Girl* album charms with the appeal of the singer's vintage material," the industry bible wrote of the song. "With the aid of Lynne and Petty, the songwriting and production on this one are first-rate. That voice will undoubtedly continue to live on."

With "You Got It" tearing up charts around the world, *Mystery Girl* hit stores on January 31.

"The late Roy Orbison's first album of all-new material in ten years, *Mystery Girl* cloaks the epic sweep and grandeur of his classic sound in meticulous, modern production—the album encapsulates everything that made Orbison great, and for that reason it makes a fitting valedictory," *Rolling Stone* said of the unexpected posthumous release.

Featuring ten songs and six producers, the album has a remarkably unified sound, with Roy's spine-tingling bel canto heightening the drama of even the most straightforward tune, and *Mystery Girl* soon became his best-selling album ever. But neither was it Roy's only album

I WAS ALL RIGHT FOR AWHILE

I COULD SMILE FOR AWHILE

BUT I SAW YOU LAST NIGHT

YOU HELD MY HAND SO TIGHT

Opposite: Classic shot of Roy in England in 1964 with his custom made Orbison Guitar and strap.

235

WHEN YOU SAID, "SO LONG"

LEFT ME STANDING ALL ALONE

ALONE AND CRYING, CRYING

CRYING, CRYING

Opposite: Barbara and Roy, London, April 1, 1969.

on the US charts. On January 28, *The Traveling Wilburys, Vol. 1* reached the Number 3 position on *Billboard*'s Top 200 Albums chart, making Roy the first artist since Elvis to have two albums in the Top 10 at the same time.

In the midst of that incredible chart success worldwide, "Crying" by Roy and k.d. lang won a Grammy for Best Country Vocal Collaboration on Wednesday, February 22. It was Roy's third Grammy.

To top it off, *Rolling Stone* published its long-awaited interview with Roy as its cover story. In it Roy talked freely about his state of mind, his records, his past, and his future. "In the three months before his death, the usually private but unfailingly polite Orbison had been generous with his time, inviting *Rolling Stone* to his recording and mixing sessions, his concerts, his comfortable, unostentatious house high in the hills overlooking the beach at Malibu," author Steve Pond wrote. "The final session took place over breakfast at a restaurant just down the beach from the pier where he'd once spoken to actor Martin Sheen about playing the lead in the movie version of the autobiography Orbison wanted to write. 'I guess I'll give the book a try now,' he said, finishing off his meal and smoking from a pack of Camels that he later left behind so that Barbara wouldn't get upset."

Memories of Roy from some of his closest friends abounded. Johnny Cash wrote about Roy in his autobiography, "I miss Roy. I miss him coming over for breakfast. He had total recall, you know. Around Roy, you didn't dare tell a story about something in which he'd been involved without asking, 'Is that the way it was, Roy?' He'd tell you exactly why you were wrong or right. He could repeat twenty-year-old conversations word for word. He could tell you what you were wearing. It was almost scary. Roy was just my buddy, but sometimes I'd look at him and wonder."

He also shared a wonderful story about a run-in with Wesley that took place not long after Roy's passing:

Wesley is still within our circle. A few years ago I started seeing him leaning against the fence bordering the place where his brothers died, where the home of his childhood once stood. One day I stopped and asked him what he was looking at. "Oh, I like to come up here sometimes and look at this lot," he said. "It gives me a little comfort." Well, I told him, there were some mighty good fruits there and whenever the fruit was ripe he should just go on in and help himself. Bring a basket. "Okay," he said. "Thank you, I will."

It was June who got the idea to give him more than the fruit. I agreed, and without any further fuss we signed the lot over to him free and clear. Now when I see him

leaning on the fence I know he's thinking about the house he wants to build there someday, and I don't feel like I lost a thing in the deal. I feel like old Roy smiled down and said, "Thank you, John."

Roy Orbison Day was declared in Texas on what would have been Roy's fifty-third birthday, April 23, 1989, while Roy was all over the charts. "You Got It," "Crying," and "California Blue" were mainstays of rock and country radio, and videos of "California Blue" and "A Love So Beautiful," starring Winona Ryder, were in heavy rotation on MTV and VH1.

With demand for Roy's music at a high not experienced since the days of "Oh, Pretty Woman," the *Roy Orbison and Friends: A Black and White Night* album, which followed the enormous success of the home video in April 1988, was released in October. And when the 1990 Grammys came around the following February 21, "You Got It" was nominated for Best Pop Vocal Performance, Male and *The Traveling Wilburys, Vol. 1*, was nominated for Album of the Year as well as Best Rock Performance by a Duo or Group with Vocal, for which the supergroup took home the prize, Roy's fourth Grammy. His fifth Grammy would come the following year, when the single of "Oh, Pretty Woman," from *Roy Orbison and Friends: A Black and White Night* won for Best Vocal Performance, Male.

In 1990, the Wilburys would reconvene for a second album, dedicated, like Petty's *Full Moon Fever*, to Roy, but some of the magic was missing.

Meanwhile, after suffering from the shock of Roy's sudden death for some time, Barbara realized that it was for her to carry on his legacy. Not wanting to let all of their hard work go to waste or, more important, perhaps, to let down the man she loved so much, she took on the job of managing Roy's estate and posthumous career with care and gusto.

"After Roy passed in 1988, of course I was aware that there were more songs," she said in 1992. "Because Roy, for the last four years of his life, had written for the album *Mystery Girl*. We had talked about the next album, but for the last three years I really didn't want to face another album. I really didn't want to listen to those songs. You know, because when I hear them, I know where Roy was emotionally, and the songs are bits of him and they are bits of me, or about me, so I just couldn't face it."

By taking unfinished songs recorded by Roy in 1987 and 1988 and overdubbing new background tracks to them, a new album, *King of Hearts*, was released in October 1992. It featured demos recorded at Will Jennings's house ("We'll Take the Night," "Love in Time"), a few finished studio tracks ("Wild Hearts," "Careless Heart," "Coming Home," and the duets with

I THOUGHT THAT I WAS OVER YOU

BUT IT'S TRUE, SO TRUE

I LOVE YOU EVEN MORE THAN I DID BEFORE

Opposite: Roy Orbison, promotional shot, 1970.

239

YES, NOW
YOU'RE GONE

AND FROM THIS
MOMENT ON

I'LL BE CRYING,
CRYING

CRYING, CRYING

YEAH, CRYING,
CRYING

OVER YOU

k.d. lang ("Crying" and "You Are the One," recorded especially for the album), and a couple of tracks that were finished by Jeff Lynne ("Heartbreak Radio" and "I Drove All Night").

Roy hit the Top 10 again with "I Drove All Night," and "Crying" with k.d. lang peaked at number 13 on the UK charts. But with Roy once again relegated to the "Oldies" bin, the album barely broke the Top 200 in the United States, though it did mean that, like his onetime labelmate Elvis Presley, Roy had charted in five consecutive decades.

Not surprisingly, a steady stream of releases followed, further cementing Roy's place in the history of rock and roll. The impeccable Bear Family boxed set of Roy's music recorded between 1956 and 1965, and *The Soul of Rock and Roll*, a wonderful collection featuring rare and unreleased tracks, were worthy additions to Roy's formidable catalog.

Then, twenty-three years to the day after Roy's death, on December 6, 2011, after helming Roy's posthumous career with such a loving touch and after a brave battle with pancreatic cancer, Barbara Orbison died at the age of just sixty-one, leaving his legacy in the hands of his three remaining sons.

Roy's boys quickly set about furthering Roy's name with an excellent deluxe version of *Mystery Girl*, a spectacular box set of his MGM albums—which included an unreleased album entitled *One of the Lonely Ones*—plus a greatest-hits album entitled *The Ultimate Collection* and a thirtieth anniversary edition of *Black and White Night*. Each made its mark on the charts, proving the timelessness of Roy's music.

"I never sing to the microphone, I'm singing through all the mechanics to the people listening," Roy said in 1976. "Even in the recording studio, I imagine people who are listening. I'm singing to real people, not the mechanics of recording or the corporate structure of the business."

That dedication to his fans remains one of the things that sets Roy apart and accounts for the new fans he makes, even almost thirty years after his death.

Roy Orbison is remembered by his legions of fans as much for his ballads of lost love as for his barn-burner rockers. In the music community, he is revered for his songwriting innovations, which defied convention, influenced generations of acolytes, and advanced popular music with their melodic, rhythmic, and lyrical sophistication.

But of course it is Roy's voice, more than anything else, that he is remembered for.

"He sounded like he was singing from an Olympian mountaintop," fellow Wilbury Bob Dylan once said of Roy's remarkable range. Built on a powerful delivery that seems so effortless and that was at once tender and soft as a springtime breeze, Roy's voice rings out to this day, inspiring new generations and creating new fans with each passing year, just as it did when the first strains of "Ooby Dooby" hit the airwaves of rural Texas, all those many years ago.

ACKNOWLEDGMENTS

Writing this book was a bittersweet project. We would, of course, have preferred that our dad were here to tell his story for himself. There were many times when we wished that we could have turned to him, or Barbara or Claudette, not to mention the many people close to them that we've lost along the way, for help and support. But we were determined to tell the real story of Dad's life once and for all and, as we read back through the manuscript during the editorial process, we came to feel confident that their guidance had been with us all along.

Of course, this project was a massive undertaking, and to get it right we called on the many people who knew and loved our dad to help.

First and foremost, we'd like to thank our coauthor, Jeff Slate, for taking all the information and research we threw at him and creating a narrative that does Dad justice. We'd met Jeff during the promotion of the *Mystery Girl* reissue and knew immediately that his knowledge of and love for our dad was genuine and that, as a songwriter and musician himself, he would bring something special to the project. We weren't wrong, as I'm sure you'll agree.

We'd also like to thank Marcel Riesco, who for ten years scoured the world and amassed a formidable collection of press clippings and memorabilia from throughout our dad's life, as well as original interviews from many of the people who were key to his story. Marcel is also a musician, and the inspiration that he drew from our father's work made a huge impression on all of us. Without his tireless efforts, this book would not have been possible.

Our manager, Chuck Fleckenstein, and everyone at Roy's Boys—Sara Beal, Luke Chalk, Chelsie Lykens, Michael Rollman, and our former colleague Jen Pappas—deserve our deepest thanks, too. That goes ditto for our lawyers, Michael Frisch and Jonas Herbsman; our business managers, LeeAnn Hard and Lana Lanis; our PR team, Bob Merlis, Ben Merlis, and Amy Treco-Block; our archivists, Derek Neill and Hazel Neill; and our teams at Sony Legacy and Universal Records, as well as our music publishers, Kobalt and Sony/ATV. Every day they work tirelessly to make sure that our dad's legacy is preserved, promoted, and enriched in ways both big and small. Their help in making this book a reality was indispensable.

Lynn Johnston, our literary agent, has been an invaluable source of help throughout this project. She was always available, always willing to assist in crafting ideas, and never shy about telling us when we'd gone astray. But, most of all, her guidance proved extraordinary both in developing the story we wanted to tell and in marketing it within the industry.

At our publisher, Center Street, our editor, Kate Hartson, deserves a big thank you, as does her editorial assistant, Grace Tweedy Johnson. Their patience, support, and dedication to this project went far above and beyond. Their entire team—especially Patsy Jones and Sarah Falter—as well as the designers Timothy Shaner and Christopher Measom at Night & Day Design, deserve our eternal thanks.

There were many folks who touched our dad's life, and whose life touched his. For those who are still with us, we know you carry him with you every day. For those who are no longer with us, it felt wrong to leave you out. So thanks to the all of you, for everything: Kathy Anderson, David Malloy, Jim Malloy, Billy Burnette, Steve Cropper, Chuck Turner, Boudleaux and Felice Bryant, Del and Carolyn Bryant, R. A. and David Lipscomb, the Teen Kings, Johnny Cash, Elvis Presley, Poppa Holifield, Sam Phillips, Bob Neal, the Everly Brothers, Acuff-Rose Music, Fred Foster, Joe Melson, Bill Dees, Bobby Goldsboro, Jeff Lynne, Tom Petty, Bob Dylan, Bruce Springsteen, Bono, T Bone Burnett, k.d. lang, Elvis Costello, Mike Utley, Tom Waits, Bonnie Raitt, Jennifer Warnes, J. D. Souther, Jackson Browne, Steven Soles, James Burton, Ron Tutt, Glen D. Hardin, Jerry Scheff, Joe and Marjorie Walsh, George and Olivia Harrison, Ringo and Barbara Starr, Neil Young, John Fogerty, Linda Ronstadt, Van Halen, Don McLean, Raul Malo, the Mavericks, Brandi Carlile, Chris Isaak, Richard Dodd, John Carter and Ana Cristina Cash, Terry Elam, John Mason, Jeff Ayeroff, Jim Zwickel, Norman Petty Studios, Sun Studio, RCA Studios Nashville, Monument Studios, US Recording Studios, Jim Keltner, Benmont Tench, Mike Campbell and the crew at Mike Campbell's Garage, Friar Park, Rumbo Records, MGM Motion Pictures, all the producers, engineers, and backing bands, light men, roadies, and bus drivers, as well as all the singers, songwriters, bands, and aspiring musicians who cover our dad's music and keep the dream alive, and especially Roy fans everywhere. This book is for you.

Finally, and most important, we'd like to thank our families. To Emily Orbison, Cameron Davidson, Åsa, Roy III, and Bo Orbison, and Erika Orbison, you are Roy's true legacy. Every day we draw our strength and inspiration from you. We hope you are as proud of this book as we are.

Above: Barbara Orbison and Roy's Boys unveil the Roy Orbison star on the Hollywood Walk of Fame in Hollywood, CA, January 29, 2010.

by Marcel Riesco

	LABEL/CAT. #	RELEASE DATE
SINGLES		
The 1950s		
Trying to Get to You/Ooby Dooby	Je-Wel 101	03/1956
Ooby Dooby/Go Go Go	Sun 242	05/1956
Rock House/You're My Baby	Sun 251	09/1956
Sweet and Easy to Love/Devil Doll	Sun 265	03/1957
So Long, Good Luck, Goodbye/ Trying to Get to You (Weldon Rogers but B-side plays Roy's version)	Imperial 5451	1957
Chicken Hearted/I Like Love	Sun 284	12/1957
Seems to Me/Sweet and Innocent	RCA 7-7381	09/1958
Almost Eighteen/Jolie	RCA 47-7447	12/1958
Paper Boy/With the Bug	Monument 45-409	9/1959
Uptown/Pretty One	Monument 45-412	11/1959
The 1960s		
Only the Lonely/Here Comes That Song Again	Monument 45-421	05/1960
Blue Angel/Today's Teardrops	Monument 45-425	08/1960
I'm Hurtin'/I Can't Stop Loving You	Monument 45-433	12/1960
Sweet and Easy to Love/Devil Doll	Sun 353	12/1960
Running Scared/Love Hurts	Monument 45-438	03/1961
A Million Teardrops/ I'm in a Blue, Blue Mood (Conway Twitty single; Roy appears on B-side)	MGM 13011	05/1961
Crying/Candy Man	Monument 45-447	07/1961
Dream Baby/The Actress	Monument 45-456	01/1962
The Crowd/Mama	Monument 45-461	05/1962
Working for the Man/Leah	Monument 45-467	09/1962
Paper Boy/Here Comes That Song Again	Monument CSx-1 (special)	1962
In Dreams/Shahdaroba	Monument 45-806	01/1963
Falling/Distant Drums	Monument 45-815	05/1963
Blue Bayou/Mean Woman Blues	Monument 45-824	08/1963
Pretty Paper/Beautiful Dreamer	Monument 45-830	11/1963
It's Over/Indian Wedding	Monument 45-837	04/1964
Oh, Pretty Woman/Yo Te Amo Maria	Monument 45-851	08/1964
Goodnight/Only with You	Monument 45-873	02/1965
(Say) You're My Girl/Sleepy Hollow	Monument 45-891	06/1965
Ride Away/Wondering	MGM K 13386	08/1965
Let the Good Times Roll/Distant Drums	Monument 45-906	09/1965
Crawling Back/ If You Can't Say Something Nice	MGM K 13410	10/1965

	LABEL/CAT. #	RELEASE DATE
Let's Swing the Jingle for Coca-Cola (60-second cut by Roy)	Coca-Cola n/a	1965
Breakin' Up Is Breakin' My Heart/Wait	MGM K 13446	01/1966
Twinkle Toes/Where Is Tomorrow	MGM K 13498	03/1966
Lana/Our Summer Song	Monument 45-939	06/1966
Too Soon to Know/ You'll Never Be Sixteen Again	MGM K 13549	07/1966
Communication Breakdown/ Going Back to Gloria	MGM K 13634	11/1966
So Good/Memories	MGM K 13685	02/1967
MGM Celebrity Scene Promo Set: (5 singles, cue sheet, bio, and jukebox title strips)	MGM CS 9-5 (DJ)	04/1967
Ride Away/Crawling Back	MGM K 13756	
Breakin' Up Is Breakin' My Heart/ Too Soon to Know	MGM K 13757	
Communication Breakdown/ Twinkle Toes	MGM K 13758	
Going Back to Gloria/Sweet Dreams	MGM K 13759	
You'll Never Be Sixteen Again/There Won't Be Many Coming Home	MGM K 13760	
Cry Softly Lonely One/Pistolero	MGM K 13764	06/1967
She/Here Comes the Rain Baby	MGM K 13817	10/1967
Born to Be Loved By You/Shy Away	MGM K 13889	01/1968
Walk On/Flowers	MGM K 13950	06/1968
Heartache/Sugar Man	MGM K 13991	09/1968
My Friend/ Southbound Jericho Parkway	MGM K 14039	03/1969
Penny Arcade/ Tennessee Owns My Soul	MGM K 14079	08/1969
The 1970s		
She Cheats on Me/ How Do You Start Over Again	MGM K 14105	01/1970
So Young/If I Had a Woman Like You	MGM K 14121	04/1970
Ooby Dooby/Go Go Go	Sun 8	09/1970
Rock House/You're My Baby	Sun 12	09/1970
Sweet and Easy to Love/Devil Doll	Sun 16	09/1970
Chicken Hearted/I Like Love	Sun 23	09/1970
(Love Me Like You Did It) Last Night/ Close Again	MGM K 14293	08/1971
God Love You/Changes	MGM K 14358	01/1972
Running Scared/Love Hurts	Monument Records ZS7-8900	04/1972

	LABEL/CAT. #	RELEASE DATE
Crying/Candy Man	Monument Records ZS7-8901	04/1972
Leah/Working for the Man	Monument Records ZS7-8902	04/1972
Mean Woman Blues/Blue Bayou	Monument Records ZS7-8903	04/1972
Pretty Paper/Beautiful Dreamer	Monument Records ZS7-8904	04/1972
Only the Lonely/Uptown	Monument Records ZS7-8906	04/1972
Dream Baby/I'm Hurtin'	Monument Records ZS7-8907	04/1972
The Crowd/In Dreams	Monument Records ZS7-8908	04/1972
Oh, Pretty Woman/It's Over	Monument Records ZS7-8910	04/1972
Falling/Distant Drums	Monument GS 1904	n/a
Blue Angel/Paper Boy	Monument GS 1915	n/a
Remember the Good/		
Remember the Good (DJ only)	MGM K 14413	04/1972
Remember the Good/Harlem Woman	MGM K 14413	04/1972
Remember the Good/		
If Only for a While	MGM K 14413	05/1972
Memphis, Tennessee/		
I Can Read Between the Lines	MGM K 14441	09/1972
Blue Rain/Sooner or Later	MGM K 14552	05/1973
I Wanna Live/		
You Lay So Easy on My Mind	MGM K 14626	08/1973
Sweet Mamma Blue/Heartache	Mercury 73610	08/1974
Sweet Mamma Blue/		
Heartache (different label)	Mercury 73610	08/1974
Hung Up on You/Spanish Nights	Mercury 73652	02/1975
It's Lonely/Still	Mercury 73705	09/1975
Belinda/No Chain at All	Monument ZS8-8690	03/1976
I'm a Southern Man/Born to Love Me	Monument 45-200	09/1976
Drifting Away/Under Suspicion	Monument 45-215	04/1977
Easy Way Out/Tears	Asylum 46048	05/1979
Poor Baby/Lay It Down	Asylum 46541	09/1979

The 1980s

	LABEL/CAT. #	RELEASE DATE
That Lovin' You Feelin' Again		
(with Emmylou Harris)/		
Craig Hundley Track (released with		
two different labels)	Warner WBS49262	06/1980
Birth of Rock and Roll (Carl Perkins)/		
Rock and Roll (Fais-Do-Do)		
(picture sleeve)	America/Smash 884 760 7	1986
Sixteen Candles (Jerry Lee Lewis)/		
Rock and Roll (Fais-Do-Do)	America/Smash 884 934 7	1986
Class of '55 (Carl Perkins)/		
We Remember the King	America/Smash 888 142 7	1986
In Dreams/Leah	Virgin 7 99434	05/1987
Crying (with k. d. lang)/Falling	Virgin 7 99388	11/1987
Handle with Care/Margarita	Wilbury/WB 7 27732	10/1988
Handle with Care/Margarita		
(Traveling Wilburys limited edition)	Wilbury/WB 7 27732W	10/1988

	LABEL/CAT. #	RELEASE DATE
You Got It/The Only One	Virgin 7 99245	01/1989
End of the Line/Congratulations	Wilbury/WB 7 27637	01/1989
She's a Mystery to Me/		
Dream Baby (live)	Virgin 7 99227	03/1989
You Got It/Crying	Virgin 7 99245	04/1989
California Blue/In Dreams	Virgin 7 99202	06/1989
(All I Can Do Is) Dream You		
(single remix promo)	Virgin PRCD2843	circa 07/1989
Oh, Pretty Woman (edited version live)/		
Claudette	Virgin 7 99159	10/1989

The 1990s

	LABEL/CAT. #	RELEASE DATE
Empty Cup/A True Love Goodbye		
(Clovis demos-bootleg release)	Clovis Label (bootleg)	1990
I Drove All Night	MCADS 54419	06/1992
Crying/Oh, Pretty Woman/Falling/		
She's a Mystery to Me	VUSCD 63	1992
Heartbreak Radio (promo)	DPRO 12731	10/1992
Heartbreak Radio/Blue Angel/		
Claudette/Lana	VUS 7243	10/1992
Heartbreak Radio/In Dreams/		
You Got It/Dream Baby	VUS 7243	10/1992
Pretty Paper	Virgin 708761158526	1996

The 2000s

	LABEL/CAT. #	RELEASE DATE
Oh, Pretty Woman/Crying (collectible		
single in box with t-shirt)	Sony Legacy 887654394873	02/2013

EPs/MINI LPs

The 1960s

	LABEL/CAT. #	RELEASE DATE
Crying/Our Summer Song/		
Let's Make A Memory/Lana/		
Loneliness/Nite Life (6 pack)	Monument MSP-2	1962
In Dreams/Lonely Wine/Shahdaroba/		
Dream/Blue Bayou/Gigolette (6 pack)	Monument MSP-003 1	1963
All I Have to Do Is Dream/		
Beautiful Dreamer/My Prayer/		
No One Will Ever Know/Sunset/		
House Without Windows (6 pack)	Monument MSP-003 2	1963
In Dreams (mini LP)	Monument SSP-503	1964
More of Roy Orbison's Greatest Hits		
(mini LP)	Monument SSP-506 1	1964
More of Roy Orbison's Greatest Hits		
(mini LP)	Monument SSP-506 2	1964
Demand Performances	MSP-010 1	1964
Demand Performances	MSP-010 2	1964
Orbisongs Volume One (mini LP)	Monument SSP 512	1965

	LABEL/CAT. #	RELEASE DATE
Roy Orbison Swings the Jingle (90-, 60-, 30-, and 10-second ads by Roy)	Coca-Cola TX-97	1965
Roy Orbison's Greatest Hits (mini LP)	Monument SSP 515	1967
The Classic Roy Orbison (mini LP)	MGM SLM 4347	1967
Early Orbison (mini LP)	Monument SSP 526	1967
More of Roy Orbison's Greatest Hits (mini LP)	Monument SSP 527	1967

LPs/CDs

The 1960s

	LABEL/CAT. #	RELEASE DATE
Lonely and Blue	Monument SM 14002	01/1961
Roy Orbison at the Rock House	Sun LP 1260	1961
Crying	Monument SM 14007	01/1962
Roy Orbison's Greatest Hits	Monument SM 14009	08/1962
Portrait of a Fool and Others (Conway Twitty, feat. Roy in 1 track)	MGM SE 4019	1962
Orbiting with Roy Orbison and Bristow Hopper (comp.)	Pickwick SDLP-164	1963
Roy Orbison's Greatest Hits (reissue of M 14009) (mono)	Monument MLP 8000	1963
Roy Orbison's Greatest Hits (reissue of SM 14009)	Monument SLP 18000	1963
In Dreams	Monument SLP 18003	07/1963
Demand Performances (Monument compilation)	Monument SLP 18010	1963
More of Roy Orbison's Greatest Hits	Monument SLP 18024	07/1964
Early Orbison	Monument SLP 18023	10/1964
Special Delivery from Baby Bare, Joey Powers, and Roy Orbison	RCA Camden CAS 820	1964
There Is Only One Roy Orbison	MGM SE 4308	08/1965
Orbisongs	Monument SLP 18035	11/1965
The Orbison Way	MGM SE 4322	02/1966
The Very Best of Roy Orbison (purple and blue cover)	Monument SLP 18045	07/1966
The Classic Roy Orbison	MGM SE 4379	09/1966
Roy Orbison Sings Don Gibson	MGM SE 4424	01/1967
The Fastest Guitar Alive	MGM SE 4475	06/1967
Cry Softly Lonely One	MGM SE 4514	10/1967
Roy Orbison's Many Moods	MGM SE 4636	05/1969
The Original Sound of Roy Orbison	Sun 113	1969

The 1970s

	LABEL/CAT. #	RELEASE DATE
The Great Songs of Roy Orbison	MGM SE 4659	02/1970
Hank Williams the Roy Orbison Way	MGM SE 4683	08/1970
The Big O (cancelled, not released)	MGM SE 4753	not released
Zigzag (movie soundtrack)	MGM 1 SE 21st	1970

	LABEL/CAT. #	RELEASE DATE
Roy Orbison Sings	MGM SE 4835	06/1972
All-Time Greatest Hits of Roy Orbison	CBS PZ 31484	1972
Memphis	MGM SE 4867	11/1972
A History: Monument Records Corp.	Monument/CBS AS25	1972
Milestones	MGM SE 4934	09/1973
I'm Still In Love with You	Mercury SRM 1045	09/1975
The Living Legend of Roy Orbison (double LP, mail order only)	Candlelite P2-12946	1975
Regeneration	Monument MG 7600	11/1976
All-Time Greatest Hits of Roy Orbison (reissue)	Monument MP 8600	1976
Roy Orbison's Greatest Hits	Monument MC 6619	1977
In Dreams	Monument MC 6620	1977
More of Roy Orbison's Greatest Hits	Monument MC 6621	1977
The Very Best of Roy Orbison	Monument MC 6622	1977
Miriam (Jessie Colter, feat. Roy in 1 track)	Capitol 11583	1977
Living Legend Soundtrack	(few copies made)	1978
Laminar Flow	Asylum 6E 198	05/1979

The 1980s

	LABEL/CAT. #	RELEASE DATE
Roadie (movie soundtrack)	Warner Bros 2HS 3441	06/1980
Roy Orbison Live in Concert (cassette and 8-track only)	Big O Records & Tapes	03/1981
My Spell on You	Hits Unlimited 233 0	1982
Pirates and Poets (Bertie Higgins, feat. "Leah" with Roy)	Kat Family Records FZ 38587	1983
Live at Gilley's (radio promo copies only)	Westwood One #LG83-49	12/1983
Last Mango in Paris (Jimmy Buffett, feat. Roy in 1 track)	MCA 5600	06/1985
Smile (Larry Gatlin & Gatlin Brothers, feat. Roy in 1 track)	Columbia FC 40068	1985
Class of '55 (Jerry Lee Lewis, Johnny Cash, and Carl Perkins)	America/Smash AR LP100	05/1986
Class of '55	Polygram 830 002-1	05/1986
Class of '55 (interview album)	America/Smash AR/LP100 1	1986
The Great Roy Orbison	Silver Eagle SE 1046	1986
Blue Velvet (movie soundtrack)	Varese Sarabande STV81292	1986
In Dreams: The Greatest Hits	Virgin 90604 1	05/1987
Hiding Out (movie soundtrack)	Virgin 790661-1	11/1987
Less Than Zero (movie soundtrack)	Def Jam/Columbia SC44042	11/1987
For the Lonely	Rhino 71493	01/1988
All-Time Greatest Hits of Roy Orbison Volume 1	CBS 44348	09/1988
All-Time Greatest Hits of Roy Orbison Volume 2	CBS 44349	09/1988
Traveling Wilburys Volume 1	Wilbury 1 27576	10/1988

	LABEL/CAT. #	RELEASE DATE
Mystery Girl (promo canvas CD package, white with embossed letters)	Virgin promo	01/1989
Mystery Girl	Virgin 791058 1	01/1989
Mystery Girl (with free 12" Crying)	Virgin 2576	1989
Classic Roy Orbison 1965–1968	Rhino R2 70711	04/1989
Our Love Song	CBS AK 45113	05/1989
Best Loved Standards	CBS AK 45114	05/1989
Rare Orbison	CBS AK 45115	05/1989
The All-Time Greatest Hits of Roy Orbison	CBS AGK 45116	05/1989
Laminar Flow (CD release)	Electra/Wea 198-2	06/1989
Polaroy (promo for A Black and White Night)	Virgin CD PRCDPolaroy	1989
A Black and White Night Live	Virgin 91295	10/1989
The Sun Years	Rhino R2 70916	11/1989
The Singles Collection 1965–1973	Polydor 839234-2	1989

The 1990s

	LABEL/CAT. #	RELEASE DATE
The Legendary Roy Orbison	CBS CD Box Set A4K46809	09/1990
Lonely and Blue	CBS A 21427	1990
Crying	CBS A 21428	1990
In Dreams	CBS A 21429	1990
Rare Orbison II	CBS AK 45404	1990
The Fastest Guitar Alive	CBS AK 45405	1990
Pretty Woman (soundtrack)	EMI # 93492	03/1990
Roy Orbison/Little Richard	RCA 9969 2 R	1990
Live in Texas 1987 (Bootleg, 1986 concert in Houston, TX)	RFCD 1193	n/a
The Other Side of Roy Orbison (Roy Orbison Volume 7)	TNT 14293/14441	1991
Best of His Rare Classics	Curb 77481	06/1991
White Knuckle Scorin' ("I Drove All Night" only)	MCA	12/1991
Mystery Girl	Virgin 86103	06/1992
King of Hearts	Virgin 86520	10/1992
Shades of Roy Orbison	Sony A24991	1994
Lonely and Blue	Sony WK 75049	1995
Crying	Sony WK 75050	1995
In Dreams	Sony WK 75051	1995
Super Hits	Columbia 67297	09/1995
In Dreams: Greatest Hits	Orbison Records ROGH 1000	1996
The Very Best of Roy Orbison	Virgin 42350	03/1997
Combo Concert	Orbison Records HCC19650	1997
Interview CD	Orbison Records	1997
End of Violence (features "You May Feel Me Crying")	Outpost Records	1997
Black and White Night	Orbison Records ROBW7891-2	1997
The All-Time Greatest Hits of Roy Orbison	DCC Monument GZS 1118	1997
Live at the BBC	Mastertone 8224	02/1998
16 Biggest Hits	Sony Legacy 69738	02/1999
Roy Orbison: The Anthology	Orbison Records ORB3805-2	1999
Official Authorized Bootleg (box set)	Orbison Records ORB3803-2	1999
A Black and White Night (remastered)	Orbison Records ORB3813-2	1999

The 2000s

	LABEL/CAT. #	RELEASE DATE
Live at Austin City Limits	Orbison Records ORB3812-2	2000
The Complete Sun Sessions	Varese Sarabande 3020662332	06/2001
Lost and Found (Teen Kings live on TV)	Varese Sarabande	2001
MGM Singles Collection 1965–1973 (mail order only)	Orbison Records Mail Order	2002
Island Bound (Bertie Higgins CD features remix of "Leah" with Roy)	Sony Special Products 54667	2003
Black and White Night	Legacy 78150	02/2006
The Essential Roy Orbison	Legacy/Sony 90696 2	03/2006
Lonely and Blue	Legacy/Sony 85572 2	08/2006
Crying	Legacy/Sony 85574 2	08/2006
In Dreams	Legacy/Sony 85573 2	08/2006
Traveling Wilburys Collection (2 CDs/DVD)	Rhino R2 167868	06/2007
Traveling Wilburys Collection (3 LPs)	Rhino RH1 224316	12/2007
The Soul of Rock and Roll (4 CD boxed set)	Legacy/Monument 5537 2	09/2008
Roy Orbison: The Last Concert (digital download only)	Orbison Records	12/2008
Roy Orbison: The Last Concert	Eagle Records EAGCD409	08/2010
Living Legend (DVD with bonus soundtrack)	MVD Visual 5092	01/2011
The Monument Singles Collection (2 CDs/DVD)	Sony Legacy 784158	04/2011
In Dreams: Greatest Hits	Sony Legacy 888837597425	09/2013
The Monument Vinyl Box	Legacy/Monument 88883761091	11/2013
The Last Concert: 25th Anniversary	Roy's Boys/Legacy 88843 00678-2	12/2013
Mystery Girl Deluxe	Sony Legacy 886976070328	05/2014
The MGM Years	Universal 4721354	12/2015
There Is Only One Roy Orbison (Part of boxed set sold individually)	Universal 4721355	12/2015
The Orbison Way (Part of boxed set sold individually)	Universal 4723291	12/2015
The Classic Roy Orbison (Part of boxed set sold individually)	Universal 4723292	12/2015
Roy Orbison Sings Don Gibson (Part of boxed set sold individually)	Universal 4723293	12/2015
The Fastest Guitar Alive (Part of boxed set sold individually)	Universal 4745830	12/2015

	LABEL/CAT. #	RELEASE DATE
Cry Softly Lonely One (Part of boxed set sold individually)	Universal 4723295	12/2015
Roy Orbison's Many Moods (Part of boxed set sold individually)	Universal 4723296	12/2015
The Big O (Part of boxed set sold individually)	Universal 4723298	12/2015
Hank Williams the Roy Orbison Way (Part of boxed set sold individually)	Universal 4723297	12/2015
Roy Orbison Sings (Part of boxed set sold individually)	Universal 4723300	12/2015
Memphis (Part of boxed set sold individually)	Universal 4723301	12/2015
Milestones (Part of boxed set sold individually)	Universal 4723302	12/2015
MGM B-Sides & Singles (Part of boxed set sold individually)	Universal 4723305	12/2015
One of the Lonely Ones	Universal 4723304	12/2015
The Ultimate Collection	Legacy 889853688715	10/2016
Black & White Night 30	Legacy 88985404832	02/2017
A Love So Beautiful: Roy Orbison with the Royal Philharmonic Orchestra	Legacy 88985441541	11/2017

IMPORTS OF IMPORTANCE

RCA Sessions: Roy Orbison/ Sonny James (German import)	Bear Family BCD 15407	1987
The Sun Years 1956–1958 (German import)	Bear Family BCD 15461	1989
Covers (Canada import)	Stardust 27777	1989
The Sun Years (Holland)	MPV 5502	1989
Mystery Girl (Japan)	Mobile Fidelity UDCD 555	1991
I'm Still In Love with You (German import)	Mercury 838 433-2	n/a
The Big O: The Original Singles Collection (UK)	Monument/Sony 492743 2	10/1998
Sweets for Sweden	Virgin Sweden	1999
Essential Sun Collection (UK)	Recall SMDCD 181	1999
100% Roy Orbison	Virgin Sweden	2000
Orbison (7 CD boxed set plus book, German import)	Bear Family BCD 16423	03/2001
Die Besten Sterben Jung: Roy Orbison Songs in German (import)	Bear Family BCD 16774	08/2005
Roy Rocks (German import)	Bear Family BCD 15916	03/2006
Roy Orbison at the Rock House (UK)	Snapper UK SNAP296	06/2009
Roy Orbison: The Last Concert (UK vinyl)	LETV032LP	09/2011
The Monument Singles Collection (2 LP set, Holland)	Music on Vinyl MOVLP350	11/2011
Roy Orbison and the Teen Kings (UK)	Charly LP1050	03/2012

	LABEL/CAT. #	RELEASE DATE

SELECT INTERNATIONAL RELEASES OF IMPORTANCE

SINGLES

Australia

Evergreen/Love Star	London HL-1990	1962
There Won't Be Many Coming Home/ City Life	London HL-2277	1967
Still/Circle	Mercury-6167335	1975

Belgium

Lonely Wine/Gigolette	London 5483	1964

Germany

San Fernando/Mama	London DL 20 726	1963
Almost Eighteen (Johnny Kendall and the Heralds overdubs)/Jolie	RCA 47-9587	1964
The Comedians/The Comedians (live)	Virgin/Topac 113.081	1990

Holland

Lana/Dance	London FL 2044	n/a

Italy

Sweet and Innocent/Seems to Me	RCA 45N 0761	n/a
Almost Eighteen/Jolie	RCA 45N 0799	n/a
Blue Bayou (different version)/ Mean Woman Blues	London 45-HL 1499 (picture sleeve)	n/a

Spain

Dream You/Dream You	Virgin SP Roy 1	n/a

UK

Borne On The Wind/What'd I Say	London HLU 9845	02/1964
Pretty Paper/Our Summer Song	London HLU 9930	11/1964
Lana/House Without Windows	London HLU 10051	06/1966
There Won't Be Many Coming Home/ Going Back To Gloria	London HLU 10096	11/1966
Break My Mind/How Do You Start Over	London HLU 10294	11/1969
Wild Hearts/Wild Hearts (instrumental)	ZTT ZTAS9	05/1985
Wild Hearts/Wild Hearts (instrumental)– Cannes Edition (black die-cut sleeve)	ZTT/Island; ZTAS 9	051985
Wild Hearts/Wild Hearts (inst)/Ooby Dooby/ Wild Hearts (extended version)	ZTT 12ZTAS9	08/1985
Wild Hearts/Wild Hearts (inst)/ Ooby Dooby/Crying (live)	ZTT ZTAS9	08/1985

	LABEL/CAT. #	RELEASE DATE

EPs

UK

	LABEL/CAT. #	RELEASE DATE
Hillbilly Rock (triangular centre)	London RES 1089	09/1957
Hillbilly Rock (round centre)	London RES 1089	1958
Only The Lonely	London REU 1274	12/1960
Roy Orbison (Uptown)	London REU 1354	03/1963
In Dreams	London REU 1373	06/1963
Sweet and Easy To Love	Ember EP 4546	1964
Tryin' To Get You	Ember EP 4563	1964
It's Over	London REU 1435	08/1964
"Oh, Pretty Woman"	London REU 1437	12/1964
Roy Orbison's Stage Show Hits	London REU 1439	021965
Devil Doll	Ember EP 4570	1965
Love Hurts	London REU 1440	061965
Roy Orbison & The Teen Kings (Fan Club bootleg 7" record)	Stars Inc. S.I. 100	Mid 1970s
Darkness/Party Heart/ How are Things in Paradise/Yes	CBS XPS 178 (promo only)	1983
Are You Ready? — Teen Kings	Roller Coaster RCEP 117	1995

LPs

Canada

	LABEL/CAT. #	RELEASE DATE
Covers	Stardust 27777	1989

Germany

	LABEL/CAT. #	RELEASE DATE
RCA Sessions: Roy Orbison/ Sonny James	Bear Family BCD 15407	1987
The Sun Years 1956-1958	Bear Family BCD 15461	1989
Roy Orbison in Deutschland (12" single)	Bear Family BFM 15352	1989
The Big O: The World's Best Singer	Do It Records Do It 002	1989
Welcome to the Birthday Party	Do It Records Do It 007	1990
I'm Still In Love With You	Mercury 838 433-2	n/a
Orbison (7 CD boxed set plus book)	Bear Family BCD 16423	03/2001
Die Beste Sterben Jung: Roy Orbison Songs in German	Bear Family BCD 16774	08/2005
Roy Rocks	Bear Family BCD 15916	03/2006

Holland

	LABEL/CAT. #	RELEASE DATE
Big O Live at the S.N.C.O (Semi-stereo 30 cm LP)	Arcade Nedrof SLP 001	n/a
The Sun Years	MPV 5502	1989
The Monument Singles Collection (2 LP set)	Music on Vinyl MOVLP350	11/2001

New Zealand

	LABEL/CAT. #	RELEASE DATE
There is Only One Roy Orbison (different cover)	World Record Club SLZ 8482	n/a

Sweden

	LABEL/CAT. #	RELEASE DATE
Sweets for Sweden	Virgin Sweden	1999
100% Roy Orbison	Virgin Sweden	2000

UK

	LABEL/CAT. #	RELEASE DATE
The Exciting Sounds Of Roy Orbison	Ember NR 5013	06/1964
"Oh, Pretty Woman"	London HAU 8207 (mono only)	11/1964
The Big O	London SHU 8406	03/1970
Connoisseur's Roy Orbison Volume 1 (Fan Club Mono 30 cm LP)	Texan Star 001	1972
Roy Orbison Returns (Dutch-British Fan Club 25 cm LP)	Big O Records 101 (mono)	1973
Focus On Roy Orbison (double set)	London FOSU 15/16	05/1976
The Other Side Of Roy Orbison (Fan Club 30 cm LP. Mono)	Texan Star 002	1976
Connoisseur's Roy Orbison Volume 2 (Fan Club 30 cm LP. Re-issued on 25 cm)	Texan Star 003	1977
The Roy Orbison Collection (2 LP set with bonus EP #XPS 178)	CBS MNT 10041 (plus XPS 178)	1983
The Sun Years (2 LP set)	Charly CDX 4	1984
Problem Child	ZU ZAZZ Z 2006	1984
The Big O: The Original Singles Collection	Monument/Sony 492743 2	10/1998
Essential Sun Collection	Recall SMDCD 181	1999
Roy Orbison At The Rock House	Snapper UK SNAP296	06/2009
Roy Orbison: The Last Concert (vinyl)	LETV032LP	09/2011
Roy Orbison and the Teen Kings	Charly LP1050	03/2012

Der Original-Hit Nr.1 aus USA

ROY ORBISON

Pretty Woman

Yo To Amo Maria

LP TRACK LISTS by Marcel Riesco

LONELY AND BLUE (Monument SM 14002), January 1961
Only the Lonely (Know the Way I Feel), Bye-Bye Love, Cry, Blue Avenue, I Can't Stop Loving You, Come Back to Me (My Love), Blue Angel, Raindrops, (I'd Be) A Legend in My Time, I'm Hurtin', Twenty-Two Days, I'll Say It's My Fault

ROY ORBISON AT THE ROCK HOUSE (Sun LP 1260), 1961
This Kind of Love, Devil Doll, You're My Baby, Trying to Get You, It's Too Late, Rock House, You're Gonna Cry, I Never Knew, Sweet and Easy to Love You, Mean Little Mama, Ooby Dooby, Problem Child

CRYING (Monument SM 14007), January 1962
Crying, The Great Pretender, Love Hurts, She Wears My Ring, Wedding Day, Summersong, Dance, Lana, Loneliness, Let's Make a Memory, Nite Life, Running Scared

ROY ORBISON'S GREATEST HITS (Monument SM 14009), August 1962
The Crowd, Love Star, Crying, Evergreen, Running Scared, Mama, Candy Man, Only the Lonely, Dream Baby, Blue Angel, Uptown, I'm Hurtin'

IN DREAMS (Monument SLP 18003), July 1963
In Dreams, Lonely Wine, Shahdaroba, No One Will Ever Know, Sunset, House Without Windows, Dream, Blue Bayou, (They Call You) Gigolette, All I Have to Do Is Dream, Beautiful Dreamer, My Prayer

MORE OF ROY ORBISON'S GREATEST HITS (Monument SLP 18024), July 1964
It's Over, Blue Bayou, Indian Wedding, Falling, Working for the Man, Pretty Paper, Mean Woman Blues, Lana, In Dreams, Leah, Borne on the Wind, What'd I Say

EARLY ORBISON (Monument SLP 18023) October 1964
The Great Pretender, Cry, I Can't Stop Loving You, I'll Say It's My Fault, She Wears My Ring, Love Hurts, Bye Bye Love, Blue Avenue, Raindrops, Come Back to Me (My Love), Summersong, Pretty One

OH, PRETTY WOMAN (London SHU 8207), November 1964
Oh, Pretty Woman, Yo Te Amo Maria, It's Over, Indian Wedding, Borne on the Wind, Mean Woman Blues, Candy Man, Falling, Mama, The Crowd, Distant Drums, Dream Baby (How Long Must I Dream)

THERE IS ONLY ONE ROY ORBISON (MGM SE 4308), August 1965
Ride Away, You Fool You, Two of a Kind, This Is Your Song, I'm in a Blue, Blue Mood, If You Can't Say Something Nice, Claudette, Afraid to Sleep, Sugar and Honey, Summer Love, Big As I Can Dream, Wondering

ORBISONGS (Monument SLP 18035), November 1965
Oh, Pretty Woman, Dance, (Say) You're My Girl, Goodnight, Nite Life, Let the Good Times Roll, (I Get So) Sentimental, Yo Te Amo Maria, Wedding Day, Sleepy Hollow, Twenty-Two Days, (I'd Be) A Legend in My Time

THE ORBISON WAY (MGM SE 4322), February 1966
Crawling Back, It Ain't No Big Thing, Time Changed Everything, This Is My Land, The Loner, Maybe, Breakin' Up Is Breakin' My Heart, Go Away, A New Star, Never, It Wasn't Very Long Ago, Why Hurt the One Who Loves You

THE VERY BEST OF ROY ORBISON (Monument SLP 18045), July 1966
Only the Lonely, Crying, Running Scared, It's Over, Candy Man, Oh, Pretty Woman, Blue Angel, In Dreams, Dream Baby, Mean Woman Blues

THE CLASSIC ROY ORBISON (MGM SE 4379), September 1966
You'll Never Be Sixteen Again, Pantomime, Twinkle Toes, Losing You, City Life, Wait, Growing Up, Where Is Tomorrow, (No) I'll Never Get Over You, Going Back to Gloria, Just Another Name for Rock and Roll, Never Love Again

ROY ORBISON SINGS DON GIBSON (MGM SE 4424), January 1967
(I'd Be) A Legend in My Time, (Yes) I'm Hurting, The Same Street, Far Far Away, Big Hearted Me, Sweet Dreams, Oh, Such a Stranger, Blue, Blue Day, What About Me, Give Myself a Party, Too Soon to Know, Lonesome Number One

THE FASTEST GUITAR ALIVE (MGM SE 4475), June 1967
Whirlwind, Medicine Man, River, The Fastest Guitar Alive, Rollin' On, Pistolero, Good Time Party, Heading South, Best Friend, There Won't Be Many Coming Home

CRY SOFTLY LONELY ONE (MGM SE 4514), October 1967
She, Communication Breakdown, Cry Softly, Lonely One, Girl Like Mine, It Takes One (to Know One), Just Let Me Make Believe, Here Comes the Rain, Baby, That's a No No, Memories, Time to Cry, Only Alive *(London LP includes extra track: Just One Time)*

ROY ORBISON'S MANY MOODS (MGM SE 4636), May 1969
Truly, Truly, True, Unchained Melody, I Recommend Her, More, Heartache, Amy, Good Morning Dear, What Now My Love, Walk On, Yesterday's Child, Try to Remember

THE GREAT SONGS OF ROY ORBISON (MGM SE 4659), February 1970
Breakin' Up Is Breakin' My Heart, Cry Softly Lonely One, Penny Arcade, Ride Away, Southbound Jericho Parkway, Crawling Back, Heartache, Too Soon to Know, My Friend, Here Comes the Rain, Baby

THE BIG O (London SHU 8406), 1970 *(Not a US release)*
Break My Mind, Help Me Rhonda, Only You, Down the Line, Money, When I Stop Dreaming, Loving Touch, Land of a Thousand Dances, Scarlet Ribbons, She Won't Hang Her Love Out (on the Line), Casting My Spell, Penny Arcade

HANK WILLIAMS THE ROY ORBISON WAY (MGM SE 4683), August 25, 1970
Kaw-Liga, Hey Good Lookin', Jambalaya (On the Bayou), (Last Night) I Heard You Crying in Your Sleep, You Win Again, Your Cheatin' Heart, Cold, Cold Heart, A Mansion on the Hill, I Can't Help It (If I'm Still In Love with You), There'll Be No Teardrops Tonight, I'm So Lonesome I Could Cry

Discography

ROY ORBISON SINGS (MGM SE 4835), June 1972
God Love You, Beaujolais, If Only for a While, Rings of Gold, Help Me, Plain Jane Country (Come to Town), Harlem Woman, Cheyenne, Changes, It Takes All Kinds of People, Remember the Good

THE ALL-TIME GREATEST HITS OF ROY ORBISON (CBS PZ 31484), 1972
Disc 1: Only the Lonely, Leah, In Dreams, Uptown, It's Over, Crying, Dream Baby, Blue Angel, Working for the Man, Candy Man
Disc 2: Running Scared, Falling, Love Hurts, Shahdaroba, I'm Hurtin', Mean Woman Blues, Pretty Paper, The Crowd, Blue Bayou, Oh, Pretty Woman

Memphis (MGM SE 4867), November 1972
Memphis, Tennessee, Why a Woman Cries, Run, Baby, Run, Take Care of Your Woman, I'm The Man on Susie's Mind, I Can't Stop Loving You, Run the Engines Up High, It Ain't No Big Thing (But It's Growing), I Fought the Law, The Three Bells, Danny Boy

Milestones (MGM SE 4934), September 1973
I Wanna Live, You Don't Know Me, California Sunshine Girl, Words, Blue Rain (Coming Down), Drift Away, You Lay So Easy on My Mind, The World You Live In, Sweet Caroline, I've Been Loving You Too Long (To Stop Now), The Morning After

I'M STILL IN LOVE WITH YOU (Mercury SRM 1045), September 15, 1975
Pledging My Love, Spanish Nights, Rainbow Love, It's Lonely, Heartache, Crying Time, Still, Hung Up on You, Circle, Sweet Mamma Blue, All I Need Is Time

REGENERATION (Monument MG 7600), November 1976
(I'm a) Southern Man, No Chain at All, Old Love Song, Can't Wait, Born to Love Me, Blues in My Mind, Something They Can't Take Away, Under Suspicion, I Don't Really Want You, Belinda

LAMINAR FLOW (Asylum 6E 198), May 16, 1979
Easy Way Out, Love Is a Cold Wind, Lay It Down, I Care, We're into Something Good, Movin', Poor Baby, Warm Spot Hot, Tears, Friday Night, Hound Dog Man

CLASS OF '55 — Memphis Rock & Roll Homecoming (America/Smash AR LP100), May 1986 *(With Johnny Cash, Carl Perkins, and Jerry Lee Lewis)*
Birth of Rock and Roll, Sixteen Candles, Class of '55, Waymore's Blues, We Remember the King, Coming Home, Rock and Roll (Fais-Do-Do), Keep My Motor Running, I Will Rock and Roll with You, Big Train (From Memphis)

THE GREAT ROY ORBISON (All-Time Greatest Hits) (Silver Eagle SE 1046), 1986 *(New recordings)*
Disc 1: Only the Lonely, Leah, In Dreams, Uptown, It's Over, Crying, Dream Baby (How Long Must I Dream), Blue Angel, Working for the Man, Candy Man
Disc 2: Running Scared, Falling, I'm Hurtin', Claudette, Oh, Pretty Woman, Mean Woman Blues, Ooby Dooby, Lana, Blue Bayou

IN DREAMS: THE GREATEST HITS (Virgin 90604 1), May 1987 *(New recordings)*
Disc 1: Only the Lonely, Leah, In Dreams, Uptown, It's Over, Crying, Dream Baby (How Long Must I Dream), Blue Angel, Working for the Man, Candy Man
Disc 2: Running Scared, Falling, I'm Hurtin', Claudette, Oh, Pretty Woman, Mean Woman Blues, Ooby Dooby, Lana, Blue Bayou

TRAVELING WILBURYS VOLUME ONE (Wilbury 1 27576), October 25, 1988 *(With George Harrison, Bob Dylan, Tom Petty, and Jeff Lynne)*
Handle with Care, Dirty World, Rattled, Last Night, Not Alone Any More, Congratulations, Heading for the Light, Margarita, Tweeter and the Monkey Man, End of the Line

MYSTERY GIRL (Virgin 791058 1), January 31, 1989
You Got It, In the Real World, (All I Can Do Is) Dream You, A Love So Beautiful, California Blue, She's a Mystery to Me, The Comedians, The Only One, Windsurfer, Careless Heart

ROY ORBISON AND FRIENDS: A BLACK AND WHITE NIGHT LIVE (Virgin 91295), October 23, 1989
Only the Lonely, In Dreams, Dream Baby, Leah, Move on Down the Line, Crying, Mean Woman Blues, Running Scared, Blue Bayou, Candy Man, Uptown, Ooby Dooby, The Comedians, (All I Can Do Is) Dream You, It's Over, Oh, Pretty Woman

KING OF HEARTS (Virgin 86520), October 20, 1992
You're the One, Heartbreak Radio, We'll Take the Night, Crying, After the Love Has Gone, Love in Time, I Drove All Night, Wild Hearts Run Out of Time, Coming Home, Careless Heart

MYSTERY GIRL DELUXE (Sony Legacy 886976070328), May 19, 2014
You Got It, In the Real World, (All I Can Do Is) Dream You, A Love So Beautiful, California Blue, She's a Mystery to Me, The Comedians, The Only One, Windsurfer, Careless Heart, The Way Is Love, She's a Mystery to Me, (All I Can Do Is) Dream You, The Only One, The Comedians, In the Real World, California Blue, Windsurfer, You Are My Love

ONE OF THE LONELY ONES (Universal 4723304), December 4, 2015
You'll Never Walk Alone, Say No More, Leaving Makes the Rain Come Down, Sweet Memories, Laurie, One of the Lonely Ones, Child Woman, Woman Child, The Defector, Give Up, Little Girl (in the Big City), After Tonight, I Will Always

THE ULTIMATE COLLECTION (Legacy 889853688715), October 28, 2016
Disc 1: Oh, Pretty Woman, I Drove All Night, You Got It, Crying, Only the Lonely (Know the Way I Feel), In Dreams, Love Hurts, Claudette, Blue Bayou, Dream Baby (How Long Must I Dream), Walk On, Falling, Running Scared, California Blue
Disc 2: Leah, Mean Woman Blues, Crawling Back, Ride Away, Too Soon to Know, She's a Mystery to Me, Blue Angel, It's Over, Ooby Dooby, Heartbreak Radio, Not Alone Anymore (Traveling Wilburys), Handle with Care (Traveling Wilburys)

Page i: Sheila Rock; **vi–vii**: Chelsie Lykens; **ix**: Glen Erler; **x**: Joe Horton; **1**: Ken Regan; **2**: Dick Clark Productions; **3**: Barbara Orbison; **4–6**: film stills Roy Orbison & Friends: A Black & White Night 30; **8**: Orbison Family Archives/Eastbourne; **9**: James Schnepf; **10**: Orbison Family Archives; **11**: Marcel Riesco; **12**: James Schnepf; **13**: Film Still, Black & White Night rehearsal; **14**: Virgin/"Crying" promo; **15**: film stills Roy Orbison & Friends: A Black & White Night 30; **16–18**: film still Roy Orbison & Friends: A Black & White Night 30; **19**: Michael Jacobs ; **20–22**: film stills Roy Orbison & Friends: A Black & White Night 30; **23**: James Schnepf; **26**: Orbison Family Archives; **27** Marcel Riesco/Orbie Lee Harris; **28** Marcel Riesco/Janna Frodsham; **29**: Marcel Riesco/Orbie Lee Harris; **30**: Pictorial Press Ltd/Alamy Stock Photo ; **31**: (top) Marcel Riesco/Orbie Lee Harris; **33**: (top) Marcel Riesco/Wink High School Yearbook 1950, (bottom) archival photo ; **34**: Wink High School Yearbook ; **35**: (top) Marcel Riesco, (bottom) courtesy Orbison family archives/Wink High School Yearbook; **36**: Marcel Riesco; **37**: Orbison Family Archives; **39**: Marcel Riesco/Orbie Lee Harris; **40**: Joe Horton ; **41**: Orbison Family Archives; **42**: Wink High School; **43**: Bob Neal/Stars Incorporated; **44**: Marcel Riesco/Bill Frady; **45**: Billy Pat Ellis; **46–48**: Orbison Family Archives; **49**: Shelby Singleton; **50**: Marcel Riesco/Bill Frady; **51–53**: Courtesy of the Teen Kings; **52** Orbison Family Archives; **54**: Orbison Family Archives; **56**: John Garner, Camera 5; **57**: Marcel Riesco; **58**: Norman Petty/The Roses promo shot; **59**: Estate of Norman Petty; **61** Marcel Riesco/Bill Frady; **62**: Orbison Family Archives; **63**: (top) Marcel Riesco/Orbie Lee Harris. (bottom) Marcel Riesco/Bill Frady; **64**: Orbison Family Archives; **65**: Harry Goodwin; **66**: Marcel Riesco/Bill Frady; **67**: Orbison Family Archives; **68–69**: Hulton Deutsch Archive/Getty Images New Musical Express; **70 & 73**: Joe Horton; **74–75**: Johnny Franklin ; **76**: Country Music Hall of Fame & Museum/Getty Images; **77**: (top) Country Music Hall of Fame & Museum/Getty Images, (bottom) Orbison Family Archives; **78**: Joe Horton; **79**: Marcel Riesco; **80**: Country Music Hall of Fame & Museum/Getty Images; **81–82**: Marcel Riesco; **83**: Michael Ochs Archives/ Getty Images; **84**: Joe Horton; **86–87**: Orbison Family Archives; **88**: Walden S. Fabry; **89**: (bottom) Marcel Riesco; **90–91**: Worthing Herald UK; **92**: Marcel Riesco; **94**: Margaret Finch/RO Int'l Fan Club; **95**: (top) Collection of Marcel Riesco (bottom) Orbison Family Archives; **96**: Marcel Riesco; **97**: Orbison Family Archives; **98**: (top) New Musical Express (bottom) Marcel Riesco; **99**: Orbison Family Archives; **100–101**: Orbison Family Archives; **102**: unknown newspaper clipping; **103**: David Redfern ; **104**: Orbison Family Archives; **105**: (top) Orbison Family Archives, (bottom) still from the *Roy Orbison Show*; **106**: Orbison Family Archives; **107**: Globe Photos/ZUMAPRESS.com; **108**: Orbison Family Archives; **109**: Michael Ochs Archives/Getty Images; **110–112**: Hulton Deutsch Archive; **113**: Ed Sullivan Show; **114**: Hulton Deutsch Archive/Getty Images; **115**: (top) Joe Horton (bottom) Orbison Family Archives ; **116**: Joe Horton; **117**: David Redfern; **118–119**: *The Fastest Guitar Alive* Film Still; **120**: *The Fastest Guitar Alive* studio promo image; **121**: The Sydney Morning Herald/Getty Images; **122**: Marcel Riesco; **123**: Orbison Family Archives; **124–129**: Orbison Family Archives; **130**: Michael Ochs Archives/Getty Images; **131**: Marcel Riesco; **132**: Orbison Family Archives / Roy Orbison Fan Club; **134**: Orbison Family Archives; **135**: MGM era promo ; **136**: (top) Orbison Family Archives (bottom) Murray Laden; **137**: Fastest Guitar promo materials; **138–141**: *The Fastest Guitar Alive* promo materials and lobby cards; **142**: Orbison Family Archives; **143**: Hulton Deutsch Archive/Getty Images; **144**: Orbison Family Archives; **145**: (top) Marcel Riesco (bottom) Orbison Family Archives; **146**:

Roy Orbison's famous sunglasses from the late 1980s.

Bettmann/Getty Images; **147**: Victoria & Albert Museum; **148–151**: Hulton Deutsch Archive/Getty Images; **153**: Togue Uchida; **154**: Marcel Riesco; **155**: Orbison Family Archives; **156–157**: Orbison Family Archives; **158–159**: Marcel Riesco; **160**: Michael Rougier/Getty Images; **162–163**: Marcel Riesco; **164**: Orbison Family Archives; **165**: Hulton Deutsch Archive; **166**: Central Press/Getty Images; **167**: Hulton Deutsch Archive; **168–169**: David Shoenfelt; **170**: Orbison Family Archives; **171**: Orbison Family Archives; **173**: Orbison Family Archives; **174**: Marcel Riesco; **175**: Christian Carswell; **176–177**: Orbison Family Archives; **179**: newspaper clipping Marcel Riesco; **178**: Still from Johnny Cash TV Special; **182**: Orbison Family Archives; **184**: Orbison Collection; **185**: signed still from television show, Just Our Luck; **186**: Orbison Family Archives; **187**: Gary Heery Elektra/Asylum Promo shot; **188**: Aaron Rapoport/Getty Images; **189**: Orbison Family Archives; **190–191**: David Shoenfelt; **192**: Sheila Rock; **193**: Orbison Family Archives /Bucky Barrett; **194**: Orbison Family Archives; **196**: Ann Summa; **198–199**: Orbison Family Archives; **200**: Orbison Family Archives; **201**: Ron Galella/Getty Images; **202**: Harry Benson; **205**: Alberto Tolot; **206**: Eastbourne/ Orbison Family Archives; **207**: Orbison Family Archives; **208**: Marcel Riesco; **209**: James Schnepf; **210**: Chelsie Lykens; **211**: Marcel Riesco; **212**: Art by Fantoons Animation Studio (Ittai Manero/David Calcano); **213**: (top) Orbison Family Archives (bottom) Neal Preston; **214**: (top) Marcel Riesco (bottom) Neal Preston; **215**: (top) Preston (bottom) Orbison Family Archives; **216–217**: Glen Erler; **219**: Sheila Rock; **220**: Rob Verhorst/Getty Images; **221**: Sheila Rock; **222**: Marcel Riesco; **223–227**: David Shoenfelt; **229**: James Schnepf; **230**: Orbison Family Archives; **231**: Orbison Family Archives; **233**: Joe Horton; **234**: Hulton Deutsch Archive/Getty; **237**: Hulton Deutsch Archive/Getty; **238**: Orbison Family Archives; **240**: Sheila Rock; **243**: Frederick M. Brown/Getty; **253**: Chelsie Lykens; **254**: (top) Luke Chalk (bottom) Rachel Naomi

Roy Jr., **Wesley**, and **Alex Orbison** are Roy Orbison's three sons. As Roy's Boys, the trio works tirelessly to protect and further their father's legacy. Wesley, the eldest, is a seasoned songwriter and guitar player. His song "The Only One" (cowritten with Craig Wiseman) appears on Roy Orbison's multi-platinum album *Mystery Girl*. Roy Jr. is a singer and guitar player who works out of his own professional recording studio, the Pretty Woman Studio. He enjoys spending time with his beautiful bride and their son, Roy Orbison III. Alex, a drummer by trade, began his career in music publishing at the age of 17. As copresident of Still Working Music, along with his brother Roy, Alex has overseen several top ten songs and number one hits. All three brothers reside with their families in Nashville.

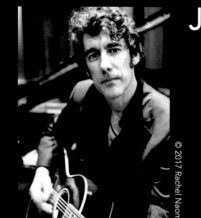

Jeff Slate is a songwriter and music journalist who regularly contributes to *Esquire*, *Rolling Stone,* and other publications. He is a lifelong fan of Roy Orbison, and recently contributed liner notes to *The Ultimate Roy Orbison* and the 50th anniversary reissue of The Beatles' *Sgt. Pepper's Lonely Hearts Club Band*. He and his partner Lynn—and their children—reside in New York City.